MCSE
THE ELECTIVES
IN A NUTSHELL

A Desktop Quick Reference

MCSE
THE ELECTIVES
IN A NUTSHELL

A Desktop Quick Reference

Michael Moncur

O'REILLY™

Beijing · Cambridge · Köln · Paris · Sebastopol · Taipei · Tokyo

MCSE: The Electives in a Nutshell

by Michael Moncur

Copyright © 1998 O'Reilly & Associates, Inc. All rights reserved.
Printed in the United States of America.

Published by O'Reilly & Associates, Inc., 101 Morris Street, Sebastopol, CA 95472.

Editor: Tim O'Reilly

Production Editor: Jane Ellin

Printing History:

> September 1998:   First Edition.

This book is printed on acid-free paper with 85% recycled content, 15% post-consumer waste. O'Reilly & Associates is committed to using paper with the highest recycled content available consistent with high quality.

ISBN: 1-56592-482-7

Table of Contents

Part 2: Internet Information Server 4.0

Part 3: Internet Explorer 4.0 Administration

Part 4: Proxy Server 2.0

Part 5: Exchange Server 5.5

Preface

The MCSE (Microsoft Certified Systems Engineer) program is a rigorous testing and certification program for Windows NT system and network administrators. MCSE candidates are required to pass four core exams and two elective exams. This book is a concise, comprehensive study guide to the areas covered on five of the most popular MCSE elective exam choices.

If you're an experienced system administrator—whether the experience is with Windows NT, UNIX, NetWare, or another system—this book will help you codify your knowledge, understand Microsoft's view of the universe, and prepare for the MCSE elective exams.

If you are a beginner, this book should also prove useful. Of course, you'll need real-world experience, which no book can provide. Depending on your technical background, you may also need help from other books or classes. Nevertheless, this book will provide a useful framework for your studies.

If you have already made some progress along the MCSE path, you probably have a number of MCSE-related books lining your shelves. While this book can't replace all of them, it can remain on your desk as a handy reference to the topics covered in the MCSE elective exams. It also includes several useful features—such as review items and practice tests—that will help you prepare to take the actual exams.

Contents

This book covers five of the most popular elective exam choices for the Windows NT 4.0 MCSE certification. This book is divided into Parts corresponding to each of the exams.

About the MCSE Exams

Introduces the MCSE and other Microsoft certifications, with information about the content of the elective exams and study tips.

Part 1, Internetworking with TCP/IP
> Covers exam 70-059, *Internetworking with TCP/IP on Microsoft Windows NT 4.0*. This exam is an MCSE elective and a requirement for the MCP+Internet and MCSE+Internet certifications.

Part 2, Internet Information Server 4.0
> Covers exam 70-087, *Implementing and Supporting Microsoft Internet Information Server 4.0*. This exam is an MCSE elective and a requirement for the MCP+Internet and MCSE+Internet certifications.

Part 3, Internet Explorer 4.0 Administration
> Covers exam 70-079, *Implementing and Supporting Microsoft Internet Explorer 4.0 by Using the Microsoft Internet Explorer Administration Kit*. This exam is an MCSE elective and an MCSE+Internet requirement.

Part 4, Proxy Server 2.0
> Covers exam 70-088, *Implementing and Supporting Microsoft Proxy Server 2.0*. This exam is an elective for the MCSE and MCSE+Internet certifications.

Part 5, Exchange Server 5.5
> Covers exam 70-081, *Implementing and Supporting Microsoft Exchange Server 5.5*. This exam is an elective for the MCSE and MCSE+Internet certifications.

The MCSE certification requires passing four required exams and two elective exams. This book's companion volume, *MCSE: The Core Exams in a Nutshell* (O'Reilly & Associates), covers all of the current required exams.

Conventions Used in This Book

Each Part within this book corresponds to a single MCSE exam and consists of five sections:

Exam Overview
> This is a brief introduction to the exam's topic and two lists of objectives to help direct your preparation. *Need to Know* lists areas you should understand in-depth because they will more than likely be on the exam. *Need to Apply* lists tasks that you should be able to perform and that you should practice during your studies. The objectives in both of these lists include cross-references into the *Study Guide*.

Study Guide
> This, the largest portion of each Part, is a comprehensive study guide for the areas covered on the exam. It can be read straight through, or referred to for areas in which you need further study.

Suggested Exercises
> This is a numbered list of exercises you can perform, usually with a small test network, to gain experience in the exam's subject areas.

Practice Test
> This section includes a comprehensive practice test in a format similar to the actual exam questions. Answers to the questions are provided with detailed explanations.

Highlighter's Index

> Here I've attempted to compile the facts within the exam's subject area that you are most likely to need another look at—in other words, those you might have highlighted while reading the *Study Guide*. This will be useful as a final review before taking an exam.

Within the *Study Guide* section, the following elements are included:

On the Exam

> These boxed tips provide information about areas you should focus your studies on for the exam.

In the Real World

> These tips provide informative asides in cases where reality and the MCSE exams don't necessarily coincide.

The following typographical conventions are used in this book:

`Constant width`

> is used to indicate keyboard keys, commands, and other values to be typed literally.

`Constant width italic`

> is used to represent replaceables within commands.

Italic

> is used for URLs, to introduce new terms, and to indicate menu and dialog box options.

Other MCSE Resources

Depending on your current knowledge and experience, you may need resources beyond this book for your MCSE studies. The one resource all MCSE candidates should be aware of is Microsoft's Training and Certification web page:

> *http://www.microsoft.com/train_cert/*

I recommend that you refer to this page regularly during your certification progress, since changes may be announced that will affect your exam choices.

A wide variety of MCSE study guides are available from other vendors, chief among them the MOC (Microsoft Official Curriculum) study guides. If you need books for further study, choose the ones that best fit your needs.

Another set of useful resources, while not specifically for the MCSE curriculum, are the various Resource Kits published by Microsoft. These are available for Internet Information Server, Internet Explorer, and Exchange Server, and go into great detail about each product. Each also includes a CD-ROM with useful utilities, some of which are described in this book.

A number of practice MCSE test programs are available. See Microsoft's web page, listed above, for information about one such program, the PEP tests. See the O'Reilly web site (listed in the next section) for links to several third-party test software providers.

How to Contact Us

We have tested and verified all the information in this book to the best of our ability. If you have an idea that could make this a more useful study tool, or if you find an error in the text or run into a question on the exam that isn't covered, please let us know by writing to us at:

O'Reilly & Associates
101 Morris Street
Sebastopol, CA 95472
1-800-998-9938 (in the U.S. or Canada)
1-707-829-0515 (international/local)
1-707-829-0104 (FAX)

You can also send messages electronically. To be put on our mailing list or to request a catalog, send email to:

nuts@oreilly.com

To ask technical questions or to comment on the book, send email to:

mcsenut@oreilly.com

or navigate to:

http://www.oreilly.com/catalog/mcselect/

and look for the Conference link.

For more information about this book and others, see the O'Reilly web site:

http://www.oreilly.com/

Acknowledgments

I would like to thank everyone involved in the production of this book and its companion volume. Tim O'Reilly, the editor of the "in a Nutshell" series, came up with the original concept and has provided much useful input as the books have evolved. Troy Mott and Katie Gardner made sure the project and I moved along smoothly, not always an easy task.

Eric Pearce provided early technical feedback that helped shape this book and its companion volume, and gave many useful comments for later drafts. The manuscript was also reviewed for technical accuracy at various stages by Walter Glenn, Mitch Tulloch, Paul Murphy, and Frank GoBell. Their input helped make this a better book.

Thanks also goes to the O'Reilly production staff: Jane Ellin, the production editor; Mike Sierra, who converted the book and provided much-needed tools support; Nancy Priest, the interior designer; Edie Freedman, who designed the cover; Seth Maislin, the indexer; Nicole Gipson Arigo and Sheryl Avruch for quality control; and Robert Romano, who provided the figures.

Finally, I would like to thank Brian Gill, David Rogelberg, and Sherry Rogelberg of Studio B for their help with this project. As always, thanks goes to my family and friends for their support, particularly my wife, Laura.

About the MCSE Exams

Microsoft's MCSE (Microsoft Certified Systems Engineer) program is rapidly gaining popularity as Windows NT is used for more networks. While Novell's CNE program was previously considered the necessary credential for network administrators, it's quickly losing ground to the MCSE program.

You must pass six exams to attain the MCSE certification: four required exams and two electives. This volume covers the current versions of several of the most popular elective exams. The core exams are covered by *MCSE: The Core Exams in a Nutshell*, also from O'Reilly & Associates.

This chapter describes the MCSE and other certification credentials offered by Microsoft, summarizes the exams covered in this book and its companion volume, and provides information about the examination process.

Microsoft Certification Programs

Microsoft offers several certification options with varying levels of difficulty, from the MCP (one exam) to MCSE+Internet (nine exams). The following sections describe each certification in detail.

On the Exam

For several of these programs, you are able to choose between two or more exams covering different versions of a software product. Since older exams are eventually retired, I recommend taking the exam for the most current product. This book and its companion volume cover the most recent exam currently available for each product.

The descriptions of certification programs and their requirements in the sections below are current at the time of this writing. For a list of the current requirements for these and other certifications, see Microsoft's Certification Online web site:

http://www.microsoft.com/train_cert/

MCP (Microsoft Certified Professional)

The MCP certification only requires passing a single exam. Depending on the exam, you are certified as an MCP with that specialty. You can attain multiple MCP certifications; in fact, you will attain several in the process of earning the MCSE certification.

In the past, the MCP certification was available only for certain exams. Microsoft has recently revised the program. You can now earn an MCP certification by passing any current (not scheduled to be retired) exam. The one exception is Exam 70-058, *Network Essentials*, which counts toward the MCSE but does not earn an MCP certification.

MCP+Internet (MCP with Internet Specialty)

Microsoft recently enhanced the MCP program to include a new certification category: MCP with a specialty in the Internet. This certification requires passing three specific exams dealing with Windows NT and the Internet. The current exams include the following:

- Exam 70-067: Implementing and Supporting Microsoft Windows NT Server 4.0
- Exam 70-059: Internetworking with TCP/IP on Microsoft Windows NT 4.0 (covered in Part 1)
- Exam 70-087: Implementing and supporting Microsoft Internet Information Server 4.0 (covered in Part 2)

The first of these exams is one of the MCSE requirements, and is covered in *MCSE: The Core Exams in a Nutshell*. The remaining exams are MCSE electives, and are covered in this book.

MCP+Site Building (MCP with Web Site Specialty)

Microsoft's newest addition to the range of certification choices is MCP+Site Building, an MCP certification that specializes in web site building. This certification requires passing two exams on Web-related topics. Currently, the two exams can be chosen from the following:

- Exam 70-055: Designing and Implementing Web Sites with Microsoft FrontPage 98
- Exam 70-057: Designing and Implementing Commerce Solutions with Microsoft Site Server 3.0, Commerce Edition
- 70-152: Designing and Implementing Web solutions with Microsoft Visual InterDev 6.0

MCSE (Microsoft Certified Systems Engineer)

The MCSE certification is currently the most sought-after credential for network administrators, and is the subject of this book. The MCSE requires passing six exams: four core requirement exams and two electives.

Core Requirement Exams

The core MCSE exams include the following:

- Exam 70-058: Networking Essentials
- Choose one of these desktop operating system exams:
    - Exam 70-073: Implementing and Supporting Windows NT Workstation 4.0
    - Exam 70-064: Implementing and Supporting Windows 95
    - Exam 70-098: Implementing and Supporting Windows 98
- Exam 70-067: Implementing and Supporting Microsoft Windows NT Server 4.0
- Exam 70-068: Implementing and Supporting Microsoft Windows NT Server 4.0 in the Enterprise

MCSE: The Core Exams in a Nutshell covers all of these exams with the exception of the Windows 98 exam, which was not yet available at the time of this writing.

Elective Exams

You can choose your two MCSE electives from a pool of available exams. We have chosen five of the most popular electives, all related to the Internet, for this book. The following is the complete list of the currently available elective exams:

- Exam 70-059: Internetworking with TCP/IP on Windows NT 4.0 (covered in Part 1)
- Exam 70-087: Implementing and Supporting Microsoft Internet Information Server 4.0 (covered in Part 2; Exam 70-077, IIS 3.0, is also accepted)
- Exam 70-079: Implementing and Supporting Microsoft Internet Explorer 4.0 by Using the Internet Explorer Administration Kit (covered in Part 3)
- Exam 70-088: Implementing and Supporting Microsoft Proxy Server 2.0 (covered in Part 4)
- Exam 70-081: Implementing and Supporting Microsoft Exchange Server 5.5 (covered in Part 5)
- Exam 70-086: Implementing and Supporting Microsoft Systems Management Server 2.0
- Exam 70-026: System Administration for Microsoft SQL Server 6.5 or 70-028: System Administration for SQL Server 7.0
- Exam 70-027: Implementing a Database Design on Microsoft SQL Server 6.5 or 70-029: Implementing a Database Design on SQL Server 7.0
- Exam 70-085: Implementing and Supporting Microsoft SNA Server 4.0

- Exam 70-056: Implementing and Supporting Web Sites Using Microsoft Site Server 3.0

This book covers the first five exams listed, which are among the most popular choices due to their focus on Internet-related issues.

MCSE+Internet (MCSE with Internet Specialty)

Until recently, the MCSE certification, with six exams, was the most advanced networking certification offered by Microsoft. The latest addition to the program is the MCSE+Internet, or MCSE with a specialty in the Internet. This is basically a combination of the MCSE and MCP+Internet certifications.

The MCSE+Internet certification requires a total of nine exams: seven core requirements, and two electives. The required exams include the following:

- Exam 70-058: Networking Essentials
- Choose one of these desktop operating system exams:
    - Exam 70-073: Implementing and Supporting Microsoft Windows NT Workstation 4.0
    - Exam 70-064: Implementing and Supporting Microsoft Windows 95
    - Exam 70-098: Implementing and Supporting Microsoft Windows 98
- Exam 70-067: Implementing and Supporting Microsoft Windows NT Server 4.0
- Exam 70-068: Implementing and Supporting Microsoft Windows NT Server 4.0 in the Enterprise
- Exam 70-059: Internetworking with Microsoft TCP/IP on Microsoft Windows NT 4.0
- Exam 70-087: Implementing and Supporting Microsoft Internet Information Server 4.0 (covered in Part 2; Exam 70-077, IIS 3.0, is also accepted)
- Exam 70-079: Implementing and Supporting Microsoft Internet Explorer 4.0 by Using the Internet Explorer Administration Kit (covered in Part 3)

The first four core exams are the same as the required exams for the MCSE certification, and are covered by this book's companion volume. The TCP/IP, Internet Information Server, and Internet Explorer exams are covered by this book.

The two electives can be chosen from the following exams, the first two of which are covered by this book:

- Exam 70-088: Implementing and Supporting Microsoft Proxy Server 2.0 (covered in Part 4)
- Exam 70-081: Implementing and Supporting Microsoft Exchange Server 5.5 (covered in Part 5)
- Exam 70-026: System Administration for Microsoft SQL Server 6.5 (or 70-028 for SQL Server 7.0)
- Exam 70-027: Implementing a Database Design on Microsoft SQL Server 6.5 (or 70-029 for SQL Server 7.0)

- Exam 70-056: Implementing and Supporting Web Sites Using Microsoft Site Server 3.0

- Exam 70-085: Implementing and Supporting Microsoft SNA Server 4.0

If you plan to pursue the MCSE+Internet certification after completing the MCSE, be sure your MCSE electives are chosen to correspond with required or elective exams for the MCSE+Internet; otherwise, you may end up taking more than 9 exams total.

MCSD (Microsoft Certified Solution Developer)

This certification is aimed at software developers rather than network administrators. Microsoft has recently revised the MCSD program. The new certification requires three required exams and one elective. The required exams include the following:

- Exam 70-100: Examining Requirements and Defining Solution Architectures

- Choose one of the following desktop application development exams:

  - Exam 70-016: Designing and Implementing Desktop Applications with Microsoft Visual C++ 6.0

  - Exam 70-176: Designing and Implementing Desktop Applications with Microsoft Visual Basic 6.0

- Choose one of the following distributed application development exams:

  - 70-015: Designing and Implementing Distributed Applications with Microsoft Visual C++ 6.0

  - 70-175: Designing and Implementing Distributed Applications with Microsoft Visual Basic 6.0

The elective exam can be chosen from various exams related to programming languages and databases. For more information, see Microsoft's web site:

http://www.microsoft.com/mcp/

MCT (Microsoft Certified Trainer)

The MCT certification is for individuals who intend to teach Microsoft's authorized courses on the MCP and other exams. To become an MCT, you must first register with Microsoft and prove that you have attended a class in instructional skills, or that you are an experienced trainer. (Microsoft holds instructor training courses for this purpose.)

After being approved as an MCT, you have to be separately approved to teach each MCP exam. To do this you must pass the exam and any related exams, and may be required to attend a Microsoft Official Curriculum (MOC) course for each subject you wish to teach.

Refer to Microsoft's MCT web site for details about the MCT program:

http://www.microsoft.com/train_cert/mct/

MCSE Elective Exams

The MCSE is the most popular of the MCP programs. It requires six exams: four core requirement exams and two elective exams. You can pick the elective exams from a variety of choices, five of which are covered in this book.

The MCSE electives covered in this book are described in the sections below.

Internetworking with TCP/IP

TCP/IP (Transmission Control Protocol/Internet Protocol) is a suite of protocols widely used by the Internet and UNIX systems, and increasing in popularity as a framework for Windows networks.

Exam 70-059, *Internetworking with Microsoft TCP/IP on Microsoft Windows NT 4.0*, covers all aspects of TCP/IP under Windows NT 4.0. This includes the basics, such as IP addressing and the protocols that make up the TCP/IP suite, as well as specific information about using TCP/IP protocols and services under Windows NT. Part 1 of this book covers this exam.

Internet Information Server 4.0

Microsoft's Internet Information Server (IIS) is a versatile web and FTP server for use on the Internet or local networks. While version 2.0 of IIS is included with Windows NT Server, version 4.0 is now available from Microsoft as part of the Windows NT Option Pack.

Exam 70-087, *Implementing and Supporting Microsoft Internet Information Server 4.0*, tests your knowledge of IIS, including planning, installation, management tasks, security, and troubleshooting. This exam is covered in Part 2 of this book.

Internet Explorer 4.0 Administration

The Internet Explorer Administration Kit, available for download from Microsoft, is a set of tools that allow custom packaging and installation of Internet Explorer 4.0, Microsoft's current web browser.

Exam 70-079, *Implementing and Supporting Microsoft Internet Explorer 4.0 by Using the Microsoft Internet Explorer Administration Kit*, covers all of the features of IE 4.0 as well as the additional capabilities provided by the Administration Kit. This exam is covered in Part 3.

Proxy Server 2.0

Proxy servers allow access to the Internet from corporate networks or other environments while providing security, caching, and other features. Microsoft Proxy Server, currently at version 2.0, is Microsoft's implementation of a proxy server.

Exam 70-088, *Implementing and Supporting Microsoft Proxy Server 2.0*, covers the use of Proxy Server for corporate networks or Internet Service Providers (ISPs). Part 4 of this book covers this exam.

Exchange Server 5.5

Microsoft Exchange Server, part of the BackOffice package, is a dedicated email server. Exchange clients are included with Windows NT, Windows 95, and Windows 98.

Exam 70-081, *Implementing and Supporting Microsoft Exchange Server 5.5*, covers installation, administration, security, and other aspects of Exchange Server. This exam is covered in Part 5 of this book.

The Examination Process

All of the MCSE exams are similar in format, and a certain amount of preparation will help you pass any of them. The following sections look at ways to prepare for the exams and the actual process of taking the exams.

Choosing Exams

Before beginning the certification process, you should choose the required and elective exams you will take, and the order in which you will take them. Here are some thoughts on making these choices.

Required Exams

There are a limited number of choices for the MCSE requirements. The three exams you can actually choose between are the NT Workstation, Windows 95, and Windows 98 exams. These each have their advantages:

*   The Windows 95 or Windows 98 exam will be easier to pass if you already have experience with these systems. In addition, Windows 95 and 98 are more widely used on desktops than NT Workstation.

*   The NT Workstation exam covers some more difficult topics, but you'll need to learn most of these topics for the NT Server exam regardless of your desktop exam choice.

The NT Workstation exam is the most popular choice; it's a good foundation for the other MCSE exams, most of which are centered on Windows NT.

Having decided which desktop exam to take, you can decide which order to take the core exams in. You can take the exams in any order, but the logical choices for a first exam are Network Essentials or the desktop OS exam (NT Workstation or Windows 95/98), since these are generally the easiest.

While the Network Essentials exam covers more basic and fundamental topics, your experience may be more in line with the desktop OS exam. For example, someone who has worked as a Windows NT network administrator for a year would find the NT Workstation exam easy to pass.

On the other hand, the same person would most likely need to study for the Network Essentials exam, because they probably don't have experience with network topologies and protocols other than those used in their employer's network.

There is also a potential career advantage to passing a desktop OS exam first, since these exams result in an MCP certification. If you are trying to start a career quickly, the MCP may help you qualify for a job in network administration or technical support. (Aside from financial advantages, having a job that requires day-to-day work with Windows NT will be very helpful in passing the remaining MCSE tests.)

Once you've passed the Network Essentials exam and a desktop OS exam, you will probably want to take the remaining exams in order: NT Server, then NT Server in the Enterprise.

Elective Exams

There are many more choices for elective exams. Your choice of two elective exams should be based on three considerations:

- Which topics do you already have experience with, or plan to learn?
- Which topics will be most useful in your career?
- Which exams provide other certification options? For example, choosing the TCP/IP and IIS exams will give you the MCP+Internet certification as well as the MCSE, and prepare you for the MCSE+Internet certification.

While choosing easier exams, or those you have experience with, can get you the MCSE certification faster, choosing more specialized topics can help you stand out from other certified applicants in your career pursuits.

Preparing for Exams

The exams currently cost $100 apiece to take, and the cost applies whether you pass or fail. Thus, it's a good idea to prepare as thoroughly as possible before attempting to take an exam. It's best to concentrate on a single exam at a time.

This book and its companion volume will obviously be helpful in preparing for exams. Depending on your understanding of the subject matter, it may be useful to study other materials. Microsoft's documentation, such as the Windows NT Resource Kits, the online books, and the help files included with various utilities, may be helpful.

It is also very important to have real-world experience with the items covered in each exam. It's nearly impossible to pass a Microsoft exam just by studying. You should have access to a network with a minimum of two Windows NT computers to experiment with; access to a larger network would be even more useful.

A number of free practice exams are available, including the PEP test free for download from Microsoft. These are not comprehensive and may not cover all of the exam topics, but can be a good barometer of your preparedness. Commercial tests are available from several third-party companies. A practice test is also included in each Part of this book.

Scheduling and Payment

Microsoft's exams are administered by Sylvan Prometric. Call (800) 755-3926 to schedule an exam. Online registration is also available at the Prometric web site (*www.prometric.com*).

You can register entirely over the phone with a credit card. If you pay by check, you must first mail the check to Sylvan Prometric, then call to schedule the exam. Call the number listed above for the address to send payments to.

Your registration ID is your social security number, or a number assigned by Prometric if you are outside the U.S. Use this number in all communications with them, and write it on any checks you send.

You usually need to schedule an exam at least 24 hours in advance. Once you've scheduled an exam, you must call 24 hours before the scheduled time if you wish to cancel or reschedule.

How the Exams Work

You take the exams at a local Sylvan Prometric testing center. The tests are administered by computer. Most of the answers are multiple choice, but many are complex and include detailed scenarios and diagrams. Some of the newer exams include simulation questions, requiring you to perform a task with a simulated utility.

You are given a set time limit for the test (usually 1.5 hours) and must answer a number of questions (between 40 and 100). You can mark questions to return to later if you're not sure of the answers, with the exception of the simulation questions.

When you complete the exam, you are shown a review screen allowing you to examine and change your answers for any of the questions. When you are finished, you are given a passing or failing score. Each exam has its own pass/fail percentage between 60% and 85%.

The questions generally fall into four categories, described below.

Single Answer

These are basic multiple-choice questions requiring a single answer, and are generally the easiest. Here is an example:

How many nodes can be used on a single segment in an Ethernet 10Base2 network?

a. 1

b. 32

c. 30

d. 90

Answer: C

These questions often address facts and figures included in the exam objectives. While these are relatively easy questions, many of them are worded to be confusing or to encourage jumping to conclusions. Be sure to read the questions carefully and double-check your answer.

Multiple Answer

These are multiple-choice questions where one or more of the answers is correct, and you must choose all that apply. The following is an example:

Which network connectivity devices operate at the physical layer of the OSI model? (select all that apply)

a. Hubs

b. Routers

c. Transceivers

d. Repeaters

Answer: **A, C, D**

These questions can be tricky. While they often address the same type of definitions and facts as the simpler questions, the multiple answers increase the possibility of mistakes. In addition, these questions often describe a network and ask you to answer questions based on its configuration.

Rather than look for one or more obvious answers to these questions, you may find it useful to consider them a series of true/false questions, and evaluate each of the possible choices separately. Otherwise, it's easy to overlook a correct answer.

Be sure to read these questions carefully. Many of them explicitly state the number of correct answers, such as "Check the 3 items that apply." If you mark the incorrect number of items, the question is considered incorrect.

Scenario

These questions present a scenario about a need or problem, and the steps taken to resolve it. You have to determine whether the solution meets the main result or the optional results. Here is a sample of this type of question:

You are installing a network in a training room, to be used temporarily for a period of 30 days. You must connect 10 workstations running Windows NT Workstation and 2 servers running Windows NT Server.

Required result: The network must have a transmission speed of 10 Mbps or higher.

Optional result: The network should be inexpensive.

Optional result: The network should be easy to install.

Solution: Install 10Base2 Ethernet in a bus topology.

Answer:

a. The solution meets the required result and both of the optional results.

b. The solution meets the required result and only one of the optional results.

c. The solution meets the required result only.

d. The solution does not meet the required result.

Correct Answer: **A**

These are the most complex questions, and can be difficult. They present a complex scenario which you will need to analyze and understand before you answer the question.

As with the previous type of question, these are best regarded as a series of true/false questions. Analyze the scenario and the proposed solution, then compare the required result and the optional results to see which ones are satisfied.

Be sure to double-check your answers to these questions—not only to check your work, but to ensure that you've selected the choice that matches the appropriate set of results.

It is also helpful to look for key phrases in these questions. For example, the question above mentions that the network is temporary, and one of Ethernet 10base2's strong points is that it can be quickly set up and taken down. The 10 Mbps transmission speed mentioned in the required result is also an indication that Ethernet is the correct choice.

Most of these questions come in sets of two or more questions using the same scenario and different proposed solutions. You may find it helpful to examine all of the questions for a scenario before answering them.

Simulation

Some of the newest exams include simulation questions. These provide a simulated version of a utility, and require you to perform a task (for example: create a user or copy a file). Simpler simulations show a dialog from a utility and ask you to click the appropriate button for a particular function.

These questions should be easy if you are experienced with the exam's subjects. You cannot mark these questions to return to them later, so be careful to perform the task correctly the first time.

Test-Taking Tips

It's best to study and prepare for one test at a time. Schedule the test on a day when you won't be under stress due to your job or other factors, and give yourself plenty of time to study for the test. Rest well the night before, and review your test preparation materials (such as this book) one last time before taking the test.

Use test preparation software, or have someone ask you questions, to be sure you're prepared for the test. Don't be satisfied if you merely know 95% of the topics the exam covers. As few as 5–10 incorrect answers can lead to a failing score, and you will make mistakes.

Since the MCSE exams are timed, pacing is important for success. The testing program includes Forward and Back buttons to review the questions and change your answers if necessary; in addition, you can check a box to highlight a question for later review.

Using these tools, a good strategy is to first review all of the questions, answering those you are sure of. Then take a second pass through the questions, answering all you can. Mark the questions that you may be able to answer with more time.

The exam scoring process does not deduct points for wrong answers, so it's beneficial to guess rather than leaving an answer blank. You can usually eliminate some of the choices to make your guess more educated. Be aware of the time limit and set aside the last 5–10 minutes to double check your answers and guess if necessary.

Don't let the scenario questions take too much of your time: remember, they count for the same score as the other types of questions. You may wish to mark these and come back to them later.

You may not bring any material (papers, calculators, books, etc.) into the exam room with you. However, you are allowed to use the Windows Calculator program for some exams. You are also provided with a writing surface (usually a dry-erase board, but pencil and paper are available upon request). If you have memorized critical items for the test, it may be helpful to write these down when you enter the testing room for reference during the exam.

If you should fail a test, ask the test administrator for a detailed report. This lists the topics of the questions you missed, and will be useful for further study. In addition, write down the questions you remember having trouble with so you can study those areas more carefully.

Continuing Education

To maintain your MCSE certification, you must continue to meet the MCSE requirements as they are updated by Microsoft. Existing exams are often retired or replaced with new versions, and exams for new products are added.

Retired Exams

Microsoft usually retires (discontinues) an exam when the product it refers to becomes obsolete, or is replaced by a new version. For example, the Windows NT 3.51 exams are scheduled to be retired when Windows NT 5.0 is released.

When one of the exams you took for the MCSE is retired, you are given time (usually six months to a year) to take a new exam to keep your certification. This can be the exam for a new version of the same product, or another exam in the same category (i.e., elective exam).

When you need to take the new version of an exam to replace a retired exam, Microsoft usually offers a 50% discount if you take the new exam within 6 months.

New Exams

Microsoft periodically releases new exams. These may cover new products, or new versions of old products. Microsoft may require that new exams be taken for MCSEs to retain their certification status.

If you take a new version of an exam you passed the previous version of within three months after it is released, you are given a 50% discount on the price.

Beta Exams

When a new exam is first developed, it is offered as a beta exam. These exams are available for 50% of the normal price. They include a large list of questions; after the beta period, most of these questions will be compiled into the real exams.

You receive credit for passing a beta exam, but you don't receive the results immediately; they are sent to you by mail after the beta period ends. Microsoft uses the results to develop the scoring to be used in the final version of the exam.

PART 1

Internetworking with TCP/IP

Exam Overview

The TCP/IP protocol suite is a set of standards, most initially developed for UNIX systems, that form the foundation of the Internet. These standards were designed to be platform-independent, and allow for easy networking between Windows NT, UNIX, NetWare, and other systems.

Microsoft's MCSE Exam 70-059, *Internetworking with Microsoft TCP/IP on Microsoft Windows NT 4.0*, covers TCP/IP in general, and the Windows NT implementation of TCP/IP in particular. If you're familiar with TCP/IP from the UNIX world, be aware that this test tends to focus on many of the Microsoft-specific aspects of TCP/IP—WINS, NetBIOS over TCP/IP, and the various Windows NT utilities.

The TCP/IP exam is one of the most popular MCSE elective exams due to its obvious application to the Internet. It is generally considered one of the more difficult exams, probably because of the complexity of IP addressing, subnet masking, and the various protocols. Along with the facts outlined in this chapter, you should have some experience planning, configuring, using, and trouble-shooting all aspects of TCP/IP under Windows NT to pass the exam.

In order to prepare for this chapter and the TCP/IP exam, you should have studied for and passed the Network Essentials, Windows NT Server, and Windows NT Server in the Enterprise exams, all of which are covered in *MCSE: the Core Exams in a Nutshell*. You should understand network browsing, Windows NT domains, domain synchronization, and RAS (remote access services).

Objectives

Need to Know	Reference
TCP/IP services and their functions	"Installing TCP/IP Services" on page 23

Need to Know	*Reference*
Layers of the DOD Reference model and their associated protocols	"TCP/IP Protocols" on page 24
IP addressing basics and address classes	"IP Addressing" on page 27
How subnetting and supernetting work	"Subnet Masking" on page 28
Various name resolution methods, including NetBIOS methods	"Name Resolution" on page 40
Differences between Static and Dynamic routing	"IP Routing" on page 50
SNMP components and terms	"Simple Network Management Protocol (SNMP)" on page 55
Functions of command-line utilities	"Command-Line Utilities" on page 58

Need to Apply	*Reference*
Install TCP/IP on Windows NT computers.	"Installing and Configuring TCP/IP" on page 20
Choose an appropriate subnet mask for a network.	"Subnet Masking" on page 28
Calculate the ranges of IP addresses for subnets.	"Subnet Masking" on page 28
Configure DHCP Scopes.	"Dynamic Host Configuration Protocol (DHCP)" on page 34
Create a HOSTS file for a server.	"The HOSTS File" on page 40
Install and configure a DNS server using Windows NT.	"Domain Name Service (DNS)" on page 40
Configure and maintain WINS servers.	"Windows Internet Name Service (WINS)" on page 44
Configure replication for WINS servers.	"WINS Replication" on page 47
Create an LMHOSTS file for NetBIOS resolution.	"The LMHOSTS File" on page 49
Configure Windows NT to act as a static or dynamic IP router.	"Configuring IP Routing" on page 53
Configure support for IP printing.	"IP and UNIX Printing" on page 53
Install, configure, and use SNMP	"Simple Network Management Protocol (SNMP)" on page 55
Monitor IP counters with Performance Monitor	"Performance Monitor" on page 57

Study Guide

This chapter includes the following sections, which address various topics covered on the TCP/IP MCSE exam:

TCP/IP Basics

Introduces the TCP/IP protocol suite and describes how to install TCP/IP and related services on a Windows NT computer.

TCP/IP Protocols

Describes the four layers of the DOD model, and the TCP/IP protocols and services that operate at each layer.

IP Addressing

Describes the IP addressing specifications, the classes of IP addresses, and protocols that translate between IP addresses and hardware addresses.

Dynamic Host Configuration Protocol (DHCP)

Introduces DHCP, a protocol which maintains a pool of available IP addresses and dynamically allocates them to clients.

Name Resolution

Discusses the name resolution processes for NetBIOS names and Internet-standard IP host names.

IP Routing

Describes static and dynamic IP routing and the protocols involved, and explains how to install these features under Windows NT.

IP and UNIX Printing

Describes Windows NT's support for UNIX-standard printing protocols, which can be used to send jobs to UNIX printers, or accept jobs from UNIX clients.

Simple Network Management Protocol (SNMP)

Describes SNMP, a versatile client-server protocol for network management, troubleshooting, and monitoring.

Optimization and Troubleshooting
    Introduces a variety of command-line protocols useful in diagnosing prob-
    lems with TCP/IP networking, and describes Windows NT utilities for
    monitoring and optimizing TCP/IP communications.

TCP/IP Basics

The TCP/IP protocol suite is named for two of its most important protocols: TCP
(Transport Control Protocol) and IP (Internet Protocol). The other protocols in the
TCP/IP suite include many of the protocols used on the Internet.

TCP/IP is the default network protocol for UNIX systems, and is becoming popular
as a protocol for Windows NT and NetWare networks, including those uncon-
nected to the Internet or UNIX servers.

Most of the TCP/IP protocols were created by the Internet Activities Board (IAB),
which consists of two task forces: the IETF (Internet Engineering Task Force) and
the IRTF (Internet Research Task Force). Most Internet protocols begin their lives
as RFCs, or Request for Comments. These documents are created to propose new
protocols or standards.

RFCs that have become standards are still referred to with an RFC number. RFC
numbers are mentioned here for many of the protocols described in this chapter.
The full text of RFCs is available from this URL:

   http://www.internic.net/ds/rfc-index.html

On the Exam

You do not need to know exact RFC numbers for the TCP/IP MCSE exam,
but you should be familiar with the RFC process and be aware of which
protocols are Internet standards.

Installing and Configuring TCP/IP

The installation process for Microsoft TCP/IP is the same for NT Workstation or NT
Server. To install TCP/IP, select the Protocols tab in the Network control panel.
Select *Add* and specify *TCP/IP Protocol.*

The TCP/IP Properties dialog, shown in Figure 1-1, contains options that are used
to configure various aspects of TCP/IP. The dialog is divided into five property
sheets. The properties in each sheet are described briefly in the sections below as
a general reference; more detailed descriptions for these settings and the subjects
they refer to can be found throughout the remainder of this chapter.

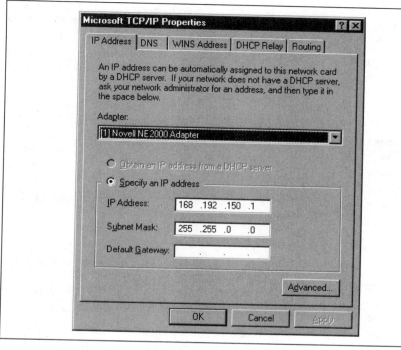

Figure 1-1: The TCP/IP Properties dialog

IP Address

The options listed here relate to IP addressing, described in the "IP Addressing" section of this chapter.

Adapter

Choose a network interface to set TCP/IP options for.

Obtain an IP address from a DHCP server

If selected, communicates with a DHCP (Dynamic Host Configuration Protocol) server to obtain the remaining information in this category.

Specify an IP address

If selected, the items below should be manually specified.

IP Address

The IP address assigned to the selected adapter.

Subnet Mask

The subnet mask corresponding to the IP address.

Default Gateway

The IP address of the default gateway (router).

DNS

The options listed here relate to DNS (Domain Name Service), described in the "Name Resolution" section of this chapter.

Host Name (optional)
  The host name to be used for DNS. If unspecified, the Windows NT computer name is used.

Domain (optional)
  The DNS domain name the computer belongs to.

DNS Server Search Order
  A list of IP addresses for DNS servers that the computer's name can be resolved by.

Domain Suffix Search Order
  A list of domain suffixes that can be added to a local computer name to form fully qualified DNS domain names.

WINS Address

The options in this category relate to WINS (Windows Internet Name Service), described in the "Name Resolution" section of this chapter.

Adapter
  Choose the network interface card that the following options apply to.

Primary WINS Server
  The IP address of the first WINS server to search when resolving a NetBIOS name.

Secondary WINS Server
  The server specified here by IP address is searched if a name is not resolved by the primary WINS server.

Enable DNS for Windows Resolution
  If selected, names the WINS server is unable to resolve are passed to a configured DNS server.

Enable LMHOSTS Lookup
  If selected, the LMHOSTS file is used to look up names not found by the WINS server.

Import LMHOSTS
  Specifies the location of the LMHOSTS file for the above option.

Scope ID
  Specifies an optional NetBIOS scope ID for the local computer.

DHCP Relay

The options here relate to DHCP routing and the DHCP Relay Agent, described in the "Dynamic Host Configuration Protocol (DHCP)" section of this chapter.

Seconds threshold
  Specifies the timeout before a DHCP request that has not been answered will be rejected.

Maximum hops

Specifies the maximum number of network hops a DHCP request can travel before being discarded.

DHCP Servers

Specify DHCP servers to forward requests to. Servers will be tried in order until a response is received.

Routing

The single option in this category is described in the "IP Routing" section of this chapter.

Enable IP Forwarding

Enables IP routing. This specifies static routing by default, or dynamic routing if the RIP for Internet Protocol service is installed.

Installing TCP/IP Services

Along with the TCP/IP protocol suite itself, Windows NT includes a variety of services that provide additional functions for a TCP/IP network. Most of these services are specific to Windows NT Server.

Select the *Add* option in the Services tab of the Network control panel to install TCP/IP services. The services included with Windows NT Server are listed in Table 1-1. These services are described in the remainder of this chapter.

Table 1-1: TCP/IP Services

Service	Description
Microsoft DHCP Server	Supports Dynamic Host Configuration Protocol, which dynamically allocates IP addresses to clients.
DHCP Relay Agent	Allows routing of DHCP data
Microsoft DNS Server	Supports Domain Name Service (DNS), which translates IP host names to IP addresses
Microsoft TCP/IP Printing	Supports printing to UNIX and TCP/IP printers
RIP for Internet Protocol	Supports dynamic routing with RIP (Router Information Protocol)
SNMP Service	Supports network management and monitoring via Simple Network Management Protocol
Windows Internet Name Service (WINS)	Translates NetBIOS names to IP addresses

---

On the Exam

Microsoft Windows NT Server 4.0 also includes version 2.0 of Internet Information Server (IIS), which provides FTP, World Wide Web, and Gopher services for Internet and Intranet use. IIS is the topic of its own MCSE exam, and is covered in Part 2, *Internet Information Server 4.0.*

TCP/IP Protocols

The TCP/IP protocol suite includes a wide variety of protocols that are in common use on the Internet, and are also supported by Windows NT. These include its namesake protocols, TCP (Transmission Control Protocol) and IP (Internet Protocol).

The various protocols that comprise the TCP/IP suite are organized according to the DOD (U.S. Department of Defense) reference model. The DOD model is similar to the 7-layer OSI (Open Systems Interconnect) model typically used with Windows NT, but condenses the process into four layers. Figure 1-2 shows how the DOD model layers correspond to OSI layers.

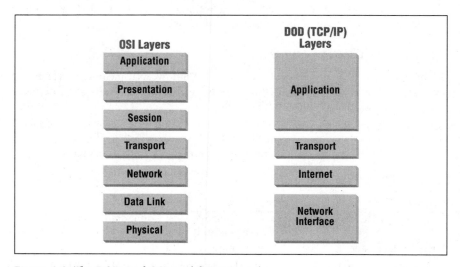

Figure 1-2: The DOD and OSI models compared

The four layers of the DOD model are Network Interface, Internet, Transport, and Application. The following sections describe each layer and give descriptions of the major protocols that act at each layer.

The Network Interface Layer

The Network Interface layer is responsible for the physical transmission of data. This layer includes protocols that deal with the specific networking topologies and media used in the network. Table 1-2 describes some common network interface layer protocols.

Table 1-2: Common Network Interface Layer Protocols

Protocol	Network Type
Ethernet	LANs using coaxial or twisted-pair cable
Token Ring	LANs using coaxial or fiber-optic cable

Table 1-2: Common Network Interface Layer Protocols (continued)

Protocol	Network Type
FDDI	LANS using high-speed fiber-optic cable
PPP (Point-to-Point Protocol)	Dial-up Internet connections
X.25	Dedicated WAN connections
Frame Relay	Dedicated WAN connections

The Internet Layer

The Internet layer deals with communication between networks (routing), and also provides a common interface for upper-layer protocols. This layer includes IP (Internet Protocol) and a variety of other protocols for network communication and routing. The protocols in this layer are described in the following sections.

On the Exam

The Internet layer also includes the routing protocols, RIP and OSPF. These are described in detail in "Dynamic Routing," later in this chapter.

IP (Internet Protocol)

IP, described in RFC 791, is the most important protocol in the Internet layer. IP collects segments of data from the higher-layer protocols (TCP or UDP) and combines them into packets, or *datagrams*.

IP datagrams include *IP addresses* to identify the originating host and the destination host. IP addresses provide a software addressing scheme that simplifies network routing.

ARP (Address Resolution Protocol)

The ARP protocol, defined in RFC 826, translates IP addresses into hardware (MAC) addresses. A complementary protocol, RARP (Reverse Address Resolution Protocol), translates hardware addresses to IP addresses. Both of these protocols are explained in detail later in this chapter.

DHCP (Dynamic Host Configuration Protocol)

DHCP is a client-server protocol that dynamically allocates IP addresses. A DHCP server maintains a pool of available IP addresses; clients request an address when they boot. DHCP is explained in detail later in this chapter.

ICMP and IGMP

ICMP (Internet Control Message Protocol) is a simple protocol used mainly for diagnostic purposes on IP networks. ICMP is defined in RFC 792. A typical use of ICMP is the ping command, described later in this chapter. This command sends an ICMP message called an Echo Request to a server to determine if it is functioning. The server, if available, responds with an Echo Reply message.

IGMP (Internet Group Management Protocol) is a similar protocol, but its messages refer to groups of nodes rather than individual nodes. IGMP is used by routers for *multicasting*, or broadcasting to multiple nodes.

The Transport Layer

The Transport layer, also called the host-to-host layer, provides a layer of abstraction in communication between hosts, and provides applications with a consistent interface independent of hardware and routing. The two host-to-host layer protocols, TCP and UDP, are explained in the sections below.

TCP (Transmission Control Protocol)

TCP is defined in RFC 793. TCP is a connection-oriented protocol: before any data is sent, a connection, or *virtual circuit*, is established between the originating host and the destination.

TCP accepts blocks of data from an application at the process/application layer, and breaks the data down into segments, which are sequenced for later reassembly. These packets are then processed by IP and sent over the network. The TCP protocol at the receiving end reassembles the segments into their original form for use by the application.

TCP is reliable, and is considered a *full-duplex* protocol: after each segment is sent, the receiving end's TCP protocol returns a handshake, or acknowledgment. If the acknowledgment is negative, the segment is re-sent. The price for reliability is high bandwidth, and a significant processing overhead.

UDP (User Datagram Protocol)

UDP is defined by RFC 768. UDP is a connectionless protocol: no virtual circuit is established between the source and destination. The destination does not know that UDP data is coming until the first segment arrives.

As with TCP, UDP accepts large blocks of data from the process/application layer and breaks them into segments. Segments are sequenced for later reassembly, but are not necessarily sent in the proper sequence, or even all over the same route.

UDP provides no handshaking, and is thus considered an unreliable protocol. However, it has a very low overhead in network bandwidth and processing, and is ideal for situations where speed is crucial and occasional errors are tolerable (such as streaming audio).

On the Exam

Although reliability and virtual circuits are separate criteria, some exam questions may be based on the assumption that connection-oriented protocols are reliable and connectionless protocols are unreliable.

The Application Layer

The Application layer includes protocols that do actual work for users. Because the complexities of the network are handled by the other layers, these protocols are generally platform-independent. Most of these protocols require server software on one machine and client software on another. The following are common Application layer protocols and services:

Telnet
> Emulates a terminal and allows you to access a host machine. UNIX machines typically support this service.

FTP (File Transfer Protocol)
> Allows for two-way file transfer between network nodes.

TFTP (Trivial File Transfer Protocol)
> A simpler (and less widely supported) file transfer protocol.

HTTP (Hypertext Transfer Protocol)
> A simple protocol used by the World Wide Web to transfer documents and files from a server to clients. Most web documents are in the HTML (Hypertext Markup Language) format.

NFS (Network File System)
> Allows file systems on remote machines to be accessed as local drives. This is similar to the drive mapping feature on Windows NT networks.

SMTP (Simple Mail Transport Protocol)
> Allows transfer of email between computers and networks.

NNTP (Netnews Transfer Protocol)
> Transmits messages for USENET news discussion groups.

SNMP (Simple Network Management Protocol)
> Allows for statistical analysis and troubleshooting on a TCP/IP network. SNMP is supported by Windows NT, and is described in detail later in this chapter.

IP Addressing

TCP/IP packets identify their destination with an IP address. The IP addressing scheme in use today was originally defined by the IETF in RFC 791.

An IP address is a 32-bit number that uniquely identifies a machine in the internetwork. The address is divided into four bytes, or *octets*. IP addresses are usually represented in dotted decimal format, such as 128.110.121.6. However, addresses often make more sense in binary format.

An IP address is actually composed of two addresses: a network address and a host address. The location of the boundary between these addresses depends on the network class, explained below. All machines on a particular network have the same network address, and must have unique host addresses.

Classes of IP Addresses

The original IETF standard defined five IP address classes, lettered A through E. Only classes A, B, and C are in wide use today, and these are the only classes supported by Microsoft's TCP/IP implementation. The main difference between the three supported classes is the number of bytes used for the host and network addresses, as described in Table 1-3.

Table 1-3: Classes of IP Addresses

Class	Network/ Host Bytes	Number of Networks	Number of Hosts per Network
A	1/3	126	16,777,214
B	2/2	16,382	65,534
C	3/1	2,097,150	254

The three classes were designed to accommodate a wide range of networks, ranging from a small number of networks with large numbers of hosts (Class A) to a large number of networks with small numbers of hosts (Class C).

Network addresses are usually referred to with full four-byte IP addresses. For example, in the class C network address 209.68.11.152, the entire network is referred to as 209.68.11.0, and the host is referred to as 209.68.11.152.

The actual number of hosts and networks for each class is limited by the fact that each class is assigned a specific leading bit pattern, and thus a range of decimal addresses for the first byte. Table 1-4 lists the ranges and corresponding leading bit patterns for each class.

Table 1-4: IP Address Class Ranges

Class	Leading Bits	First Byte Range
A	0	1–126
B	10	128–191
C	110	192–223

On the Exam

For the TCP/IP MCSE test, you should be able to recognize the class of an IP address by looking at its first byte; you should memorize the values in Table 1-4. You should also be able to divide an address into its host and network addresses based on its class.

Subnet Masking

You can add flexibility to the host/network addressing scheme by using *subnet masking*. This technique steals two or more bits from the host address, and uses

---

these bits to divide the network into smaller networks, or subnets. These subnets can communicate via a router.

The subnet mask itself is, like the IP address, a 32-bit number. This number is applied to the binary IP address with a logical AND operation to determine the network address. In simpler terms, bits set to 1 in the subnet mask indicate the network address, and bits set to 0 indicate the host address.

When you have not divided the network into subnets, the default subnet mask for the class is used. The default subnet masks are shown in Table 1-5.

Table 1-5: Default Subnet Masks

Class	Default Subnet Mask
A	255.0.0.0
B	255.255.0.0
C	255.255.255.0

To divide the network into subnets, you can dedicate two or more bits to the subnet address by adding corresponding bits set to 1 to the subnet mask. The number of subnets available is 2^n-2, where n is the number of bits used for the subnet address. It is necessary to subtract 2 because the binary subnet address cannot be all ones or all zeros.

Depending on the number of subnets you have allocated, a different number of host addresses is available; the maximum number of hosts decreases as you increase the number of subnets. The maximum number of hosts is $2^{(x-n)}-2$, where x is the total number of available bits for subnet and host addresses: 24 for Class A, 16 for Class B, or 8 for Class C. The subnet masks available for all three classes of network are illustrated in Table 1-6.

On the Exam

For the TCP/IP MCSE exam, you will be expected to know the number of available subnets and available hosts for a particular subnet mask, and thus determine the appropriate subnet mask to use for a given need. You can calculate this using the formulas above and the techniques in the next section.

Table 1-6: Class A, B, and C Subnet Masks

Subnet Address Bits	Mask Ends With	Address Block	Subnets	Class C Hosts	Class B Hosts	Class A Hosts
2	192	64	2	62	16,382	4,194,302
3	224	32	6	30	8190	2,097,150
4	240	16	14	14	4094	1,048,574
5	248	8	30	6	2046	524,286

Table 1-6: Class A, B, and C Subnet Masks (continued)

Subnet Address Bits	Mask Ends With	Address Block	Subnets	Class C Hosts	Class B Hosts	Class A Hosts
6	252	4	62	2	1022	262,142
7	254	2	126	(Invalid)	510	131,070
8	255	1	254	(Invalid)	254	65,534

You cannot use more than 6 bits for the subnet address in a Class C network, because you would be left with no available host addresses.

Techniques for Subnetting

While you should now have an understanding of the subnetting process and the reasons for doing so, you should also understand the process of implementing subnets. The following procedure describes a technique for determining a subnet mask and calculating the IP address ranges to be used for clients.

On the Exam

The following instructions refer to the information in Table 1-6. Rather than memorizing this table for the TCP/IP exam, consult the *Suggested Exercises* section for instructions on recreating it on paper. The instructions also include alternatives that do not use the table.

---

1. Based on the number of physical network segments, determine the subnet mask to use. For example, suppose you are dividing a Class C network into 5 segments, with 20 nodes on each segment. Based on Table 1-6, a subnet mask of 255.255.255.224 would allow for 6 subnets with 30 hosts. This value can also be calculated without the table:

    a. Convert the number of physical segments to binary. In this example, 5 becomes 101. Since this number requires three bits, you will need three bits for the subnet mask.

    b. Form an 8-bit binary octet by placing bits set to 1 in the number of positions you calculated above, and adding bits set to zero to complete the octet. In this example, the result would be 11100000.

    c. Convert the result to decimal; this is the last octet of the subnet mask. Since the example is a Class C network, the mask is 255.255.255.224.

    d. To calculate the number of subnets available (which may be greater than the number you needed) use the formula 2^n-2, where n is the number of subnet mask bits; in this example, the number is 2^3-2, or 6. The formula for the number of Class C hosts is $2^{(8-n)}$-2; in this example, 2^5-2, or 30.

2. Each of the subnets will have its own range of IP addresses. To calculate these, use the value in the Address Block column of the table. In our

example, the value is 32, and the base address for the first subnet would end in 32 (for class B or C, 32.0 or 32.0.0). To calculate this value without the table, follow these steps:

    a. Using zeros for the first bits and one for the last, write down the lowest value for the number of subnet mask digits; for this example, 001.

    b. Add zeros to fill in the 8-bit octet. For this example, 00100000. Convert this number to decimal, giving the interval (in the example, 32).

3. Add the Address Block value to form subsequent addresses until you have one for each subnet. Since there are six subnets in the example, the last octet of the base addresses would be 32, 64, 96, 128, 160, and 192.

4. The range of IP addresses for clients in each subnet begins with the base address, and ends with the next base address minus one. In our example, the first range would be 32 to 63, but since this is a Class C address and a network address of all binary ones or zeros is not allowed, the first range is 33 to 62, the second is 65 to 94, and so on.

How Subnets Work

Clients use the subnet mask value to determine whether to send packets to a router for machines on different subnets, or directly to the destination for machines on the same subnet. This is done with a binary AND function.

A binary AND is performed by comparing each of the bits in two values. If both values are 1, the result is 1; if the values are 0, or if they differ, the result is 0. The client first performs an AND with its own IP address and the subnet mask. Using the example above, the calculation for a client with IP address 192.168.0.33 is shown in Table 1-7.

Table 1-7: AND Calculation

Description	IP Address	Binary Address
My address	192.168.0.33	11000000.10101000.00000000.00100001
Subnet mask	255.255.255.224	11111111.11111111.11111111.11100000
AND result	192.168.0.32	11000000.10101000.00000000.00100000

The result is the base address for the subnet's range of IP addresses. The client then performs the same operation with the destination address; if the result is the same, the machines are on the same subnet. If the result is different, the machines are on different subnets, and the resulting base address is used to route the packets.

Supernetting

Occasionally you may require the opposite of subnetting. For example, you may have three class C networks, and wish to address them as one large network. This can be accomplished using a process called *supernetting*.

To use supernetting, you steal bits from the last network address octet and use them as part of the host address. For example, the default Class C subnet mask is

255.255.255.0. To support three Class C addresses, you will need two extra bits, so the subnet mask to use is 255.255.252.0.

To calculate a mask for supernetting, AND the values of the last network address octets. For example, suppose our three Class C addresses are 132.124.4.0, 132.24.5.0, and 132.24.6.0. The last network address octets are 4, 5, and 6, or in binary 100, 101, and 110.

An AND operation with these three values results in 100. Use these three bits as the last bits of the subnet mask network address octet, with the remaining bits set to 1. In this example, the octet would be 11111100. In decimal this is 252, so the subnet mask is 255.255.252.0.

Supernetting only works if the addresses are consecutive and fall in the correct range; be sure the addresses are assigned specifically for this purpose. If the AND technique described above results in all ones, supernetting cannot be used. Also, this technique only works if the routers support supernetting.

Many of the routers used in today's Internet backbones use CIDR (Classless Inter-Domain Routing), a system that uses a supernetting technique to treat groups of IP addresses assigned to the same organization as the same network.

On the Exam

Supernetting is not stressed on the TCP/IP exam, but you should understand how to calculate a supernet mask and understand that a group of consecutive IP addresses are required.

Reserved IP Addresses

As mentioned above, certain addresses and ranges are not available for use. These values are reserved for various purposes, as described in Table 1-8.

Table 1-8: Reserved TCP/IP Addresses

Reserved Address	Description
0.0.0.0	Reserved for use by the RIP protocol
127.0.0.1	Loopback—packets are sent back to the local machine without using the network
255.255.255.255	Broadcasts to all nodes on the network
Network address all 0s	Refers to "this network only"
Network address all 1s	Broadcast (all networks)
All zeros in node address	Refers to "this node"
All ones in node address	Broadcast (all nodes)
First bytes 224-239	Multicasting addresses (Class D)
First bytes 240-254	Reserved for future use (Class E)

IP Address Assignments

If your network is not connected to the Internet or is hidden from the Internet by a firewall or proxy server, you can assign IP addresses in any way you see fit; in fact, you can even break the class addressing rules given above, although doing so can cause problems with routing.

If your network is directly connected to the Internet, you must obtain a registered IP network address from InterNIC (the Internet Network Information Center), the agency that assigns IP addresses and domain names. Further information about registration is available at this URL:

http://www.internic.net/

With the exploding popularity of the Internet, it is now virtually impossible to obtain a Class A or Class B address, and Class C addresses are becoming scarce. Because of this, InterNIC is now rather strict about issuing addresses.

For small company networks with Internet connectivity, one alternative is to connect to the Internet through an ISP (Internet Service Provider). The ISP may allocate you a small block of IP addresses, or may assign them dynamically as machines on your network connect to the Internet.

Address Resolution Protocol (ARP)

The ARP protocol is used to translate IP addresses into hardware (MAC) addresses. The ARP protocol is defined in RFC 826. The translation process is called *IP address resolution.*

How ARP Works

ARP is handled by default as part of Microsoft TCP/IP, and no additional server software is necessary. The ARP process is simple:

1. Each host has a local ARP cache. The IP address is first searched for in that cache. If found, no network communication is necessary.

2. If the destination IP address is on the local subnet, the client sends an ARP packet as a broadcast to the local network to resolve the address.

3. If the address is not local, the route table is checked for a path to the remote subnet. If found, the hardware address of the default gateway is retrieved from the ARP cache.

4. If the remote gateway is not listed in the cache, an ARP broadcast is sent asking for the hardware address of the gateway.

5. Any machine that recognizes the IP address sent in the ARP packet as its own sends a reply directly to the client specifying its hardware address.

6. Once the reply is received, the IP address and hardware address are added to the local ARP cache. The TTL (time to live) of objects in this cache is two minutes by default in NT Server. If the same IP address is resolved a second time, the TTL is increased to ten minutes.

You can exert some control over the local ARP cache using the **arp** command-line utility, described at the end of this chapter.

Reverse ARP (RARP) uses a similar process to resolve hardware addresses to their corresponding IP addresses. Since the hardware address is known, reverse ARP requests are sent directly to the destination rather than as a broadcast.

On the Exam

You should know the purpose of the ARP and RARP protocols for the TCP/IP MCSE exam. You should not need to know the exact steps involved in ARP resolution.

Dynamic Host Configuration Protocol (DHCP)

DHCP (Dynamic Host Configuration Protocol) provides an alternative to manually assigning IP addresses to computers. DHCP automatically assigns, or *leases*, IP addresses to hosts from a centrally managed pool. Windows NT fully supports this standard, and NT hosts can be configured to act as DHCP servers or clients.

In the Real World

DHCP is an extension of the BootP protocol defined in RFC 951, and is itself described in RFCs 1531, 1533, 1534, 1541, and 1542.

DHCP provides obvious advantages over manual address assignment: there is less administrative hassle, and new machines can be added to the network without assigning dedicated IP addresses. In situations where all machines on the network are not used at once, DHCP allows a small pool of addresses to serve a larger number of machines.

Along with IP addresses, DHCP can be configured to send the appropriate DNS and WINS server addresses and default gateway addresses to Windows NT clients. This greatly simplifies the process of adding a new client.

DHCP is simple to install and practical for use in all but the smallest networks. Its disadvantages include the necessity of managing the address pool, the potential for conflicts between DHCP-assigned and manually-assigned addresses, and the lack of a consistent address needed for some client applications. (Addresses can be reserved for specific clients, as described below.)

On the Exam

As an extension of the BootP protocol, DHCP requests are not passed through a router unless it has been specifically configured to forward them. The DHCP Relay service, described in this section, provides an alternative for routers without BootP forwarding.

How DHCP Works

DHCP clients and servers communicate with various messages, defined by RFC 1531. Communication is via UDP, and uses ports 67 and 68. When a DHCP client initializes, the following process occurs:

1. The client broadcasts a DHCPDISCOVER message, requesting an IP address lease from any DHCP server. This message includes the client's MAC address and NetBIOS name. If there is no response to the discover message, it is rebroadcast at intervals until a response is received.

2. Any DHCP servers that receive the message respond with DHCPOFFER messages. These messages include the DHCP server's IP address, an available IP address, its corresponding subnet mask, and the lease's duration in hours. DHCP servers reserve the offered addresses for a period of time and await a request.

3. The client selects one of the offered leases (in NT, always the first one offered) and sends the server a DHCPREQUEST message, which includes the client's MAC address, the offered IP address, and the server's IP address.

4. The DHCP server responds to the request by broadcasting a DHCPACK (acknowledgment) message if the requested address is still available. In this case, the client is now ready to access the network, and the DHCP server marks the address as unavailable to other clients. If the address is no longer available, the server sends a DHCPNAK (negative acknowledgment) message, and the client begins the process again with a DHCPDISCOVER message.

5. After 50 percent of the IP address lease duration given in the offer message has expired, the client attempts to renew the lease by sending another DHCPREQUEST message directly to the DHCP server. If there is no response, the renewal request is rebroadcast after 87.5 percent of the lease has expired, and any available server can respond.

6. If the address is still available, the DHCP server responds with DHCPACK, and a new lease period begins. If the address has become unavailable, the server responds with DHCPNAK; in this case, the client restarts the discovery process after the lease period expires.

The DHCP server releases an IP address, making it available to other clients, when the lease duration expires without a renewal, when a renewal request is denied, or when the client sends a DHCPRELEASE message.

On the Exam

For the TCP/IP MCSE exam, you should be familiar with the basics of the DHCP process and the functions of a DHCP server. You should not need to know the exact steps involved or the message names.

Windows NT clients store their assigned IP addresses in the registry; other clients use a file for the purpose. When the client reinitializes, it first attempts to request the address stored from a previous session.

Configuring a DHCP Server

The DHCP Server service is included with Windows NT Server, but is not installed by default. To install it, open the Network control panel, select the Services tab, press the Add button, and select *Microsoft DHCP Server.*

The machine you use as a DHCP server cannot be a DHCP client; its IP address, subnet mask, and default gateway must be configured manually.

When you install the DHCP Server service, the DHCP Manager utility is added to the Administrative Tools menu. This utility allows you to manage DHCP options and create and modify *scopes*, or pools of available IP addresses.

Creating a Scope

You must define at least one scope for each DHCP server. To define a scope, choose *Create* from the Scope menu in DHCP Manager. The Create Scope dialog is shown in Figure 1-3.

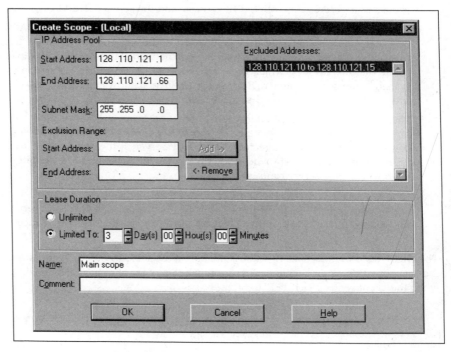

Figure 1-3: The Create Scope dialog

Enter the following information to create a scope:

Start Address and End Address

      Specify the range of addresses to be assigned by this server. This range should not conflict with any manually configured addresses, or with ranges on any other DHCP servers.

Subnet Mask

Specify the subnet mask corresponding to the address range. This subnet mask will be sent to the client along with an IP address.

Excluded Addresses

Add ranges or individual addresses to this list to exclude them from the scope. These addresses will never be offered by the DHCP server. If an address within the range is used by a DHCP, DNS, or other server that requires a consistent address, it should be excluded here and assigned manually.

Lease Duration

Choose *Unlimited* for infinite-length leases, or specify a lease duration for the addresses in the scope. The default is 3 days.

Name and Comment

Specify a name to identify the scope, and optionally an additional comment.

To enable a scope, choose *Activate* from the Scope menu. Windows NT offers to activate the scope automatically when you first create it.

Client Reservations

You can create a reservation for clients that will use DHCP but need a consistent address. To create a reservation in DHCP Manager, highlight the scope and choose *Add Reservations* from the Scope menu. Specify these options in the Add Reserved Clients dialog:

IP Address

The IP address to be reserved for the client. This must be a non-excluded address in the scope's range.

Unique Identifier

The hardware (MAC) address of the client workstation.

Client Name

A unique name to identify the client here. This does not need to correspond to the client's computer name.

Client Comment

An optional comment.

DHCP Options

The DHCP Options menu in DHCP Manager allows you to specify values for various options defined by the DHCP standard. These options are generally used to send additional information to the client, such as the address of a DNS server.

You can set options for all scopes (*Global*), the current scope (*Scope*), or for a reserved client. To use an option, activate it and set a value. Although you can set values for the full list of DHCP options and even define your own options, a limited set of options are recognized by Windows clients. These are described in Table 1-9.

Table 1-9: Common Numeric DHCP Options

Option Number	Option Name	Value Type	Description
003	Router	Array of IP addresses	Preferred routers (gateways) in order of preference
006	DNS Servers	Array of IP addresses	Available DNS servers in order of preference
044	WINS/NBNS Servers	Array of IP addresses	Available WINS servers in order of preference
046	WINS/NBT Node Type	Byte	WINS Node type; see "NetBIOS Name Resolution" below
047	NetBIOS Scope ID	String	Identifier for NetBIOS over TCP/IP

On the Exam

The DHCP options are not emphasized in the MCSE exam, but you should be aware that they are available and can be set for a server, a scope, or an individual client.

Configuring DHCP Clients

When you install TCP/IP on a Windows NT workstation, you can choose the *Enable Automatic DHCP Configuration* option to support DHCP. Since DHCP uses broadcasting, you do not need to specify DHCP server addresses.

To enable DHCP after *TCP/IP* is installed, highlight *TCP/IP* in the Protocols tab of the Network control panel, choose *Properties,* and select the *Obtain an IP address from a DHCP server* option.

Although DHCP generally works well without intervention, the IPCONFIG command-line utility provides several options that may be useful for debugging DHCP problems at the client. See the "Optimization and Troubleshooting" section at the end of this chapter for a summary of this utility.

Maintaining the DHCP Database

A DHCP server keeps a set of database files in the \systemroot\system32\dhcp directory. This is a standard database in Microsoft's JET format, the format used by Microsoft Access. The database is normally maintained and backed up automatically, but you may find it useful to backup, restore, or compact the database.

Backing up DHCP Data

The DHCP database is automatically backed up once per hour to the \systemroot\system32\dhcp\backup\jet directory. You can copy the files in this directory to another location to retain a backup.

You can modify the database backup interval by changing this registry key:

```
HKEY_LOCAL_MACHINE\SYSTEM\CurrentControlSet\Services\
DHCPServer\Parameters\BackupInterval
```

Restoring DHCP Data

The DHCP server automatically attempts to restore a backup if it detects a problem with the database. You can manually trigger this restore process by setting this registry key to 1:

```
HKEY_LOCAL_MACHINE\SYSTEM\CurrentControlSet\Services\
DHCPServer\Parameters\Restore Flag Option
```

Alternately, manually copy the files in \systemroot\system32\dhcp\backup\jet to replace the files in \systemroot\system32\dhcp.

Compacting DHCP Data

Compacting the DHCP database removes space occupied by deleted entries, and reduces the size of the file on disk. In Windows NT 4.0, the system automatically compacts the database periodically. In earlier versions, you must do so manually.

You must stop the DHCP server with the Services control panel or the net stop dhcpserver command before compacting, and restart it afterward with the control panel or net start dhcpserver.

To compact the database, change the current directory to \systemroot\system32\dhcp and use the command jetpack dhcp.mdb temp.mdb. The second filename is used temporarily and deleted.

DHCP Relay Agent

DHCP works between subnets if the router supports BootP routing, as defined in RFC 1542. Most modern routers can be configured to forward BootP and DHCP broadcasts. If you use multiple subnets, you can either configure a separate DHCP server for each subnet, or arrange for DHCP broadcasts to be routed or forwarded.

You can also use a server on each subnet in addition to routing; this allows a remote DHCP server to offer an address when a local server is not responding. When two subnets are configured in this way, Microsoft recommends that each server's scope include 75% of the available IP addresses for its own subnet, and 25% of those for the remote subnet. Remember not to duplicate any addresses between the two scopes.

Windows NT Server 4.0 includes DHCP Relay Agent, a feature that allows clients on a subnet without a DHCP server to use DHCP by forwarding requests to another subnet.

DHCP Relay Agent is installed by default in Windows NT Server. To configure the relay agent, select the DHCP Relay tab in the TCP/IP Properties dialog and specify the IP address of the remote DHCP server. The computer will then monitor DHCP broadcasts in the local subnet and forward them to the appropriate address. You only need to enable the relay agent on one computer per subnet.

Name Resolution

TCP/IP supports *host names*, or alphanumeric aliases corresponding to particular IP addresses. These provide a user-friendly alternative to IP addresses, and can be used in most places an IP address would be accepted.

When you attempt to access a remote machine via its host name, a process called *host name resolution* occurs. Windows NT clients use the following methods, in order, to attempt to resolve an IP host name:

1. The name is compared with the local host name.
2. The HOSTS file is checked for an entry corresponding to the host name.
3. Any configured DNS servers are queried.
4. A WINS server is queried, if available.
5. A NetBIOS B-node broadcast is sent.
6. The LMHOSTS file is checked.

Steps 1–3 deal with TCP/IP host name resolution. If these methods fail, the client attempts to use the NetBIOS resolution methods in steps 4–6. The following sections explain the various types of name resolution in detail.

The HOSTS File

The simplest method of host name resolution uses the HOSTS file. This is a lookup table formatted as an ASCII text file, and stored in \winnt\system\ drivers\etc\HOSTS. This file follows the format of the HOSTS file in BSD UNIX 4.3.

The HOSTS file lists IP addresses, each followed by one or more host names to act as aliases for that address, separated by spaces or tabs. The # symbol begins a comment. The following is a simple example of a HOSTS file:

```
# HOSTS file
# (This is a comment)
127.0.0.1       localhost       # Loopback to local host
192.168.0.1     thismachine     # alias to my actual address
209.68.11.152   starling        # A frequently-used host
```

Entries in the HOSTS file are resolved very quickly, and do not require connection to a name server, so this file is convenient to use for hosts that you will frequently access via ftp, telnet, or other utilities.

Domain Name Service (DNS)

DNS is a standard for host name resolution that was first developed for UNIX, and is defined by RFCs 1034 and 1035. DNS is the standard for name resolution on the Internet, and is also used locally in many networks. Windows NT machines can act as DNS clients or servers.

A DNS client sends a host name to the server, and receives an IP address in response. Host names can range from simple machine names on a local network to subdivided names such as *cc.utah.edu* used on the Internet. Internet host names use a host name, a domain name, and a top-level domain name (TLD). The most common TLDs are listed in Table 1-10. An entire host name with its TLD is referred to as a FQDN, or *fully qualified domain name.*

Table 1-10: Top-Level Domain Names

Domain	Purpose
COM	Commercial organizations
EDU	Educational institutions
ORG	Organizations (usually non-profit)
NET	Internet service providers
GOV	U.S. Government organizations
MIL	U.S. Military organizations
INT	International organizations
US, CH, and other country codes	Geographic domains

As with IP addresses, the InterNIC assigns domain names for use on the Internet, with the exception of the geographic domains. InterNIC also maintains the Internet's primary DNS servers, which relay information to local DNS servers on sites throughout the world.

Configuring DNS

Windows NT Server 4.0 includes a full-featured DNS server. To install it, select the Services tab in the Network control panel. Choose *add*, and select the *Microsoft DNS Server* entry.

After the DNS server is installed, you can use the DNS Manager utility in the Administrative Tools menu to configure the DNS server. You must first add the DNS server's IP address to the list with the New Server command in the DNS menu.

The DNS configuration consists of a number of zones, or DNS databases. At installation, the Cache zone is the only one available. This zone automatically caches the results of DNS requests, and is searched first.

To set up DNS for your network, first create a new zone, and choose *Primary* as the zone type. You can then create domain entries, host entries, and resource records under the zone.

If you are using multiple DNS servers, you can create Secondary zones. These are read-only replicas of existing zones, and can be used to create redundancy between the servers.

To configure a Windows NT client to use DNS, select the Protocols tab in the Network control panel. Highlight *TCP/IP*, select *Properties*, and select the DNS tab. Here you can specify the local machine's DNS name and domain, and provide a list of DNS servers to search. You can also configure DHCP to send the addresses for DNS servers to clients (using option 006).

The DNS Database

The DNS server stores its information in simple ASCII database files. Each zone has a corresponding filename with a DNS extension. You specify this filename when creating the zone.

Each DNS file includes a SOA (Start of Authority) record, specifying administrative information for the zone, followed by a number of records describing the hosts and other entries in the zone. It's possible to edit this file manually, but the DNS Manager utility supports all of the options available in the file.

The DNS database files are stored in the \systemroot\system32\dns directory. You can view them with a text editor or back them up, even while the DNS server is running.

DNS and WINS

If the DNS server is unable to resolve a name in one of its zone databases, it can optionally access a WINS server (explained below) to resolve the name as a NetBIOS name.

To enable this feature, select *Properties* from the DNS menu in DNS Manager. Select the WINS Lookup tab, select the *Use WINS Resolution* option, and add at least one WINS server to the list.

While Windows NT clients can query a WINS server themselves if the DNS server can't resolve a name, this feature of the DNS server allows other clients (such as UNIX machines) to resolve NetBIOS names using standard DNS.

NetBIOS Name Resolution

The NetBIOS API provides support for the naming scheme used by Windows networking: computer names, domains, and workgroups. Windows NT includes NetBIOS over TCP/IP (NBT), a service that allows NetBIOS communications and name resolution through TCP/IP. NBT is based on the specifications in RFCs 1001 and 1002.

After the HOSTS file and DNS fail to locate an IP host name, Windows NT clients attempt to use NetBIOS resolution. NetBIOS names have their own rules for domain resolution, and their own name server service (WINS). When an application supports NetBIOS directly, NetBIOS resolution methods are used before host name resolution.

The steps involved in NetBIOS name resolution depend on the client's NetBIOS node type, or name resolution mode. The following are the five possible node types and their name resolution methods:

B-node (broadcast)

These nodes send a broadcast (NetBIOS name query) to the entire local subnet when they need to resolve a name. The broadcast is repeated three times if necessary. Each machine on the subnet compares the NetBIOS name in the broadcast with its own name. If a machine finds a match, it sends a reply (NetBIOS name query response) to the original node, and the NetBIOS session is established.

Enhanced B-node

This is Microsoft's nonstandard version of the B-node method, and is Windows NT's default if a WINS server is not used. The broadcasts are sent as in the previous method. If no response is received from any machine on the local subnet, the client searches its local LMHOSTS file (explained later in this section) for an entry corresponding to the name.

P-node (peer-to-peer)

This type of node sends a NetBIOS name query message directly to a defined WINS server (described later in this section). No further resolution attempts are made.

M-node (mixed)

These nodes first attempt to use B-node broadcasts. If no response is received, they send a query to a WINS server. Primary and secondary WINS servers are tried, if specified in the client's configuration.

H-node (hybrid)

These nodes use the opposite of the M-node method: they first send a query to the defined WINS servers. If there is no response or the response is negative, they resort to B-node broadcasts. This is Windows NT's default method when a WINS server is available, and minimizes network traffic.

On the Exam

You should be familiar with these node types for the TCP/IP MCSE exam. Windows NT machines are always either Enhanced B-nodes or H-nodes.

When an application attempts to resolve a NetBIOS name, the following steps are performed under Windows NT:

1. The local NetBIOS name cache is checked.

2. A WINS server is queried, if available.

3. A B-node broadcast is sent.

4. The LMHOSTS file is checked for an entry with the NetBIOS name.

5. The HOSTS file is checked.

6. A DNS server is queried, if available.

Steps 1–4 of this process comprise NetBIOS resolution. If these fail, host name resolution (steps 5–6) is attempted. The processes involved in NetBIOS resolution are described in detail in the following sections.

Windows Internet Name Service (WINS)

The P-node, M-node, and H-node methods of NetBIOS name resolution can make use of an NBNS (NetBIOS Name Service) server. Microsoft's implementation of NBNS is called WINS, or Windows Internet Name Service. A properly configured WINS server allows clients to avoid bandwidth-heavy B-node broadcasts.

How WINS Works

Several processes, each involving a type of message sent between the client and the server, make up WINS resolution:

1. When a client initializes, it sends a NAME REGISTRATION REQUEST message to its defined primary WINS server. If it does not receive a response, it sends the same request to its secondary WINS server.

2. If the server hasn't already registered the same name to another client, it sends a POSITIVE NAME REGISTRATION RESPONSE message, specifying a TTL (time to live) indicating how long the name will remain registered. Windows NT's default TTL is 6 days. Otherwise the server sends an END-NODE CHALLENGE message, and the client must challenge the already-registered node.

3. After 50 percent of the TTL has expired, the client attempts to renew the registration by sending a NAME REFRESH REQUEST message. If the response is positive, a new TTL is specified.

4. When the client needs to resolve a NetBIOS name, it sends a NAME QUERY REQUEST message to the server. The server replies with a positive response if the name is registered, or a negative response if the name is not found.

5. When the client shuts down, it sends a NAME RELEASE REQUEST to the server, and receives a NAME RELEASE RESPONSE releasing the name. The client stops using the name, and the server removes it from the WINS database.

On the Exam

You should not need to know the exact WINS process or message names for the TCP/IP MCSE exam. However, you should be familiar with the basic process and when broadcasts or point-to-point messages are used. You should also know the default TTL (6 days) and that a renewal is requested after 50% of the TTL.

Configuring WINS

Windows NT and Windows 95 clients can specify primary and secondary WINS server IP addresses in their TCP/IP configuration. The WINS server addresses can also be sent via DHCP by setting two options in the DHCP scope:

044 WINS/NBNS Servers

Specify the IP addresses of primary and secondary WINS servers.

046 WINS/NBNS Node Type

Specify type 0x8, meaning H-node type.

Any Windows NT server can act as a WINS server. Microsoft recommends two servers, and two fast servers can service roughly 10,000 WINS clients. WINS clients access servers strictly by IP address, so a WINS server machine must have an address dedicated, or at least reserved via DHCP.

In the Real World

Although a WINS server can theoretically service about 5000 clients, it's usually more practical to use more than one for large networks (or use DNS). However, WINS servers can be used across routers.

As with other services, the WINS server is installed from the Network control panel. Select the Services tab, choose *Add*, and select *Windows Internet Name Service*.

The WINS Manager utility in the Administrative Tools menu is used to manage the configuration of the WINS server. Select *Add WINS Server* from the Server menu to add your WINS servers to be managed.

To change the WINS server's configuration, select *Configuration* from the Server menu in WINS Manager. Figure 1-4 shows the configuration dialog, including advanced options. The following options are available:

Renewal Interval

The TTL value sent to clients. Defaults to 144 hours (6 days).

Extinction Interval

The time that elapses after a client releases a name before it is marked as extinct (unused). Defaults to 144 hours (6 days).

Extinction Timeout

The time that elapses after a name is marked extinct and before it is purged from the database. Defaults to 144 hours (6 days).

Verify Interval

The interval at which all non-local names will be verified. Defaults to the minimum, 576 hours (24 days).

Pull Parameters

The *Initial Replication* option controls whether pull partners are polled immediately when the WINS server starts, or when a change has been made to partnership options. *Retry Count* specifies the number of polling attempts to be made at each pull interval.

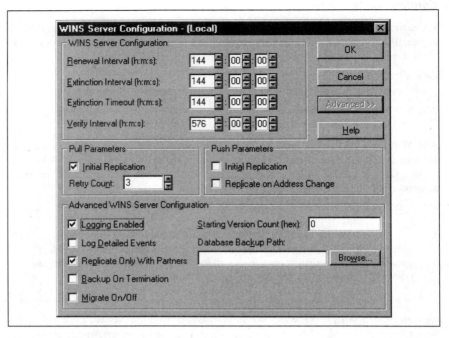

Figure 1-4: The WINS Server Configuration dialog

Push Parameters

The *Initial Replication* option controls whether an update is sent to push partners immediately upon initialization or a change to partnership options. The *Replicate on Address Change* option specifies whether a client address change in the database causes a replication.

Logging Enabled

If selected, WINS events are logged in the \systemroot\system32\wins\jet.log file.

Log Detailed Events

If selected, the jet.log file entries are more verbose, possibly slowing down the WINS server.

Replicate Only With Partners

If selected, only WINS servers listed in the server's Replication Partners list can send or request updates.

Backup on Termination

If selected, a backup of the WINS database is created in the path specified by the *Database Backup Path* option when the WINS service is stopped.

Migrate On/Off

If selected, static entries in the database can be treated as dynamic entries if they conflict with a new entry.

Starting Version Count
> Specify a version number for the database; if this number is above the corresponding numbers on other servers, the current server's records are replicated to those servers.

Database Backup Path
> The path used for the *Backup on Termination* option.

On the Exam

For the TCP/IP MCSE exam, you should be familiar with all of the above settings, and should have experience installing and configuring a WINS server under Windows NT.

WINS Replication

The Windows NT WINS server includes support for automatic database replication between servers. The replication scheme uses a system of *partners*:

- *Push partners* automatically send updates to partner servers whenever changes are made to the WINS database. This provides for the best database synchronization.

- *Pull partners* periodically poll partner servers and receive updates for any changes since the previous polling. This system works best over wide-area links where constant synchronization updates would inflate bandwidth.

On the Exam

For the TCP/IP MCSE exam, you should know when to use push and pull partners. Pull partners update at a timed interval, and are thus best for slower links. Push partners update when an update is needed, and are best for faster links.

To configure WINS replication, choose *Replication Partners* from the Server menu in WINS Manager. This dialog includes a list of partners for the current server. The *Replicate Now* button causes all partners to be contacted for updates immediately. In addition, the following options are available for each listed partner:

Replication Options
> Select whether the server is a push partner, pull partner, or both.

Configure (Push)
> Displays properties for a push partner. The only modifiable property is *Update Count*; this is the number of changes that must be made to the WINS database before an update is sent.

Configure (Pull)

Displays properties for a pull partner. You can set the *Start Time* field to schedule a daily replication, or set the *Replication Interval* field for periodic updates. The default configuration polls for updates every half hour.

Send Replication Trigger Now

Causes the push or pull process to begin immediately. If the *Push with Propagation* option is selected, the push update is flagged to be sent on from partner servers to their corresponding partners immediately.

WINS Proxies

Windows NT includes the *WINS Proxy Agent*, a service that forwards non-WINS name resolution requests to a WINS server. This is used to support name resolution on a subnet without its own WINS server. The Proxy Agent monitors broadcasted B-node requests and forwards them to a WINS server in another subnet. One or two computers per subnet can be configured to act as WINS proxies.

In the Real World

If you use a router or bridge between subnets and enable the transmission of broadcasts, the WINS proxy service is not required; however, this causes a substantial amount of network traffic, and should be avoided.

No further configuration is needed on the B-node client; it sends its usual broadcast for name registration, and the WINS proxy registers the name with the WINS server. When the B-node client attempts to resolve a name, it does so with a broadcast; the WINS proxy receives the broadcast and queries the WINS server to provide a response.

To enable the WINS proxy on a client, you must modify the registry. Set the EnableProxy value to 1 in this key:

```
HKEY_LOCAL_MACHINE\SYSTEM\CurrentControlSet\Services\
NetBT\Parameters
```

The WINS Database

The WINS server keeps a database in the \systemroot\system32\WINS\ WINS.MDB file. This is a JET database, similar to that used for DHCP. The Mappings menu in WINS Manager includes several functions dealing with the database:

Show Database

Displays the contents of the WINS database. You can sort or filter the database view, or show entries owned by a particular WINS server.

Initiate Scavenging

Performs a cleanup operation on the database. Entries marked for deletion are removed from the database.

Static Mappings

Provides support for non-WINS clients on the network. You can manually specify name and IP address for these machines. The Import button in this dialog adds static mapping entries from a file in the LMHOSTS format.

Backup Database

Copies the contents of the WINS directory to the directory of your choice.

Restore Local Database

Restores the WINS database from the backup directory you specify. This action stops the WINS server, and does not restart it; you will need to start it with the Services control panel or the net start wins command.

As with the DHCP database, you can compact the WINS database to conserve space. To do this, stop the WINS server with the Services control panel or the net stop wins command. Switch to the \systemroot\system32\wins directory, then type this command:

```
jetpack wins.mdb temp.mdb
```

The second filename is temporary, and is deleted when the process is complete. After the compacting process is complete, restart the WINS service with the Services control panel or the net start wins command.

The LMHOSTS File

The LMHOSTS file is consulted if a negative response is received from a B-node broadcast (Enhanced B-node) or from a WINS server (H-node). This file is similar to the HOSTS file, but uses IP addresses and NetBIOS names. To enable the LMHOSTS file, select the Enable LMHOSTS Lookup option in the WINS tab of the TCP/IP Properties dialog.

LMHOSTS is a standard ASCII file stored in the \\systemroot\system32\drivers\etc\. Windows NT includes a sample LMHOSTS file, stored in the same directory as LMHOSTS.SAM. The following is an example of a simple LMHOSTS file:

```
168.192.150.1      East1      # this is a comment
168.192.150.2      East2      #PRE   # see below
168.192.150.6      North1
```

Entries in the LMHOSTS file can be suffixed with #PRE to indicate that they are to be directly loaded into the local NetBIOS cache for fast resolution. Entries suffixed #DOM are domain entries, which can be used to support network browsing and domain authentication.

The LMHOSTS file supports a rudimentary form of remote name resolution through the use of block inclusion. Entries from the LMHOSTS file on a remote server can be included using the following syntax:

```
BEGIN_ALTERNATE
#INCLUDE \\East1\public\lmhosts
END_ALTERNATE
```

The files you include are searched only if no match was found in the local LMHOSTS file. If more than one remote LMHOSTS file is included in this fashion, they are searched in order; if a name is resolved by one file, the remaining files will not be searched.

On the Exam

For the TCP/IP MCSE exam, you should be familiar with the format of the LMHOSTS file, its purpose, and the differences between HOSTS and LM-HOSTS. The LM in LMHOSTS stands for LAN Manager, the networking standard developed by Microsoft and IBM that originated NetBIOS.

IP Routing

An IP router, or *gateway*, is a device that has more than one network adapter, and is thus connected to multiple subnets. Routers can pass packets between the subnets, allowing them to act as a contiguous network. Routers can be either dedicated hardware devices or software services on hosts.

On the Exam

You may remember from the Network Essentials exam that a "gateway" was defined as a higher-layer device that translates between protocols. If the term is used in the TCP/IP exam, however, it is most likely intended as a synonym for "router."

Any Windows NT workstation or server has the capability of acting as an IP router if it has multiple network interfaces attached to two or more subnets. This type of node is referred to as a *multihomed* computer.

There are two basic types of IP routing: *static routing* uses a fixed routing table specifying available destinations, and *dynamic routing* maintains a routing table dynamically by communicating with other routers. These are examined in the sections that follow.

On the Exam

The static and dynamic IP routing supported by Windows NT, along with static and dynamic IPX routing, are collectively referred to as the Multiprotocol Router (MPR) by Microsoft.

Static Routing

In static routing, a *route table* stores information about available destinations and the gateway (router) they can be reached through. Route tables are not networked between routers in any way, so the routes must be specified for each multihomed computer.

The route command, described at the end of this chapter, allows you to modify or display the route table. Type route print to display the current route table. The following is an example of a simple route table:

Network Address	Netmask	Gateway Address	Interface	Metric
127.0.0.0	255.0.0.0	127.0.0.1	127.0.0.1	1
168.192.0.0	255.255.0.0	168.192.150.1	168.192.150.1	1
224.0.0.0	224.0.0.0	168.192.150.1	168.192.150.1	1

The route table includes the following fields:

Network Address
> The network address of the destination network.

Netmask
> The subnet mask corresponding to the network address.

Gateway Address
> The IP address of the gateway (router) that connects to the specified subnet.

Interface
> The IP address of the interface card in the local computer that connects to the gateway.

Metric
> The number of hops (cost) for the route. This number is used to optimize routes.

On the Exam

You should be familiar with the information found in the route table for the TCP/IP MCSE exam, and should know to use the route command to modify the table. The details of the route command syntax are included in "Command-Line Utilities," later in this chapter.

Default Gateways

Each Windows NT client has a default gateway address defined in the IP Address tab of the TCP/IP Properties dialog. The Advanced button in that dialog allows a list of gateways to be listed in order of priority. The default gateway list can also be received by a DHCP client.

The default gateway is listed in the route table with a network address of 0.0.0.0. The defined gateways are used in order when no explicit route is found in the route table for a destination address.

In a network with only two subnets, you can create a functional static routing setup with only the Default Gateway parameter. Configure a multihomed computer on each subnet as a router, and enter each machine in the other's Default Gateway field. In this scheme all destinations not recognized as part of the local subnet are automatically sent to the other subnet.

Dynamic Routing

Dynamic routing uses a *routing protocol* to exchange information between routers rather than a manually configured route table. Two routing protocols are widely supported on today's networks and the Internet: RIP and OSPF. These are described in the sections below. Only RIP is currently supported by Windows NT without third-party software.

RIP (Router Information Protocol)

RIP is the most popular routing protocol in use today. RIP is a *distance vector routing protocol*, meaning that the primary information routers exchange is a measure of the distance (in *hops*, or number of intermediate nodes) between destinations, and these distances are used to calculate optimal routes.

In the Real World

RIP was formally documented in RFC 1058, and expanded in RFCs 1387–1389.

RIP keeps an internal routing table similar to the table used for static routing, but the table is maintained strictly by receiving updates from adjacent routers. The following information is maintained for each entry in the RIP database:

- *Address*: The IP address of the host or network the route points to.
- *Gateway*: The first router (gateway) that packets should be sent to in order to reach the destination.
- *Interface*: The IP address of the network adapter in the local machine that is connected to the gateway's subnet.
- *Metric*: A measure of the number of hops required to reach the destination, or *cost*. Metric values range from 1 to 15.
- *Timer*: A measure of the amount of time since the record was updated.

OSPF (Open Shortest Path First)

OSPF is a *link state routing protocol*, meaning that routing is based not only on distance but on the current status of links in the network.

OSPF is an autonomous system, meaning that all routers use the same algorithm and a copy of the same database. Each OSPF router maintains a database that keeps track of the entire routing system, and receives updates from other routers.

In the Real World

OSPF is documented in RFC 1131 (version 1) and RFC 1247 (version 2).

This protocol uses less network traffic than RIP, since OSPF routers only transmit changes to the routing table rather than periodically broadcasting the entire table.

OSPF is considered superior to RIP for most purposes, but has not yet been implemented as widely. The routing capabilities of Windows NT Server 4.0 do not currently support OSPF, although some third-party routers do support this protocol.

On the Exam

Although OSPF is not currently supported by Windows NT, you should be familiar with its purpose and its advantages for the TCP/IP MCSE exam.

Configuring IP Routing

Static routing is available by default on any multihomed Windows NT host. You can enable static routing with the *Enable IP Forwarding* option in the IP Forwarding tab of the TCP/IP Properties dialog.

After enabling IP forwarding, you can add route table entries using the route command, or use the default gateway method explained above for small networks. Static routing was the only type of routing supported in Windows NT 3.51.

Windows NT Server 4.0 includes support for dynamic routing. To install dynamic TCP/IP routing, select *Add* from the Services tab of the TCP/IP Properties dialog, and choose *RIP for Internet Protocol.*

A server with the RIP service installed and running acts as a dynamic rather than static router, and automatically exchanges routes via RIP with other routers. No specific configuration options are available for dynamic routing.

In the Real World

Although Windows NT computers can act as routers, hardware routers are usually a better choice for large and complex networks. These are more reliable, easier to configure, and often support modern routing protocols such as OSPF.

IP and UNIX Printing

Windows NT also includes support for IP printing. These features are typically used to support UNIX clients. You can configure NT clients to print to UNIX

---

printers, and configure UNIX clients to print to an NT printer. The components of IP printing are described in the following sections.

Installing the LPD Service

Windows NT Server includes the TCP/IP Printing service, which allows the NT Server to act as an LPD (line printer daemon) server, a standard for UNIX printers. Once this is configured, NT clients can print through this server to UNIX printers, and UNIX clients can print to Windows NT printers.

To install the TCP/IP Printing service, open the Network control panel. Select the Services tab. Press the Add button, and select *Microsoft TCP/IP Printing* from the list. Once the service is installed, you must restart the server before it can be used.

UNIX Print Utilities

NT Server includes implementations of the UNIX print utilities `lpr` and `lpq`, which provide command-line access to the `lpd` service. These utilities are described in the following sections.

---

lpr

`lpr [options] filename`

Sends a print job to a printer running the `lpd` service, either a UNIX server or a Windows NT server running the TCP/IP Printing service. The `filename` specified is copied to the printer; this should be a text file or a file formatted for printing.

Options

-*S host*

> Specify the host name (by IP host name or IP address) running the LPD service.

-*P queue*

> Specify the print queue within the server.

-*C class*

> Specify an optional job classification; this is printed on the initial banner page.

-*J name*

> Specify a job name for the banner page.

-*o type*

> Specify the type of file. Omit the **type** parameter for ASCII files. Use l (lower-case L) as the type for formatted printer files (such as postscript files).

-*x*

> If specified, the SunOS-compatible version of the `lpd` protocols is used. This supports SunOS 4.1.*x* and earlier versions.

-*d*

> If specified, the data file is sent to the printer before the banner page.

lpq

lpq [*options*]

Displays the current status of a print queue on an lpd server. The output includes a list of files waiting to be printed.

Options

-S host
> Specify the host name (by IP host name or IP address) running the LPD service.

-P queue
> Specify the print queue within the server.

-l

> Produces a more verbose version of the output.

Simple Network Management Protocol (SNMP)

In a complex network, it's impossible for an administrator to keep track of every aspect of every machine on the network. Network management attempts to automate this task. SNMP is the most commonly used protocol for network management.

SNMP allows the collection and display of information about the network and its nodes. SNMP was initially defined in RFC 1098, and is supported by Windows NT workstations and servers. SNMP supports two types of services:

- *Agents* run on nodes and maintain a database of information about the node in a database called the MIB (Management Information Base).

- *Management systems* are used to request, collect, view, and summarize the data from management agents.

Windows NT includes a SNMP Agent service that can be installed on any NT 3.51 or NT 4.0 system. Third-party software is required to act as the management system.

How SNMP Works

Each SNMP agent maintains a Management Information Base, or MIB. This is a hierarchical database of objects corresponding to the current status of the monitored system. There are several types of MIBs, and agents can support more than one.

The type of data available from an agent depends on the MIBs installed. Microsoft's SNMP service supports four MIBs:

- MIB II is the Internet standard SNMP MIB, defined in RFC 1213. It includes 171 objects relating to the agent system's configuration and network activity.

- LAN Manager MIB II is a database of objects specific to Microsoft networking.

- DHCP MIB is a Microsoft-specific database of objects relating to DHCP.

- WINS MIB is installed with a WINS server, and includes objects relating to WINS.

SNMP agents generally wait for requests from a management system, and respond when queried. Communication uses several messages defined in the SNMP standard, and proceeds in this fashion:

1. The manager sends a GetRequest message, requesting information from a particular MIB, or a SetRequest message, requesting that an MIB parameter be changed.

2. The SNMP agent responds with a GetResponse message containing the information requested. For a SetRequest, the GetResponse message indicates whether the action was successful.

3. If the MIB object is an array or table and has additional members, the manager sends GetNextRequest messages for each additional data item.

The one type of communication initiated by the SNMP agent is a Trap message, indicating that a monitored error condition has occurred. You determine whether traps are sent and the manager they are sent to in the SNMP agent's configuration.

SNMP supports rudimentary security in the form of community names. Each GetRequest message includes the management system's community name, and this must match the agent's community (or list of accepted communities) for the request to be honored.

On the Exam

You should know the basics of how SNMP works for the TCP/IP MCSE exam, but you should not need to know the exact process and message names. You should know how community names are used for security.

Configuring SNMP

To install the Microsoft SNMP Service, select *Add* from the Services tab of the TCP/IP Properties dialog. Select *SNMP Service*. After installation, select *Properties* to display the SNMP properties. The properties are divided into three tabbed categories, described below.

On the Exam

Although Windows NT does not include an SNMP management system, installing the SNMP service adds a variety of counters for the TCP/IP protocol to the Performance Monitor utility, as described later in this chapter.

Agents

Contact (optional)

> The contact person for the agent computer. An email address or phone number may be useful here.

Location (optional)

> A description of the physical location of the agent computer.

Service

> Choose the types of services that will be reported on. These correspond to categories of objects in the MIB.

Traps

Community Name

> The community names used when sending Trap messages to SNMP managers. Select one of the defined community names to specify trap destinations.

Trap Destinations

> A list of IP addresses to which Trap messages should be sent.

Security

Send Authentication Trap

> If selected, a Trap message is sent when an SNMP request is received with an invalid community name.

Accepted Community Names

> A list of acceptable community names for incoming SNMP packets.

Accept SNMP Packets from Any Host

> If selected, SNMP packets are accepted from any host with a valid community name.

Only Accept SNMP Packets from These Hosts

> If selected, SNMP packets are considered valid only if they come from one of the listed IP addresses. The community name is also verified.

Optimization and Troubleshooting

The following sections present some utilities that will be useful in monitoring TCP/IP performance and troubleshooting TCP/IP connectivity and configuration problems.

Performance Monitor

The Performance Monitor utility in the Administrative Tools menu is a general-purpose tool for monitoring statistics about the current server. This utility was introduced in *MCSE: The Core Exams in a Nutshell*.

If the SNMP agent service is installed as described in the "Simple Network Management Protocol (SNMP)" section above, several additional Performance Monitor objects become available. The following objects and their counters may be useful for monitoring TCP/IP performance:

Network Interface
Basic statistics relating to the network interface card. This object and the ICMP, IP, TCP, and UDP objects are added when you install the SNMP agent.

Network Segment
Includes statistics for the local subnet. This object is installed when you install the Network Monitor Agent service.

ICMP
Statistics about ICMP (Internet Control Message Protocol). The ping utility, explained below, is an example of ICMP messages.

IP
Statistics relating to Internet Protocol (IP).

TCP
Statistics relating to TCP communications, including establishment of connections.

UDP
Statistics relating to UDP datagrams.

WINS Server
Statistics about WINS queries, responses, and errors.

On the Exam

You should have experience using Performance Monitor for the TCP/IP MCSE exam, and should be familiar with the counters in the categories listed above.

Command-Line Utilities

The command-line utilities described in the sections below may be useful for troubleshooting TCP/IP connections, configurations, services such as DHCP, and host name resolution.

On the Exam

For the MCSE exam, you will not necessarily need to have all of the options for these utilities memorized, but you should know the most common options and know which utility to use for a given troubleshooting task.

---

arp

Displays or modifies information in the ARP hardware address table, used to translate between IP addresses and hardware (MAC) addresses. This utility is useful for diagnosing and debugging problems with ARP resolution.

Options

-a ip

Displays the entries in the ARP table. If an IP address is specified, only the entries relating to that address are diaplayed.

-d ip

Deletes the ARP table entry for the IP address specified.

-N server

Rather than those of the current host, displays the ARP table entries for the specified server.

-s ip physical

Adds a host to the list with the specified IP address and physical (MAC) address.

hostname

Displays the IP hostname of the current machine. No options are available.

ipconfig

Displays or modifies IP address configuration. This utility is most often used for diagnosing and debugging problems with DHCP. If used without options, ipconfig displays a summary of TCP/IP settings for each LAN adapter, including IP address, subnet mask, and default gateway.

Options

/all

Displays a detailed list of TCP/IP options. This includes more useful information, including whether DHCP is enabled, and WINS Server, Scope ID, and other data retrieved through DHCP.

/release

Sends a DHCPRELEASE message, releasing the current IP address. The client loses the ability to communicate via TCP/IP until the lease is renewed with a new address.

/renew

Forces the client to send a DHCPREQUEST message to the DHCP server, attempting to renew its lease.

nbtstat

nbtstat [options]

Displays or modifies information and statistics relating to NetBIOS over TCP/IP (NBT). Useful for troubleshooting problems with NetBIOS name resolution.

Options

-a name

Lists the NetBIOS name table (HOSTS file) for the remote machine specified by *name*.

-A address

Lists the NetBIOS name table (HOSTS file) for a remote machine specified by its address.

-c

Lists names and IP addresses in the local NetBIOS cache.

-n

Lists all of the NetBIOS names corresponding to the local machine.

-r

Displays statistics about NetBIOS resolution, including the number of names resolved by HOSTS file entries or by a WINS server.

-R

Reloads the local NetBIOS cache, replacing the current contents.

-s

Lists currently open NetBIOS sessions by name.

-S

Lists currently open NetBIOS sessions by IP address.

---

net start

net start [options]

Starts a network service. If used without options, displays a list of currently running services.

Options

service

Starts the named service. Service names relating to TCP/IP include DHCP CLIENT, FTP SERVER, SERVER, SNMP, TCPIP NETBIOS HELPER, DHCP SERVER, WINS.

---

net stop

net stop service

Stops a network service.

Options

service

Specify the service to stop. The service names listed above can be used. Type net help stop to list all available services.

---

netstat

Displays TCP/IP network statistics, or displays information about current connections. Used for troubleshooting servers or network connectivity. If used without options, displays a summary of active connections.

Options

-a

Displays a detailed list of active connections and ports.

-e

Displays statistics for ethernet adapters.

-n

Displays IP addresses rather than host names in statistics.

-p protocol

Displays information only for the specified protocol. Protocol values are tcp, udp, or ip.

-r

Displays the entries in the routing table as well as active connections and ports.

-s

Displays separate lists of statistics for each protocol.

nslookup

Queries a DNS server to resolve a host name or IP address. This command is useful to test the functionality of a DNS server or the client's DNS configuration. If used without options, nslookup enters interactive mode, as described below.

Options

-command

Goes into interactive mode, and accepts nslookup commands. Type nslookup help to list the commands. If *command* is specified, it is executed first.

hostname

Attempts to resolve the IP address corresponding to the host name.

IP address

Attempts to resolve the host name corresponding to the IP address.

server

Uses a specified DNS server instead of the default.

ping

Corresponds to the UNIX ping utility. Sends an Echo Request ICMP packet to a remote node and waits for a response. This utility is typically used to troubleshoot network connectivity.

Options

host
> The host to attempt a connection with.

-a
> Displays resolved host names rather than IP addresses.

-f
> Sends non-fragmented packets.

-i ttl
> Specify a time to live (timeout) for the ping packets.

-l size
> Specify the size of the data buffer.

-n number
> Specifies the number of packets to send.

-r number
> Records the route for the specified number of hops.

-s number
> Records time stamps for the specified number of hops.

-t
> Continues to ping the host until interrupted manually.

-w seconds
> Specifies the timeout (milliseconds) to await a reply.

---

route
route [options]

Displays routing information or maintains entries in the static routing table.

Options

add
> Adds a route to the routing table. Specify the destination IP address and the gateway address for routing.

change
> Changes an existing entry in the route table.

delete
> Deletes a route table entry. Specify the IP address.

print
> Displays the route table including the network address, subnet mask, gateway address, interface IP address, and metric (number of hops).

-f
> Flushes the routing table (deletes all routes).

-p
> When used with -a, makes the added route permanent (not lost at reboot).

---

tracert

An implementation of the UNIX `traceroute` utility. Displays the hosts that lie on the route between the current host and a specified destination. Useful for trouble-shooting routing or network connectivity.

Options

-d

Displays the route without resolving IP addresses to host names.

-h hops

Specifies the maximum number of network hosts to traverse in reaching the destination.

-j hosts

Specifies a list of hosts to specify the route along.

-w timeout

Specifies the timeout in milliseconds to wait for a reply from each intermediate host.

Optimization and Troubleshooting   63

Suggested Exercises

The TCP/IP exam includes questions about TCP/IP basics, IP addressing, and subnet masking, which you should study thoroughly. In addition, Windows NT utilities, services, and TCP/IP support are covered.

You should have a minimum of one Windows NT Server machine to prepare for this exam. Since TCP/IP is all about networking, two or more machines will be useful. You will typically need only one Windows NT Server computer to act as a server, and one or more Windows NT Workstation machines to act as clients.

Performing the following exercises will help you prepare for the TCP/IP MCSE exam:

1. For each machine in your network, perform these steps:

    a. Add TCP/IP to the list of protocols.

    b. Assign an IP address to the computer. If your network is not connected to the Internet, you can choose arbitrary addresses.

    c. Use **ping** from another computer to verify that the computers can communicate.

2. Install and configure DHCP Server on a Windows NT Server computer. Create a scope of IP addresses, and configure the client computers to request addresses from the server.

3. Configure a Windows NT computer to use DHCP Relay agent.

4. Create HOSTS files on each computer on the network with aliases for the other computers.

5. Install WINS Server on a Windows NT Server computer.

6. Configure DHCP options to assign the WINS Server address to clients.

7. Install and configure DNS server on a Windows NT Server computer.

8. Configure DHCP options to assign the DNS server address to clients.

9. Use the `route` command to create a routing table for static routing.

10. Install RIP for Internet Protocol on an NT Server computer.

11. Install the TCP/IP Printing service on an NT Server computer. Use the `lpr` command to send some jobs to a print queue, and the `lpq` command to view the queue.

12. Install the SNMP agent on a Windows NT computer.

13. Use Performance Monitor to monitor TCP/IP counters on the computer with SNMP agent installed.

Practice Test

Test Questions

1. The PPP protocol operates at which layer of the DOD model?

    a. Network Interface

    b. Transport

    c. Internet

    d. Application

2. Which of the following protocols and services work at the Internet layer of the DOD model? (select all that apply)

    a. IP

    b. FTP

    c. DHCP

    d. UDP

3. The ICMP protocol is typically used for which functions?

    a. Network management and diagnostics

    b. Transmission of non-realtime data

    c. Transmission of realtime data

    d. IP address resolution

4. Which layer of the DOD model handles routing between subnets?

    a. Transport

    b. Application

c.   Network Interface

d.   Internet

5. Which of the following protocols and services work at the Transport layer of the DOD model? (select all that apply)

   a.   TCP

   b.   ICMP

   c.   UDP

   d.   DHCP

6. Which of the following describe the TCP protocol? (select all that apply)

   a.   Connection-oriented

   b.   Unreliable

   c.   Half-duplex

   d.   Uses a virtual circuit

7. Which of the following describe the UDP protocol? (select all that apply)

   a.   Connection-oriented

   b.   Unreliable

   c.   Full-duplex

   d.   Uses a virtual circuit

8. For the IP address 128.110.121.4, what is the default subnet mask?

   a.   255.0.0.0

   b.   255.255.255.0

   c.   255.255.0.0

   d.   255.255.128.0

9. You are assigned to divide a class C IP network into subnets. You currently have 5 network segments connected by routers, which have between 20 and 30 workstations each.

   Required Result: The subnet mask chosen must support all current workstations.

   Optional Result: The subnet mask should allow expansion to 35 computers per subnet.

   Optional Result: The subnet mask should allow the addition of one new subnet (total 6).

   Solution: Use the subnet mask 255.255.255.224.

   a.   The solution meets the required result and both of the optional results.

b. The solution meets the required result and only one of the optional results.

c. The solution meets the required result only.

d. The solution does not meet the required result.

10. Which protocol translates IP addresses into MAC addresses?

    a. DNS

    b. WINS

    c. ARP

    d. RARP

11. Which class does the IP address 204.228.126.1 belong to?

    a. Class A

    b. Class B

    c. Class C

    d. Class D

12. The DHCP Relay is not needed if the router supports which feature?

    a. IP routing

    b. BootP routing

    c. DHCP addressing

    d. NetBEUI routing

13. DHCP is an extension of which protocol?

    a. DNS

    b. WINS

    c. BootP

    d. ARP

14. You are subnetting a Class C network and need to allow for up to 24 subnets. Each subnet will have 4–5 hosts. What is the appropriate subnet mask?

    a. 255.255.255.192

    b. 255.255.255.224

    c. 255.255.255.240

    d. 255.255.255.248

15. In the IP address 128.110.121.32, what is the network address?

    a. 128.0.0.0

    b. 128.110.0.0

    c. 128.110.121.0

    d. 128.110.121.32

16. A pool of IP addresses made available through a DHCP server is referred to as a:

    a.   Zone

    b.   Queue

    c.   Lease

    d.   Scope

17. To change the interval for DHCP backups, you would modify a value in:

    a.   The HOSTS file

    b.   The registry

    c.   The LMHOSTS file

    d.   The DHCP.INI file

18. Which one of the following parameters cannot be set via DHCP for a Windows NT client?

    a.   Preferred Gateway

    b.   IP Address

    c.   NetBIOS Name

    d.   Subnet Mask

19. In Windows NT host name resolution, which of the following methods is tried first?

    a.   LMHOSTS file

    b.   WINS Server

    c.   HOSTS file

    d.   DNS Server

20. Which of the following services is used to translate NetBIOS names to IP addresses?

    a.   DNS

    b.   HOSTS

    c.   WINS

    d.   ARP

21. Which service translates IP host names to IP addresses?

    a.   DNS

    b.   HOSTS

    c.   WINS

    d.   ARP

22. Which types of NetBIOS resolution use a WINS server? (select all that apply)

    a.   B-node

    b.   P-node

    c.   M-node

    d.   H-node

23. Which of the following methods are used primarily for NetBIOS name resolution? (select all that apply)

    a.   WINS

    b.   DNS

    c.   HOSTS file

    d.   LMHOSTS file

24. Which utility would you use to modify a WINS server's timeout settings?

    a.   WINS Manager

    b.   Server Manager

    c.   User Manager for Domains

    d.   Internet Services Manager

25. Which Windows NT service allows a WINS server to service B-node name resolution requests?

    a.   WINS Manager

    b.   WINS Relay

    c.   WINS Proxy Agent

    d.   Browser service

26. Which of the following is the correct command to compact a WINS server database?

    a.   jetpack

    b.   jetpack wins.mdb temp.mdb

    c.   compact wins.mdb

    d.   compact wins.mdb temp.mdb

27. By default, a Windows NT Server computer with two network cards on different subnets acts as:

    a.   A WINS server

    b.   A static router

    c.   A dynamic router

    d.   A hardware router

28. You are troubleshooting a Windows NT computer. The computer is able to successfully send data to computers on the local subnet, but cannot transmit data outside the subnet. Which configuration parameter most likely needs to be changed?

    a.   IP Address

    b.   Subnet Mask

    c.   Default Gateway

    d.   WINS Server

29. Which of the following protocols are used for communication between routers? (select all that apply)

    a.   PPP

    b.   OSPF

    c.   RIP

    d.   DNS

30. If you need to monitor a Windows NT Server computer using SNMP from a remote Windows 95 computer, which software should be installed on the NT Server computer?

    a.   SNMP Service

    b.   SNMP Manager

    c.   Performance Monitor

    d.   RIP for Internet Protocol

31. Which of the following commands displays a table of IP addresses and their corresponding hardware addresses?

    a.   ipconfig -a

    b.   arp -a

    c.   arp -ox

    d.   route -a

32. Which of the following commands causes a client computer's current IP address to be released and returned to the DHCP server's available pool of addresses?

    a.   DHCP /release

    b.   arp /release

    c.   ipconfig /release

    d.   net dhcp /release

33. Which of the following commands is typically used to test the network connection and configuration between the local machine and a remote machine?

a. net test

b. ping

c. ipconfig /test

d. echo

34. Which of the following commands is used to add an entry to the routing table in a Windows NT computer acting as a static router?

a. route add

b. ipconfig /add

c. net route add

d. RIP /add

35. Which of the following commands will query a DNS server and display the current IP address for the host name host1?

a. tracert host1

b. ipconfig /query host1

c. nslookup host1

d. dnslookup host1

36. Which Windows NT command displays a list of the nodes in the path between the local machine and a remote node?

a. nslookup

b. tracert

c. ipconfig

d. traceroute

37. When configuring a Windows NT TCP/IP client, which of the following settings require a specific IP address? (select all that apply)

a. WINS Server

b. DNS Server

c. DHCP Server

38. Which of the following servers should be assigned a dedicated or reserved IP address rather than using DHCP? (select all that apply)

a. WINS Server

b. DHCP Server

c. DNS Server

39. A group of host names and their corresponding IP addresses in the DNS Server database is called:

a. A scope

b. A segment

    c.   A zone

    d.   A group

40. In the RIP protocol, routes are chosen based on their cost, which represents:

    a.   The number of hops

    b.   The physical distance between routers

    c.   The type of LAN or WAN connection

    d.   The reliability of the routers on a route

41. Which of the following can be used to treat three consecutive Class C network addresses as a single network address? (select all that apply)

    a.   Subnetting

    b.   IP Routing

    c.   CIDR (Classless Inter-Domain Routing)

    d.   Supernetting

42. Which of the following capabilities are provided by the TCP/IP Printing service? (select all that apply)

    a.   UNIX clients can print to Windows NT printers

    b.   Windows NT clients can print to UNIX printers

    c.   NT clients can print to NT printers in other subnets

    d.   NT clients can monitor a UNIX print queue

43. Which of the following is the correct command to send an ASCII document called file1.txt to a UNIX print queue called laser2 on a server called unixserv?

    a.   lpd unixserv laser2 file1.txt

    b.   lpr -S unixserv -P laser2 file1.txt

    c.   lpd -S unixserv -Q laser2 file1.txt

    d.   lpr -S unixserv -P laser2 -o l file1.txt

44. Which of the following commands is used to send a print job to a UNIX print queue?

    a.   lpr

    b.   lpd

    c.   lpq

    d.   lprint

45. Under Windows NT Server, what is the default TTL (time to live) for a WINS name registration?

    a.   4 hours

    b.   6 hours

c. 24 hours

d. 6 days

46. Which of the following services must be installed in order to view counters under the Network Interface object in Performance Monitor?

    a. SNMP Service

    b. Network Monitor Agent

    c. TCP/IP Printing

    d. DHCP Server

47. Which of the following protocols and services is *not* supported by software included with NT Server 4.0?

    a. DHCP

    b. DNS

    c. OSPF

    d. RIP

48. Which service must be installed to support static IP routing under NT Server 4.0?

    a. RIP for Internet Protocol

    b. Static Routing Service

    c. DHCP Relay Service

    d. No service is required

49. Which of the following services can only be enabled under Windows NT 4.0 by changing the registry?

    a. DHCP Relay

    b. IP Forwarding

    c. WINS Proxy

    d. DNS client

50. Which of the following services uses a MIB (Management Information Base)?

    a. SMTP

    b. SNMP

    c. DNS

    d. DHCP

Answers to Questions

1. A. The PPP protocol operates at the Network Interface layer of the DOD model.

2. A, C. The IP and DHCP protocols operate at the Internet layer of the DOD model. FTP (choice B) is an Application-layer protocol. UDP (choice D) operates at the Transport layer.

3. A. ICMP is used for network management and diagnostics.

4. D. The Internet layer handles routing.

5. A, C. The TCP and UDP protocols operate at the transport layer.

6. A, D. TCP is a connection-oriented protocol and uses a virtual circuit.

7. B. The UDP protocol is connectionless and unreliable.

8. C. Since this is a Class B address, 255.255.0.0 is the default subnet mask.

9. B. A subnet mask of 255.255.255.224 allows 6 subnets with up to 30 hosts each. Thus, the solution meets the required result (supports the current workstations) and only one of the optional results (allow a total of 6 subnets).

10. C. The ARP protocol translates IP addresses into MAC (hardware) addresses.

11. C. The IP address 204.228.126.1 is a Class C address.

12. B. DHCP relay is not required if the router supports BootP (and thus DHCP) routing.

13. C. DHCP is an extension of the BootP protocol.

14. D. The subnet mask 255.255.255.248 allows 30 subnets with up to 6 hosts each.

15. B. This is a Class B address; therefore, the first two octets represent the network address.

16. D. A pool of IP addresses in a DHCP server is called a scope.

17. B. The DHCP backup interval is stored in the registry.

18. C. The NetBIOS name cannot be set by a DHCP server.

19. C. The HOSTS file is consulted before any of the other methods.

20. C. The WINS service translates NetBIOS names to IP addresses. DNS (choice A) is similar, but works with host names rather than NetBIOS names.

21. A. The DNS service translates host names to IP addresses. WINS (choice C) is similar, but works with NetBIOS names.

22. B, C, D. P-node (peer-to-peer), M-node (mixed), and H-node (hybrid) resolution methods use a WINS server.

23. A, D. WINS and the LMHOSTS file are NetBIOS name resolution methods.

24. A. The WINS Manager utility can be used to modify WINS timeout settings.

25. C. The WINS Proxy Agent service allows a WINS server to handle B-node NetBIOS name resolution requests.

26. B. The correct command to compact the WINS database is jetpack wins.mdb temp.mdb.

27. B. By default, a Windows NT Server computer connected to two subnets acts a static router.

28. C. Since local machines can be contacted, the most likely problem is the Default Gateway setting.

29. B, C. The OSPF and RIP protocols are used for communication between routers.

30. A. The SNMP Service, which acts as an SNMP agent, should be installed on the NT Server computer.

31. B. The arp -a command displays a list of IP addresses and hardware addresses.

32. C. The ipconfig /release command releases a leased IP address.

33. B. The ping command is typically used to test a network connection.

34. A. The route add command adds an entry to the routing table.

35. C. The nslookup host1 command returns the current IP address for the specified host name.

36. B. The tracert command displays a list of nodes between the local machine and a specified remote node.

37. A, B. The WINS Server and DNS Server settings require a specific IP address. DHCP (choice C) uses broadcasts, and does not require a specific server IP address.

38. A, B, C. WINS servers, DNS servers, and DHCP servers should have a dedicated IP address.

39. C. A group of host names and addresses in the DNS Server database is called a zone.

40. A. The cost represents the number of hops (intermediate nodes) between nodes.

41. C, D. CIDR and supernetting can be used to treat three consecutive network addresses as a single network address. IP Routing (choice B) can connect the networks, but they still use separate network addresses. Subnetting (choice A) is the opposite: it treats one network address as several.

42. A, B, D. The TCP/IP Printing service allows UNIX clients to print to NT printers, and NT clients to print to UNIX printers. NT clients can also monitor UNIX print queues. While NT clients can print to NT printers in other subnets (choice C) this is not a function of the TCP/IP Printing service.

43. B. The correct command is lpr -S unixserv -P laser2 file1.txt.

44. A. The lpr command sends a file to a UNIX print queue.

45. D. The default time to live (TTL) for a WINS registration under Windows NT Server is six days.

46. A. The Network Interface object is added to Performance Monitor when the SNMP service is installed.

47. C. The OSPF (Open Shortest Path First) routing protocol is not included with NT Server 4.0.

48. D. No additional service needs to be installed to support static IP routing. For dynamic routing, RIP (choice A) must be installed.

49. C. The WINS Proxy service requires a registry change to be enabled.

50. B. An MIB (Management Information Base) is used by the SNMP (Simple Network Management Protocol) service.

Highlighter's Index

Protocols

Network Interface Layer
Handles physical network topology and media
Protocols: Ethernet, Token Ring, PPP, etc.

Internet Layer
Handles routing and communication between networks
IP (Internet Protocol): Combines data into packets; handles IP addressing
ICMP (Internet Control Message Protocol): Network management and diagnostics
IGMP (Internet Group Management Protocol): Manages groups of nodes
Other protocols: ARP, DHCP, RIP, OSPF, etc.

Transport Layer
Allows for communications between hosts
TCP: Connection-oriented, reliable, full-duplex
UDP: Connectionless, unreliable, slightly faster transmissions

Application Layer
Supports applications and high-level services
Protocols: Telnet, FTP, HTTP, NFS, etc.

IP Addressing

IP Addresses are divided into classes. This table describes the differences between the classes:

Class	Network/ Host Octets	Leading Bits	First Byte Range	Networks	Hosts per Network
A	1/3	0	1–126	126	16,777,214
B	2/2	10	128–191	16,382	65,534
C	3/1	110	192–223	2,097,150	254

Subnet Masking

Class A default: 255.0.0.0
Class B default: 255.255.0.0
Class C default: 255.255.255.0
Number of networks: $2^{(bits)} -2$
Number of hosts (Class A): $2^{(24 - bits)} -2$
Number of hosts (Class B): $2^{(16 - bits)} -2$
Number of hosts (Class C): $2^{(8 - bits)} -2$

This table can be used to calculate subnet masks:

Subnet Address Bits	Address Block	Mask Ends With	Subnets	Class C Hosts	Class B Hosts	Class A Hosts
2	64	192	2	62	16,382	4,194,302
3	32	224	6	30	8190	2,097,150
4	16	240	14	14	4094	1,048,574
5	8	248	30	6	2046	524,286
6	4	252	62	2	1022	262,142
7	2	254	126	(Invalid)	510	131,070
8	1	255	254	(Invalid)	254	65,534

Instructions for recreating this table for use during the exam

As an alternative to learning the formulas and performing binary conversions during the exam, you can recreate the above table of subnet masks on the writing materials provided. These instructions may seem complex, but you should be able to easily recreate the table after practicing a few times. (You are also allowed to use the Windows Calculator for this test.)

1. Divide your paper into 8 rows. Write the numbers 2 through 8 down the left column to form the Subnet Address Bits column.

2. Start at the bottom of the second column with 1, and double the number as you go up (1, 2, 4, 8...) to form the Address Block column.

3. For the Subnet Mask column, start with 255 at the bottom of the third column. Subtract the Address Block value to the left to form the next row up's value, and proceed in this fashion (255 minus 1 is 254, 254 minus 2 is 252, 252 minus 4 is 248, etc.).

4. For the Subnets column, start at the top row. Each row's value is 2 to the power of the number of address bits minus 2. The powers of two double each line, so the values from the top are 4 minus 2, 8 minus 2, 16 minus 2, and so on.

5. For the Class C Hosts column, remember that the bottom two rows should be marked as invalid. The top five rows are the same as the top five rows of the Subnets column, but in reverse order.

6. You will not usually need the Class B and Class A Hosts columns. If you do, start at the bottom of the Class B column with 256 (2^8) minus 2, and continue with powers of two (512 minus 2 is 510, 1024 minus 2 is 1022, etc.). For the Class A column, start with 65536 (2^{16}) minus 2 and go up. To double-check your chart, the values in the Class C, B, and A columns for each row should end in the same digit.

DHCP (Dynamic Host Configuration Protocol)

Basics

Maintains a pool of addresses (Scope) and assigns dynamically
Uses broadcasts and one or more dedicated DHCP servers
Manage with DHCP Manager

Client Configuration

DHCP server address not required
DHCP can be used for IP address, subnet mask, default gateway, WINS Server, and DNS Server settings under Windows NT
Clients require IP address and subnet mask, either manually configured or using DHCP

Name Resolution

Host Name Resolution Order

1. Local host name

2. The HOSTS file

3. Any configured DNS servers

4. WINS (NetBIOS)

5. B-node broadcast (NetBIOS)

6. LMHOSTS file (NetBIOS)

HOSTS File

Used for host name resolution
ASCII list of names (aliases) and IP addresses
Stored in \winnt\system\drivers\etc\HOSTS
Consulted before DNS server

DNS (Domain Name Service)

Internet standard for host name resolution; requires a DNS server
Windows NT Server includes DNS Server software
Zone: defined group of names and IP addresses
Requires definition of at least one zone in database

NetBIOS Name Resolution Order

1. Local name cache

2. WINS Server

3. B-node broadcast

4. LMHOSTS file

5. HOSTS file

6. DNS Server

NetBIOS Resolution Node Types

B-node (broadcast): Sends a broadcast and waits for a response from the
appropriate node
Enhanced B-node: Checks LMHOSTS file if no response is received from
broadcast
P-node (peer-to-peer): Queries a WINS server
M-node (mixed): Sends a broadcast, and queries a WINS server if no response
H-node (hybrid): Queries WINS server if available, then uses broadcasts
Windows NT uses Enhanced B-node or H-node

LMHOSTS File

Used for NetBIOS name resolution; consulted before WINS server
ASCII list of NetBIOS names and IP addresses
Stored in \winnt\system\drivers\etc\LMHOSTS
Sample file stored in LMHOSTS.SAM
Enable from WINS tab of TCP/IP Properties

WINS (Windows Internet Naming Service)

Uses a dedicated server; WINS Server included with NT Server
Used with P-node, M-node, H-node resolution
Configure with WINS Manager utility
Clients require WINS server address
Server address can be set with DHCP

IP Printing

TCP/IP Printing Service
NT clients can print to UNIX printers
UNIX clients can print to NT printers
Supports LPD (line printer daemon) standard

IP Printing Utilities
lpr: Adds a print job to a UNIX print queue
lpq: Displays current print queue contents
These commands work for UNIX servers, or for NT servers running the TCP/
IP Printing service

IP Routing

Static Routing
Uses a routing table with network addresses and gateways
Default gateway is used when no explicit route exists

Dynamic Routing
Uses a routing protocol (RIP or OSPF)
Windows NT Server includes RIP for IP

Routing Protocols
RIP (Routing Information Protocol): Distance vector protocol; uses distance (in
hops) to choose routes
OSPF (Open Shortest Path First): Link-state protocol; not supported by default
in Windows NT

SNMP (Simple Network Management Protocol)

Components
Agents run on machines to be monitored
Agents maintain an MIB (management information base)
Management systems obtain data from agents and analyze it

Messages
GetRequest: Obtain a parameter's value from MIB
SetRequest: Set a parameter's value, if supported
Trap: Sent from agent to indicate an error condition

Command-Line Utilities

arp

Displays information and statistics for the ARP protocol.

hostname

Displays the IP host name of the local machine.

ipconfig

Displays or modifies IP address configuration. Includes options to release or renew an address obtained via DHCP.

nbtstat

Displays or modifies information and statistics relating to NetBIOS over TCP/IP.

net start, net stop

Starts or stops a network service.

netstat

Displays TCP/IP network statistics and information about current connections.

nslookup

Translates between host names and IP addresses using DNS.

ping

Sends an echo request to a host via ICMP and awaits a reply.

route

Displays routing table information; allows additions and deletions to route table entries.

tracert

Displays a list of intermediate nodes between the local host and a remote host.

PART 2

Internet Information Server 4.0

Exam Overview

The Internet, which began life as the U.S. Department of Defense's ARPANET project, is now the world's largest network, and has become hugely popular in recent years. Microsoft Internet Information Server (IIS) is a server for several common Internet services, including Web and FTP.

Microsoft's MCSE Exam 70-087, *Implementing and Supporting Microsoft Internet Information Server 4.0*, covers all aspects of IIS, from installation to trouble-shooting, from an administrator's point of view. The emphasis is on managing the server rather than creating the actual content.

IIS 4.0 is a major revision. It includes a variety of features and services that were not included in version 3.0, and replaces the Internet Service Manager with an integrated utility called Microsoft Management Console (MMC). If you are familiar with a previous version of IIS, you should install and study the new version.

In order to prepare for this chapter and the IIS exam, you should have studied for and passed the Network Essentials, Windows NT Server, and Windows NT Server in the Enterprise exams. In addition, you should study the "IP Addressing" section of Part 1, *Internetworking with TCP/IP*, if you haven't passed the TCP/IP exam.

Objectives

Need to Know	Reference
Basics of Internet protocols and services	"Internet Protocols and Services" on page 90
Types of Web content	"Web Content" on page 91
IIS components and their purposes	"Components of IIS" on page 96
Differences between IIS versions	"IIS Versions" on page 99
IIS hardware requirements and required software	"Installation Planning" on page 100

Need to Know	Reference
Differences between IIS installation methods	"Installation Methods" on page 103
Tools for managing IIS services	"IIS Administration" on page 105
Methods of running virtual servers	"Virtual Servers" on page 116
Features and purposes of Index Server, Certificate Server, Transaction Server, SMTP Service, and NNTP Service	"Managing Other Services" on page 119
Supported log file formats and their limitations	"Setting Logging Options" on page 131
Performance Monitor counters associated with IIS services	"Monitoring IIS Performance" on page 132

Need to Apply	Reference
Plan an IIS installation.	"Installation Planning" on page 100
Install IIS and related services.	"The IIS Installation Process" on page 102
Configure WWW service properties.	"Configuring WWW Services" on page 108
Create custom HTTP headers.	"HTTP Headers" on page 111
Configure FTP service properties.	"Configuring FTP Services" on page 112
Create virtual Web or FTP directories.	"Virtual Directories" on page 115
Create virtual Web or FTP servers.	"Virtual Servers" on page 116
Control access to Web and FTP directories.	"IIS Security" on page 117
Configure Microsoft Index Server and integrate it with IIS.	"Index Server" on page 119
Configure Certificate Server and issue certificates.	"Certificate Server" on page 122
Use the Transaction Explorer utility to manage Transaction Server.	"Transaction Server" on page 123
Configure and manage the SMTP service.	"SMTP Service" on page 124
Configure and manage the NNTP service.	"NNTP Service" on page 128
Set options for logging for Web, FTP, SMTP, and NNTP services.	"Setting Logging Options" on page 131
Import and create reports from log files.	"Creating Reports" on page 132
Monitor IIS and determine bottlenecks.	"Monitoring IIS Performance" on page 132
Optimize Web and FTP services.	"Optimizing IIS" on page 133
Analyze sites with Content Analyzer.	"Analyzing Web Content" on page 134
Troubleshoot common IIS problems.	"Troubleshooting Common Problems" on page 134

Study Guide

This chapter includes the following sections, which address various topics covered on the IIS MCSE exam:

IIS Basics

Introduces the Internet protocols and services supported by IIS and its related software, the types of documents typically used with IIS, and the components of IIS and the Windows NT Option Pack.

Installing IIS

Describes the process of planning an IIS installation, the hardware and software requirements, and the steps involved in the installation.

Configuring IIS

Explains the administrative tools included with IIS, and shows how to configure the web and FTP services within IIS and secure IIS resources.

Managing Other Services

Describes several other services included with IIS: Index Server, Certificate Server, SMTP Service, and NNTP Service.

Optimization and Troubleshooting

Describes the process of using IIS log files and monitoring performance with the Performance Monitor utility, and describes methods of optimizing IIS and analyzing web content.

IIS Basics

Internet Information Server 4.0 includes a variety of services for use on the Internet or local Intranets. The Windows NT 4.0 Option Pack, which includes IIS 4.0, also includes a variety of other Internet-related services.

The following sections describe the Internet standards, services, and protocols supported by IIS and related software, the types of documents typically used with IIS, and the architecture and features of IIS 4.0.

On the Exam

There are a number of significant differences between IIS 4.0 and previous versions. This chapter and the exam focus on version 4.0. If you have experience with a previous version, you should still install IIS 4.0 and study it thoroughly.

Internet Protocols and Services

The Internet began life as the U.S. Department of Defense's ARPANET project, and has since evolved into a globe-spanning network of computers including those of universities, companies, and an increasing number of individuals.

Internet services are based on the platform-independent TCP/IP protocol suite, described in Part 1, *Internetworking with TCP/IP*. The following sections describe some of the most commonly-used protocols and services.

World Wide Web

The World Wide Web (WWW) is the most well-known Internet service. Web servers act as a repository for web documents, and distribute the documents to clients using the HTTP (Hypertext Transfer Protocol) protocol. IIS acts as a web server under Windows NT.

Web clients are called *browsers*. The most popular current browsers are Microsoft Internet Explorer (IE) 4.0 and Netscape Navigator 4.0. Web documents include text, HTML (hypertext markup language), and other types described later in this chapter.

Web documents (and documents using other protocols) can be referred to with a URL, or uniform resource locator. A URL has this form:

http://site/directory/filename

The first portion of the URL, *http://*, refers to the HTTP protocol. FTP, News, and other protocols can also be specified. The remainder of the URL specifies a site name (an IP host name) and a directory and file under the site. If a filename is not specified, the directory's default document (typically default.htm or index.html) is sent to the client.

File Transfer Protocol (FTP)

FTP is a protocol that allows file transfers (uploads and downloads) between hosts on a TCP/IP network (such as the Internet). This protocol predates the WWW, and is still widely used.

FTP is also a client-server protocol. FTP servers answer requests and accept a variety of standard commands: for example, GET to download a file and PUT to upload a file. FTP clients may be simple command-based clients, or may provide a graphic interface while transmitting commands to the FTP server in the background.

An FTP server is included in IIS 4.0. In addition, Windows NT and Windows 95 include a command-line FTP utility. To use it, type `ftp` followed by the name of the site to connect to at the command prompt:

```
ftp ftp.ora.com
```

Email

While not as glamorous or graphically attractive as the Web, email is at least as popular among Internet users. Users can employ a wide variety of email clients to send text-based messages to other users. Internet email is largely distributed by two protocols:

SMTP (Simple Mail Transfer Protocol)
> Used by clients to send and receive messages, as well as between hosts to route messages to their destinations.

POP (Post Office Protocol)
> A more recent protocol, typically used by graphic email clients to transfer messages from a server for reading offline.

On the Exam

IIS 4.0 includes an implementation of the SMTP service, but does not include full email capabilities. Microsoft Exchange, covered in Part 5, *Exchange Server 5.5*, is a full-featured mail server.

Discussion Groups

A less popular aspect of the Internet is discussion groups, also called *newsgroups*. These are linked databases of messages (called *articles*) that allow non-realtime discussions, similar to email but in a public forum. A large number of newsgroups are available, including the standard USENET groups.

Rather than being stored on a central server, newsgroups use a distributed system. Each server that participates in a newsgroup stores its own copy of every message, networking with one or more other servers to receive copies of messages from other systems and distribute new messages. News servers communicate using the NNTP (Network News Transfer Protocol) protocol.

Web Content

While IIS includes Web, FTP, and a number of other services, it is primarily known as a web server, and most IIS installations exist primarily for this purpose. While the HTTP protocol can be used to transfer any type of document, several types of content are commonly used with web servers. These are described in the following sections.

On the Exam

For the IIS exam, you should be familiar with the features, capabilities, and typical uses of the following content types, and know how to deal with server issues relating to them. You do not need to know the exact commands or techniques used to create web content.

Hypertext Markup Language (HTML)

While web (HTTP) servers can be used with any type of documents, they are traditionally used for HTML (Hypertext Markup Language) documents. HTML is a language developed specifically for the Web, and integrates text, graphics, and other content.

In the Real World

HTML is a subset of SGML (Structured Generalized Markup Language), a standard language used to define elements (headers, paragraphs, etc). within a text document. While intended primarily for text, the current version of the HTML standard (4.0) includes tags for graphics, embedded programs and scripts, and other non-text content.

HTML documents are constructed with commands called *tags*. Tags are enclosed within angle brackets. Some tags can be used alone, while others are containers, requiring open and closing tags. The closing tag consists of a slash followed by the tag name. For example, an entire HTML document is enclosed by the tags <HTML> and </HTML>.

HTML tags are used to define particular types of text within a document (paragraphs, headings, etc.); to define the formatting used to display text (boldface, italic, fixed font, etc.); and for other features, such as images and links to other documents. The following is a simple example of a minimal HTML document:

```
<HTML>
<HEAD>
<TITLE>A simple document</TITLE>
</HEAD>
<BODY>
<H1>This is a heading</H1>
<P>This is the first paragraph.
Click <a href="http://www.oreilly.com/">Here</a>
to follow a link. </P>
</BODY>
</HTML>
```

HTML is a standard language maintained by the World Wide Web Consortium (W3C). The current version of the HTML standard is 4.0, and the standard continues to evolve. Internet Explorer 4.0 and Netscape Navigator 4.0 follow this new standard.

The HTML standard is intended to allow users of different browsers on different platforms to view the same document, and this is possible when the standard is followed. Older browsers on older machines, text-based browsers, and even custom software for sight-impaired users can be used to read web documents.

In the Real World

While both Microsoft and Netscape claim that their browsers support the latest HTML standard, neither is a full and precise implementation, and both browsers include support for non-standard features. Unfortunately, many web designers abandon the HTML standard and design for a particular browser, reducing the usefulness of the standard.

Java

The Java language, originally developed by Sun Microsystems, has become the Internet's de facto standard for web-based applications. Java is an object-oriented language, similar to C++, and is designed for platform independence.

Java can be used to create two types of programs: applications and applets. Applications are stand-alone programs, and applets are embedded within a web page. Applets are typically stored on a web server and referenced with the <APPLET> or <EMBED> tags in HTML.

When a Java applet is created, the Java statements are compiled into *bytecode*, a pseudo-machine code, and stored in a *class file* on the web server. The browser loads the class file when it encounters the <APPLET> tag, and executes it via the Java virtual machine. Modern web browsers further compile the bytecode into platform-specific machine code using a just-in-time compiler.

In the Real World

While Java was intended to be platform-independent, today's Java programmers have to deal with incompatibilities not only between platforms, but between browsers on the same platform. Microsoft has created their own version of the Java virtual machine, included in Internet Explorer 4.0; this version is not 100% compatible with Sun's specification for the Java language.

JavaScript and VBScript

JavaScript, developed by Netscape Corporation, is a client-side scripting language with syntax based loosely on that of Java. The script commands are embedded within an HTML web page, and are executed by the client (browser) when the page is displayed.

<table>
<tr><td>

On the Exam

Microsoft's implementation of JavaScript is called JScript, to differentiate it from Netscape's version, and is not wholly compatible with the JavaScript specification. While the two languages have much in common, IIS and IE officially support only JScript, and you will rarely find mention of JavaScript in the MCSE exams.

</td></tr>
</table>

VBScript (or Visual Basic Script) is Microsoft's alternative to JavaScript, and is a subset of the Visual Basic language. Both languages can manipulate the content of a web page using a hierarchy of browser objects.

Scripts are embedded in an HTML document between <SCRIPT> and </SCRIPT> tags. The following is an example of a simple HTML document containing a JavaScript command to display the modification date of the document:

```
<HTML>
<HEAD>
<TITLE>Simple Example</TITLE>
</HEAD>
<BODY>
<H1>JavaScript Example</H1>
<SCRIPT>
document.write("Document last modified" +
document.lastModified);
</SCRIPT>
</BODY>
</HTML>
```

ActiveX

ActiveX, Microsoft's specification for embedded applications, can also be used within web documents. ActiveX programs, called *components*, are compiled programs that can be executed within the web browser. ActiveX programs are actually a type of Windows program, and are generally platform-specific. ActiveX is supported only by Internet Explorer.

An extension of ActiveX called Component Object Model (COM) allows reusable components to be created and controlled by scripting languages, such as Active Server Pages. For example, IIS includes an IIS Admin object that can be used to modify the IIS configuration under script control.

Common Gateway Interface (CGI)

The HTML specification includes the <FORM> tag and a number of related tags, which can be used to create interactive forms within web documents. This feature is frequently used for questionnaires, order forms, and other applications that require information from the user.

After data is entered into the form, the user presses a button to submit the form contents. The data is then passed back to the server, typically to a CGI application. The CGI program can then send an HTML document in response.

CGI is not a language, but a standard for programs to be executed on web servers. In practice, CGI programs can be created as binary programs using languages such as C++, or as scripts using languages such as Perl or Active Server Pages (described in the next section).

In the Real World

Perl is a script language commonly used in UNIX systems, and is by far the most popular language for CGI programs. Perl is not directly supported by IIS, but support can be added with third-party software.

Active Server Pages (ASP)

Active Server Pages is a scripting language developed by Microsoft. Unlike Java-Script or VBScript, ASP is a server-side language: the scripts are parsed and executed by the web server, and are not sent to the browser.

ASP scripts are embedded in HTML documents, enclosed between the special symbols <% and %>. Any output generated by the script is sent to the browser as part of the HTML document, and displayed accordingly.

In the Real World

ASP is generally used as an alternative to CGI. It is a relatively simple language to use for server-side applications such as database access. Its main disadvantage is that it is proprietary to Microsoft, and supported only by IIS.

Style Sheets

HTML was originally designed as a text definition language, more concerned with content than presentation. However, the Web has evolved into a popular medium, and web designers continually look for ways to gain more control over the format, colors, and other aspects of their documents.

Style sheets are a new W3C standard that give designers precise control over document formatting, while still allowing users to override settings. A style sheet can be embedded within an HTML document or in its own document. Styles can be specified for particular elements (headings, paragraphs, etc.) and for entire documents.

Dynamic HTML

Dynamic HTML (DHTML) is a new addition to HTML that allows script control over style sheet elements and other elements. This allows portions of a page's content to be changed dynamically without redisplaying the entire page. DHTML is supported by the latest Microsoft and Netscape browsers.

In the Real World

Microsoft and Netscape both introduced technologies called Dynamic HTML at roughly the same time, and there is still some difference in the way it is supported in the different browsers.

Channels

Channels are a new form of web content, designed for information that is updated regularly; for example, news items. Channels are HTML documents that can be subscribed to by a user. Once subscribed, the user is notified when the document has changed, and can automatically update their copy of the document.

Channels are defined as regular HTML pages combined with a content definition file, or CDF. The CDF describes the content of the document and indicates how frequently it is typically updated.

Components of IIS

IIS 4.0 is available from Microsoft as part of the Windows NT 4.0 Option Pack, a bundle of supplemental software for Windows NT 4.0. The Option Pack is available for purchase with Windows NT, and is available for download or purchase from Microsoft.

The following sections examine the components of IIS 4.0 and several IIS-related components also included in the Option Pack.

On the Exam

For the IIS 4.0 exam, you should be familiar with all of the software included in the NT 4.0 Option pack, including all of the services described in this chapter.

WWW and FTP Services

The core of IIS provides World Wide Web and file transfer protocol (FTP) services. Both of these services are handled by the *inetinfo.exe* process under Windows NT. Both the FTP and HTTP (WWW) services are multithreaded services, designed to handle a number of users at the same time.

Index Server

Index Server, included with IIS 4.0, provides indexing and search features for web content. The Index Server can be configured to read and index the content of

---

some or all of the web pages made available on the server, and provides a search facility through web-based forms.

Certificate Server

The HTTP protocol is normally insecure; data is transmitted in unencrypted form, and can be read by anyone. Security has been implemented for web documents through public-key cryptography. The main secure protocol for web servers is secure socket layer, or SSL.

Secure communication relies on authentication. SSL uses digital certificates, which securely identify the source of encrypted information. Microsoft Certificate Server is an Option Pack component that allows you to issue, renew, and revoke these certificates.

Microsoft Transaction Server (MTS)

Microsoft Transaction Server (MTS) is an Option Pack component that supports transaction-based web applications. Transactions are a way of managing database access to ensure reliability and consistency. Applications can be built and managed using the Transaction Server Explorer utility.

Internet Connection Services (ICS)

Windows NT allows dial-up users to access networks through the use of Remote Access Services, or RAS. ICS is an add-on for RAS that adds support for new protocols and services.

ICS includes the PPTP (Point-to-Point Tunneling Protocol), which allows private networking over public networks: packets are encrypted, sent over a public network such as the Internet, and decrypted. This allows the formation of *virtual private networks* (VPNs): corporate networks that connect locations via the Internet, rather than using a dedicated WAN connection.

Data Access Components

When a web site is intended to allow access to a large amount of data—as is common in corporate Intranets—it is usually best to use a standard database server, such as SQL, rather than strictly web-based tools. IIS includes Microsoft Data Access Components, a collection of utilities to allow access to SQL servers and other ODBC-compliant databases. These are made available as objects, which can be manipulated through ActiveX, Active Server Pages, or other languages.

Active Server Pages (ASP)

IIS includes support for ASP, as described earlier in this chapter. If this feature is enabled, scripts are executed when web pages are requested. Microsoft Script Debugger, a utility for debugging ASP scripts, is also included.

Microsoft Message Queue (MSMQ)

Microsoft Message Queue Server (MSMQ) is an Option Pack component that provides a messaging interface for application programs. This server maintains a queue of messages, and automatically routes them between applications. MSMQ can work with MTS to enable communication between transaction-based applications.

Site Server Express

Microsoft Site Server Express, included with IIS 4.0, is a suite of utilities for managing web content and log files. The following components are included:

Content Analyzer
> A utility that analyzes web content and maps it in several ways. This utility can be used to find invalid links and create navigational tools.

Posting Acceptor
> An IIS add-on that supports the HTTP POST command, allowing users to upload web content to the server without using FTP or other tools.

Usage Import and Report Writer
> A utility that analyzes IIS log files and generates a variety of reports.

In the Real World

The HTTP POST command, supported by the Posting Acceptor service, is a standard defined in RFC 1867. In addition to Microsoft software, this protocol is supported by some versions of Netscape Communicator.

Administration Tools

IIS includes a variety of tools for managing its configuration, all described later in this chapter. These include the following:

Internet Service Manager
> This main IIS configuration utility operates within Microsoft Management Console, described below. A web-based version of Internet Service Manager that can be used remotely is also included with IIS 4.0.

Windows Scripting Host
> Allows client-side scripts written using JavaScript or VBScript to manipulate IIS configuration values.

Microsoft Management Console
> A versatile tool that can be used to manage IIS as well as other aspects of Windows NT Server.

IIS Versions

Internet Information Server has progressed through a number of versions since it was first introduced. While IIS 4.0 is the current version, several versions are currently available. These are described in the sections that follow.

IIS 2.0

IIS 2.0 is included with Windows NT Server 4.0, and can be selected for installation during the Windows NT installation process. IIS 2.0 includes FTP, web, and Gopher (a text-based service that predates the Web) services.

Personal Web Server (PWS)

PWS 2.0, a feature-limited version of IIS 2.0, is included with Windows NT Workstation 4.0. This version includes FTP, web, and Gopher services, but is limited to 10 incoming connections (as is NT Workstation itself). This server is adequate for small company Intranets.

IIS 3.0 and Index Server

IIS 3.0 is included with Windows NT Server 4.0 Service Pack 2 (SP2). SP2 is available for download from Microsoft. Index Server 1.0 is also included in SP2.

IIS 4.0

IIS 4.0 is the latest version, currently available as part of the Windows NT Server 4.0 Option Pack. IIS 4.0 runs under Windows NT Server 4.0. It can also be installed under NT Workstation or Windows 95; under these systems IIS is also known as Personal Web Server (PWS) and is limited to 10 incoming connections.

On the Exam

The IIS 4.0 exam focuses on the use of IIS under Windows NT Server, although it can be used on other platforms. The exam may refer to PWS 4.0; this is the name for the limited-capability version for NT Workstation and Windows 95.

The remainder of this chapter describes this version. IIS 4.0 includes a number of new features:

- Support for the HTTP 1.1 protocol, a new specification that allows for more efficient data transfer

- Allows support for file uploading from clients to server via the HTTP 1.1 PUT command and an alternate method defined in RFC 1867

- Supports HTTP redirection (the server can respond to a request by diverting the browser to a different server or location)

- Support for SMTP (Simple Mail Transport Service)

- Support for discussion groups with the NNTP (Net News Transport Protocol) protocol

- Support for remote administration with the IIS Admin Objects

- Allows dynamic loading and unloading of IIS components

- Includes Microsoft Management Console, a new administrative utility for IIS and other Windows NT services

- Includes support for clustering (included in the Windows NT 4.0 Enterprise Edition), allowing fault tolerance through redundant servers

- Support for SSL (Secure Sockets Layer) 3.0

On the Exam

For the IIS 4.0 MCSE exam, you should be familiar with the new features of IIS 4.0 and have experience using and configuring this version. You should also have some experience with IIS 2.0, included with NT Server. IIS 2.0 is addressed by the NT Server in the Enterprise exam, covered by *MCSE: The Core Exams in a Nutshell.*

Installing IIS

IIS is relatively simple to install, and will run on most computers that can run Windows NT. The following sections look at the hardware and software requirements of IIS 4.0, the installation process, and the steps involved in installing other components of the Windows NT 4.0 Option Pack.

Installation Planning

Unlike IIS 2.0, which comes with Windows NT Server, IIS 4.0 must be installed separately. The installation files can be downloaded from Microsoft's web site, and are available on CD as part of the Windows NT 4.0 Option Pack.

In the Real World

When you install Windows NT Server, you are given the option to install IIS 2.0. IIS 4.0 does not require any files from this previous version, so there is no need to install it before installing the new version. If you have already installed IIS 2.0, you should remove it before installing version 4.0.

Hardware Requirements

IIS 4.0 does not require a great deal of hardware beyond that required by Windows NT itself. The minimum requirements for IIS are 32 MB of RAM and a 486 processor. Microsoft's recommended minimum for an efficient IIS server is a 90-MHz Pentium or faster and 64 MB of RAM.

If your server will be heavily used, a larger amount of RAM will increase speed. Processor speed will have little effect on the server's speed unless a large amount of CPU-intensive operations (such as CGI and ASP scripts) are used.

In addition to the disk storage required by Windows NT itself, IIS requires a minimum of 50 MB of disk storage (Microsoft recommends at least 200 MB). Additional services (such as SMTP) will require more storage. In addition, the Web and other documents stored on the server will require storage.

On the Exam

The requirements listed above are for the Intel versions of Windows NT and IIS, which the exam focuses on. The requirements for the Alpha version are a 150-MHz processor (200 MHz recommended) and 48 MB of RAM (64 MB recommended).

Windows NT Configuration

Depending on the scale of your Internet/Intranet server needs, you may use a dedicated server to run IIS, or run it on an existing server. For an existing server, the Windows NT configuration may need to be changed to accommodate IIS. IIS requires the following configuration:

- The TCP/IP protocol must be installed and configured. To avoid problems, you may wish to assign the server a fixed IP address, although this is not required.

- Windows NT Service Pack 3 (SP3) must be installed before installing IIS.

- Internet Explorer 4.01 (IE4) must be installed before installing IIS. While IE is a client application, it includes several system-level DLL files that IIS 4.0 requires. In addition, IE4 is required to display some of the HTML-based configuration dialogs.

- To improve the server's speed, you may wish to move the swap file to a drive other than the system volume. However, this disables the memory dump feature, which may be useful in the event of a system crash.

Security and Fault Tolerance

IIS 4.0's security largely depends on the security of the underlying Windows NT operating system. Most of the security features can be configured after IIS is installed and running.

The one security-related change you should make before installing IIS is the use of the NTFS file system. IIS can be used on a FAT system, but does not provide any file or directory security of its own. With NTFS, anonymous access can be tightly controlled, and user-based full access can be configured.

The IIS Installation Process

Like Windows NT, IIS 4.0 includes a friendly installation program. The same program is used to install IIS and the other components of the Option pack. To install IIS, you will need a copy of the Option Pack installation files for the appropriate operating system (Windows 95, NT Workstation, or NT Server).

On the Exam

This section describes the installation of IIS 4.0 and the Option Pack under Windows NT Server 4.0. Installation is similar for NT Workstation or Windows 95, although some features will be unavailable.

Installing Required Software

Before installing IIS, you must install Windows NT Service Pack 3 and Internet Explorer 4.0. If you are installing the Option Pack from CD-ROM, these should be included on the CD; otherwise, you will need to download them from Microsoft's web site.

Service Pack 3 should be installed first. To install it, select the EXE file in the I386 directory. The SP3 installation is automatically, and does not prompt you for any information. After installation, restart Windows NT.

To install IE4, start the IE4SETUP.EXE program and follow the instructions. If you are installing IE4 strictly to allow IIS to install, you can use a Custom installation and disable the optional components.

Installation Methods

The Option Pack setup program includes three basic options: Minimum, Typical, and Custom. The first two options provide predefined combinations of components, while the Custom option allows you to select or deselect all components. Table 2-1 lists the optional features and indicates which type of installation they are available from.

Table 2-1: Components of the Option Pack

Component	Minimum	Typical
Internet Information Server (web server)	Yes	Yes
Index Server	Yes	Yes
Management Console (MMC)	Yes	Yes
Internet Service Manager	Yes	Yes
Microsoft Transaction Server (MTS)	Yes	Yes
Frontpage extensions and Posting Acceptor	Yes	Yes
Data Access Components	Yes	Yes
Active Server Pages	Yes	Yes
FTP Service	No	Yes
HTML Internet Service Manager	No	Yes
Online Documentation	No	Yes
Script Debugger	No	Yes
Site Server Express	No	No
Windows Scripting Host	No	Yes
Web Publishing Wizard	No	No
Certificate Server	No	No
SMTP Service	No	Yes
NNTP Service	No	No

On the Exam

For the IIS 4.0 MCSE exam, you should have an idea of which components are included with each type of installation, although you do not need to memorize the list above.

Installing IIS

IIS and the other components of the NT Option Pack are installed from the same setup program. Follow these steps to install the Option Pack:

1. To start the installation, run the SETUP.EXE program in the installation directory for the appropriate operating system.

2. An introductory dialog should be displayed. Press Next to continue.

3. The license agreement for IIS is now displayed. Press Accept to accept the agreement and continue the installation.

4. You are now prompted to choose an installation method (*Minimum, Typical,* or *Custom*) as described above. Choose *Custom* to allow the installation of all components.

5. If you selected Custom installation, a list of Option Pack components is now displayed. Select the components you wish to install; you can add or remove components after installation if necessary. Some components are divided into subcomponents, which you can also select or deselect.

6. You are now prompted for three directory locations: the home directory for web documents (default: \INETPUB\WWWROOT), the directory for the FTP service (default: \INETPUB\FTPROOT), and the directory the IIS files will be installed in (default: \Program Files).

7. If you chose to install Microsoft Transaction Server, you are now prompted for the directory for the MTS program files.

8. You are now prompted for a username and password for remote administration of MTS. If you select the *Local* option, administration must be done from the IIS computer; for remote administration, select *Remote* and a username and password.

9. If you chose to install Index Server, you are prompted for the default index directory. This will be used as the root for indexing and searching. By default, the WWW directory specified in step 6 is used.

10. If you chose to install the SMTP service, you are asked for a mail root directory. This defaults to \INETPUB\MAILROOT.

11. If you chose to install the NNTP service, you are prompted for a directory for the NNTP files. This directory will store news articles and other files used by the NNTP server. The default is \INETPUB\NNTPFILE.

12. If you chose to install Certificate Server, you are prompted for locations for shared files, the certificate database, and log files. You are then prompted for identification information (name, address, etc.) for the individual or organization issuing the certificates.

13. The files for IIS and the other components are now installed. This may take several minutes.

14. Press Finish to end the installation program. You must then restart the computer to start IIS and other services.

On the Exam

You do not need to know the exact list of installation steps for the IIS 4.0 MCSE exam, but you should be familiar with the installation process and the information required. Be sure to install IIS 4.0 at least once to gain experience with this process.

Configuring IIS

Once IIS is installed and the computer is restarted, the IIS services are started. You can now manage IIS and the other components of the Option Pack using a variety of tools found under the Windows NT 4.0 Option Pack menu under the Start menu. The following sections describe the administrative tools, the settings available for IIS, and other configuration tasks.

IIS Administration

IIS 4.0 includes two main administration tools: Microsoft Management Console (MMC) and the HTML-based Internet Service Manager. Additionally, WSH (Windows Scripting Host) can be used for batch administration. These are described in the following sections.

Microsoft Management Console (MMC)

MMC is an all-purpose management console for server applications. MMC can use a number of *snap-ins*, each of which allows administration of a different service. The IIS installation includes the Internet Service Manager snap-in for MMC. Other components (such as Index Server) include their own snap-ins.

On the Exam

While MMC currently allows you to manage IIS and related services, Microsoft plans to include MMC snap-ins for all components of Windows NT in future versions. This will allow the various administrative utilities (User Manager, Server Manager, etc.) to be run from a common interface.

Internet Service Manager

Internet Service Manager is the main administrative tool for IIS. This utility is an MMC snap-in. To start it, select *Internet Service Manager* from the Microsoft Internet Information Server menu under the Windows NT 4.0 Option Pack menu. This starts MMC and opens the snap-in.

The left-hand portion of the MMC screen displays a hierarchy of consoles (such as Internet Service Manager), computers, and the services running on each computer. Figure 2-1 shows the Internet Service Manager display with a computer name highlighted.

IIS allows multiple sites under a single service. For example, you can run several web sites with different IP addresses (or with different ports on the same address). These can be controlled individually, as described later in this section.

By default, one site is created for each service (FTP, NNTP, etc.). For the web services, a default site is created; in addition, an administrative site provides access to the HTML-based administration tools. This site uses a randomly-chosen port number as a security measure.

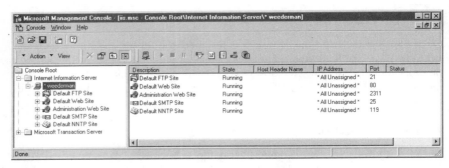

Figure 2-1: The Internet Service Manager snap-in for MMC

Web-Based Administration

IIS also includes an HTML-based version of Internet Service Manager. While there is little advantage of using this version on the local computer, it can be accessed via the Web to allow remote administration. Figure 2-2 shows the HTML version of Internet Service Manager displayed within Internet Explorer.

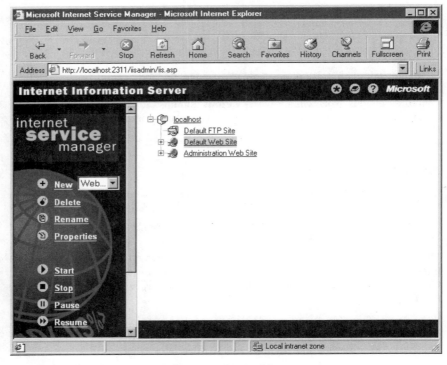

Figure 2-2: The HTML version of Internet Service Manager

You can access this version of Internet Service Manager with its entry in the Internet Information Server menu. In addition, it can be accessed through the web server using this URL:

http://hostname:port/iisadmin/iis.asp

On the Exam

Index Server (described earlier in this chapter) also includes an HTML-based administration tool.

Windows Scripting Host (WSH)

Windows Scripting Host (WSH) is a system that allows ActiveX scripting, as supported in Internet Explorer 4, to be used directly in the operating system. This allows scripting languages, such as VBScript and JavaScript, to be used for general-purpose scripting.

IIS includes a set of objects that can be used with the scripting host to control various parameters. These are organized under the IIS Admin Base Object. This object makes most of the parameters in the IIS metabase available to scripts.

On the Exam

For the IIS MCSE exam, you should know that WSH is often the fastest way to make large-scale changes to IIS configuration. For example, if you need to change the bandwidth settings for many servers in a large site, a script could be written to make all of the changes. The script could then be scheduled to change the bandwidth available at different times of the day.

The Metabase

IIS configuration is stored in the *metabase*, a database of keys and values similar to the registry. The metabase is kept in RAM while IIS is running. This database is changed when you use one of the utilities described above to modify the configuration of IIS and other services; in addition, objects in the metabase can be addressed by scripts or programs.

On the Exam

You should not need to know exact metabase keys and values for the IIS MCSE exam. The IIS 4.0 Resource Kit, available separately from Microsoft, includes a utility called MetaEdit that allows you to edit the metabase directly.

Configuring WWW Services

Internet Service Manager includes a variety of properties that control the behavior of the web server. Properties can be set at four different levels:

Master properties
> These properties are used for any new sites created. To set Master properties, right-click on the computer in Internet Service Manager. Select *Properties*; then select *WWW Service* and click Edit.

Site properties
> These properties are set for a particular site. For example, the default web site is created during the IIS installation and has its properties set to default values. To change a site's properties, right-click on the site and select *Properties*.

Directory properties
> Directories within a site can have their own properties, which override the site properties. To set directory properties, right-click on the directory and select *Properties*.

File properties
> Files within a web site can have their own properties, which override the site and directory properties. To set these properties, right-click on a file and select *Properties*.

On the Exam

Although the IIS installation creates the default web site with a default set of properties, these properties are not used to initialize new sites. The Master properties are used for this purpose.

Each of these categories includes the same basic list of properties, although only a subset of the list is available for files and directories. The properties for the WWW service are divided into a number of tabbed dialogs, or *pages*; each of these is described in its own section below.

Web Site

This property page includes basic information about the web site. The following groups of parameters are included:

Web Site Identification
> Specify a description, IP address, and port for the web site. The Advanced button allows you to enter multiple addresses and ports and specify host header names for each; this feature is used to allow multiple virtual hosts to share the same IP address and port, as described later in this chapter.

Connections
> By default, IIS allows an unlimited number of concurrent connections per web site. To limit the connections for this site, select *Limited To* and specify a

---

number of connections. You can also specify a timeout (the number of seconds a connection must remain idle before being disconnected automatically).

Enable Logging

If this option is selected, log entries are written to a file for each access to the site. Use the *Active log format* option to specify the format for the log. Log options are described in more detail later in this chapter.

Operators

This property page displays a list of users who have administrative rights for the web site, and can thus manage its configuration using Internet Service Manager. By default, the Administrator account is the only operator. Use the Add button to add users.

Performance

This property page includes three groups of parameters that affect the performance of the web server:

Performance Tuning

This option allows you to estimate the number of hits (file accesses) to the site per day. IIS attempts to optimize its performance based on this number of hits; when multiple sites are running on the same server, this parameter can be used to determine which site receives the most attention from the CPU.

Enable Bandwidth Throttling

If enabled, you can specify a number (in KB per second) to limit the bandwidth available to this site. This is useful for dividing bandwidth between multiple sites based on their importance. This setting overrides the server's main bandwidth setting (set in the computer's properties in Internet Service Manager).

Connection Configuration

This section contains a single option: *HTTP Keep-Alives Enabled*. Keep-alives are a feature of HTTP 1.1 that allows clients to keep a connection open for multiple requests, increasing client performance. The disadvantage of this feature is that it increases the number of inactive connections.

On the Exam

Turning off the HTTP keep-alives option is one way to reduce the ongoing number of connections to the IIS server without resorting to restricting the number of concurrent connections.

ISAPI Filters

This property page allows you to define ISAPI (Internet Server Application Programming Interface) programs that modify the behavior of the server. For example, Microsoft Proxy Server 2.0 (described in Part 4, *Proxy Server 2.0*) implements part of its functionality as an ISAPI extension to IIS.

Home Directory

This property page includes options relating to the web site's home directory. For a directory, the properties on this page override the web site's settings. The first option on the page specifies where the directory's content is stored:

A directory located on this computer
> This is the default setting, and refers to a directory on the local computer. If this option is used for directories, a directory structure can be created under the web site that does not necessarily parallel the file system's structure.

A share located on another computer
> If selected, the directory will act as a virtual directory, and the actual content will be read from a shared directory.

A redirection to a URL
> If selected, the browser will be redirected to a URL (this URL can be on the same server, or a different server anywhere on the Internet).

If the directory uses a local directory or share, the following options are also available:

Path
> Specify the path to the directory (a local directory path or a UNC path for a share).

Read and Write
> These options provide basic security. By default, Read access is enabled and Write access is disabled. You can modify these options for a site or for individual directories. If both NTFS and IIS permissions are set for a directory, the most restrictive of the two becomes the effective permission.

Log Access
> If selected, this site (or directory) will be included in the log file.

Directory Browsing Allowed
> Normally, if the client requests a URL that includes a directory but no filename, the default document (typically Default.htm) is returned. If this document does not exist, a list of files in the directory is returned. Deselect this option to disable this feature.

Index This Directory
> This option is used by Index Server, and specifies that the directory will be included in the index.

FrontPage Web
> If selected, the directory is made accessible to clients using Microsoft FrontPage to upload or edit files.

Documents

This property page includes the following options related to web documents:

Enable Default Document

> If selected, a default document will be returned when a client requests a URL with a directory name but no filename. You can modify the list of default documents here; the default entries are Default.htm and Default.asp.

Enable Document Footer

> If selected, the specified HTML file is appended to the end of all documents served from this directory or site. This is useful for a disclaimer, notice, or address that should appear on every page.

In the Real World

The default document name that is used in most UNIX web servers is index.html. You may wish to add this document to the list if you or your customers are using content originally created for another server.

Directory Security

This property page includes options to manage the security of the directory or site. These options are described in detail in "IIS Security," later in this chapter.

HTTP Headers

HTTP headers are sent to a web client at the beginning of each web document, and typically include information such as the page's modification and expiration dates. The options in this property page allow you to customize headers:

Enable Content Expiration

> One of the HTTP headers is the Content-Expiration header, which indicates how long a document is valid. This is used by browsers to determine whether to reload a document or use a cached copy. To enable this feature, select this option and specify a date or time period.

Custom HTTP Headers

> Allows you to configure custom headers to be included in each HTTP response. Use the Add button and specify a header name and value to add a header.

Content Rating

> Optional headers can specify rating information for web documents. This does not restrict access to any documents, but rating headers allow browsers to restrict documents if so configured. IIS supports the RSAC (Recreational Software Advisory Council) rating system.

MIME Map

> MIME (Multipurpose Internet Mail Extensions) is a standard for specifying content types (text, HTML, etc.). Browsers use the MIME type specified in an HTTP header to display the document appropriately. Press the File Types button to add file types.

Custom Errors

When a client's HTTP request results in an error, an HTTP error code is returned in an HTML document. Common HTTP errors include 404 (Not Found) and 403 (Forbidden). By default, IIS returns brief text messages indicating these errors.

Using the properties in this page, you can specify custom messages to be sent in response to error conditions. Custom errors can be specified as text messages or as locations of HTML documents.

In the Real World

Since a user who receives a "not found" error message was most likely trying to access a specific page on the site, one common use for custom errors is to include links to the main company page and frequently-used pages to assist users who may have typed an incorrect address or referred to an obsolete page location.

Configuring FTP Services

As with the WWW service properties, FTP properties can be set at different levels: master properties (used for new sites), site properties, and directory properties. FTP sites do not support file properties. The categories available in FTP properties dialogs are described in the following sections.

FTP Site

This property page allows you to define basic information about the FTP site:

Identification
Specify a description, IP address, and port number for the FTP site. Unlike web sites, FTP sites can have only a single address.

Connection
Choose unlimited connections, or specify a limited number of concurrent connections for this site. You can also specify a timeout in seconds for idle connections.

Enable Logging
Enables and specifies the format for a log of FTP accesses to the site or directory.

Security Accounts

Unlike the Web, where very few documents are secured, FTP access often requires a username and password. IIS allows access using Windows NT user accounts. The options in this page allow you to configure security for the FTP site:

Allow Anonymous Connections
> If selected, anonymous access to the FTP site is permitted. The Windows NT username and password specified here are used to access files for anonymous users. The *Allow Only Anonymous Connections* option specifies that Windows NT usernames cannot be used for access.

FTP Site Operators
> This is a list of users who are allowed administrative access to the FTP site. By default, the Administrators group is included in this list.

On the Exam

If you do not select the *Allow Only Anonymous Connections* option, users can use Windows NT passwords to access FTP data. However, the FTP protocol does not encrypt passwords, and thus may be a security risk.

Messages

This property page allows you to specify three messages sent to the user by the FTP server:

Welcome
> Displayed when a user connects to the site. This message is displayed by almost all FTP clients.

Exit
> Displayed when the user exits (logs off) the site. This message is typically not visible to users of graphical FTP clients.

Maximum Connections
> Displayed when the maximum number of connections (specified in the FTP Site Property page) has been exceeded, and the user is denied access.

Home Directory

As with the Home Directory setting for the WWW service, the FTP files can be stored in a directory on the local computer, or stored in a shared directory on another computer. The following options are included here:

Path
> Specify the local directory or UNC path to a shared directory. If a shared directory is used, the Connect As button allows you to specify a username and password for the share.

Read and Write
>	Provides basic security. You can enable the *Read* option, the *Write* option, or both for a directory or site. When this setting and NTFS permissions are both defined for a directory, the most restrictive of the two is the effective permission.

Log Access
>	If selected, accesses to the FTP site or directory are logged in the log file.

Directory Listing Style
>	Choose MS-DOS or UNIX format for directory listings. MS-DOS is the default format.

In the Real World

While IIS defaults to MS-DOS directory listing format, the UNIX format is standard on the Internet. Selecting this format will provide compatibility with the greatest number of FTP clients.

Directory Security

This page allows you to restrict access to the FTP site to a particular set of machines. First, choose whether all computers will be granted access or denied access by default. You can then specify a list of exceptions to the rule by IP address or domain name.

Managing the File System

The document directory structure available to web browsers and FTP clients can mirror an NTFS directory structure, or can be configured with virtual directories and servers that act as aliases for NTFS directories. The following sections explain how to configure and manage the IIS file system.

Setting Up Directories

Each web or FTP site configured in IIS has a root, or "home," directory. For the default web site, this location is usually \INETPUB\WWWROOT. Directories created under the home directory are available to web or FTP clients.

By default, subdirectories are shared with the same permissions as the root directory. To give a subdirectory its own set of permissions, open the directory's Properties dialog from Explorer and modify the settings in the Web Sharing tab. The permissions can also be changed from Internet Service Manager's Properties dialog.

Setting Permissions

There are two sets of permissions that affect a user's ability to read files or directories from a web or FTP client:

NTFS permissions

These are Windows NT's standard file permissions. NTFS security is available only on NTFS volumes, and can be set for all users or particular users.

IIS permissions

These are IIS's specific permissions. These permissions affect all users.

To set NTFS permissions for a directory, use the Properties dialog in Explorer. To control anonymous access, assign permissions to the IIS user (typically IUSR_ `ServerName`).

To set IIS permissions, use the options on the Directory page of the Properties dialog in Internet Service Manager. The following permissions are available for web and FTP sites and directories:

Read

Allows clients to read files from the directory.

Write

Allows clients to write files to the directory using upload (FTP) or HTTP 1.1 PUT (WWW).

Browse

(WWW only) If enabled, clients requesting the directory's URL without specifying a filename are responded to with a list of files in the directory.

Script

(WWW only) Allows the execution of server-side scripts (such as ASP scripts) from the directory.

Execute

(WWW only) Allows the execution of binary programs (EXE files). This permission also includes the Script permission.

None

(WWW only) Prevents the execution of all types of scripts and programs. This can be used to override a script permission set at a higher level.

Virtual Directories

A virtual directory appears as a subdirectory of a site's home directory, but is actually located elsewhere. The content for a virtual directory can be located on the IIS computer or another computer in the Windows NT domain.

Virtual directories work the same way for web or FTP sites. To create a virtual directory, right-click on a site and select *New*, then *Virtual Directory*. (You can also create a virtual directory under a subdirectory, or under another virtual directory.)

A wizard prompts you for information to create the virtual directory. Follow these steps:

1. Choose an alias for the directory. This is the name that the directory will appear as to web or FTP clients.

2. Select the location for the directory's files. The actual directory does not need to have the same name as the virtual directory. You can enter a UNC path or browse the network to use a shared directory.

3. You are now allowed to select or deselect each of the available permissions for the virtual directory (read, write, browse, script, and execute). Select *Finish* to create the virtual directory.

On the Exam

Virtual directories located on remote computers can be slow to access, particularly if the computer is across a slow link. In addition, if the computer containing a remote directory is down or inaccessible, the virtual directory will be unavailable to clients. The advantage of remote virtual directories is that they allow content to be created on different computers and directly published without being moved to the IIS server.

Virtual Servers

Virtual servers are separate web or FTP sites run on a single server. For example, the sites *www.site1.com* and *www.site2.com* could be run on a single server, but would appear as separate sites to clients.

The simplest method of creating virtual servers is to assign multiple IP addresses to the server computer, and register each of them with the appropriate site name. To configure this type of virtual server, create two or more web or FTP sites in Internet Service manager and choose the appropriate IP address in each of their properties.

A second type of virtual server uses HTTP 1.1 *host headers* to differentiate between two or more server names registered to the same IP address. Browsers send a header with the HTTP request indicating the server name in the requested URL, and IIS differentiates based on this header.

This method avoids the need for multiple IP addresses, with some restrictions: it works only for web sites, and requires that browsers support HTTP 1.1 to access sites directly. IIS displays a menu of servers with the same IP address to browsers that do not support HTTP 1.1.

To configure virtual servers with host headers, create one or more web sites in Internet Service Manager. In the web Site page of each site's Properties dialog, click the Advanced button, then the Add button. Specify the appropriate IP address, the port number (usually 80), and the domain name for the site.

In the Real World

HTTP 1.1 is supported by the latest Microsoft and Netscape browsers, but older browsers are still used by a significant portion of the web audience. Until HTTP 1.1 is more widely supported, you may wish to avoid using the host headers feature except in controlled environments, such as local Intranets.

IIS Security

As with Windows NT itself, security is an important part of any IIS installation. The following sections describe components of IIS security and the process of configuring them to avoid security problems.

Anonymous Access

IIS can be configured to allow anonymous access to a web or FTP site or directory; for web sites, this is the default behavior. To configure anonymous access for a web site, select the Edit button in the Directory Security property page.

Enable the *Allow Anonymous Access* option and press the corresponding Edit button to choose a user account. This user account is used for anonymous access, and its permissions affect all anonymous users.

To configure an FTP site for anonymous access, enable the *Allow Anonymous Connections* option in the Security Accounts property page. You can also edit the user name and password from this page.

Authentication

Along with anonymous access, web and FTP sites can use user account names and passwords to allow access to resources. IIS uses the Windows NT user account database.

The FTP protocol always prompts for a name and password, and any Windows NT account can be used to access FTP if the user has NTFS permissions in the FTP directory.

Web sites require a method of authentication to allow non-anonymous access. Two types of authentication are supported by IIS:

Basic Authentication
> This is the standard form of authentication supported by the HTTP protocol. It may be a security risk, since passwords are transmitted as clear (ASCII) text.

Windows NT Challenge/Response
> This is a Microsoft protocol that sends an encrypted challenge based on the password and receives an encrypted response. Since no unencrypted passwords are sent over the network, this method is more secure; however, the client must support the protocol. Currently, only Microsoft Internet Explorer (versions 3.0 and later) supports this type of authentication.

In the Real World

For IIS servers connected to the Internet, you may need to use Basic Authentication to support all browsers. One way to reduce the security risk is to configure the IIS computer as a Member Server in the Windows NT domain. This allows the server to have its own set of user accounts, and if one of these accounts is compromised the Windows NT domain's accounts will still be secure.

Restricting Access

Along with user-based restriction, IIS allows access to a site or directory to be restricted based on the client's IP address or domain name. This feature is useful for preventing local content from being available to remote sites on the Internet.

On the Exam

To restrict a range of IP addresses using this feature, you will need to use the appropriate subnet mask. For the IIS MCSE exam, you should understand how to calculate a subnet mask, as described in Part 1 of this book.

To configure IP-based access restrictions for a web site, select the Edit button in the IP Address and Domain Name Restrictions section of the Directory Security property page. The resulting dialog is shown in Figure 2-3. For an FTP site, the same options are available directly from the Directory Security property page.

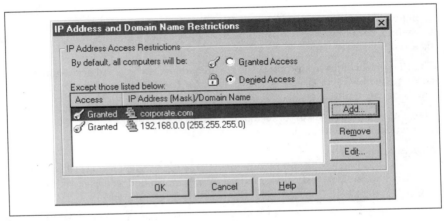

Figure 2-3: IP Address and Domain Name Restrictions

To configure access restrictions, first specify whether all computers are to be granted or denied access by default. Next, add one or more exceptions to the rule by pressing the Add button. You can specify a single computer's IP address, a network address and subnet mask for a group of computers, or a domain name.

On the Exam

The Administration web site, created when IIS is installed, has access restrictions turned on: by default, all computers are denied access, and the loopback address (127.0.0.1) is added as an exception. If you need to remotely administer the server, add one or more addresses to this list.

Encryption and Authentication

IIS supports the SSL (Secure Sockets Layer) 3.0 standard, developed by RSA Data Security, Inc. When supported by both client and server, SSL transmits all data in an encrypted form.

SSL is a *public-key* encryption scheme. This system uses two keys: a public key and a private key. Messages encrypted with the public key can only be unencrypted with the private key, and messages encrypted with the private key can only be unencrypted with the public key. This system allows the public key to be transmitted over the network without compromising security.

SSL servers use *digital certificates* to verify their identity. A digital certificate is issued by a third-party certificate authority. The certificate includes the organization's public key, and is used to verify the sender of a web page. For high-security content, client certificates can be used to authenticate clients.

To obtain a certificate from an authority, start the Key Manager utility, available from the toolbar of Internet Service Manager, and select the *Create New Key* option from the Key menu. This creates an encrypted key request based on your organization's name and other information; the request can then be sent to the authority as a text file. One popular certificate authority is VeriSign, at *www.verisign.com.*

Microsoft Certificate Server, also included with the NT Option Pack, allows you to issue digital certificates to clients or other organizations. This is explained in "Certificate Server," later in this chapter.

Managing Other Services

While IIS is primarily a web and FTP server, IIS and the Windows NT Option Pack include a variety of other components that add features to these services or act as servers for other protocols. These are explained in the following sections.

Index Server

Microsoft Index Server is a comprehensive indexing system for web documents. Index Server can be selected for installation during the Option Pack install process, or installed later.

Index Server consists of two parts: a background process that indexes documents and creates index files, and a facility for querying the index. The actual index files are stored in the catalog directory, which you selected during installation.

On the Exam

Index Server's index files use a significant amount of disk storage, usually about 40% of the total size of the documents being indexed. Be sure to plan for this storage when configuring an IIS and Index Server computer.

Managing Index Server

Index Server includes a utility called Index Server Manager, available from the Microsoft Index Server menu under the Windows NT Option Pack menu. This utility is shown in Figure 2-4. Index Server Manager is a snap-in for MMC, and has an interface similar to Internet Service Manager.

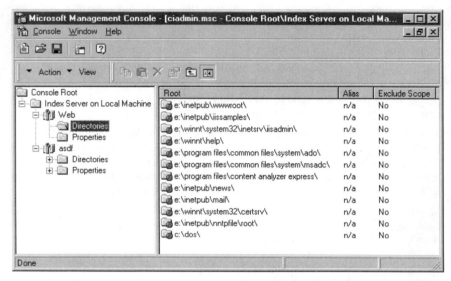

Figure 2-4: The Index Server Manager MMC snap-in

You can use the *Start* and *Stop* options in the Actions menu to start or stop the background indexing process. The entries in the hierarchy under Index Server describe each of the available catalogs; by default, a single catalog exists. Each catalog has a number of properties in the following categories:

Location

Displays the name, location, and size of the catalog. This information cannot be edited.

Web

This category includes two options. *Track Virtual Roots* specifies that virtual directories will be included in the index. *Track NNTP Roots* specifies that News directories (explained later in this chapter) will be included.

Generation

This category includes two options. *Filter files with unknown extensions* speci-fies whether Index Server will attempt to read and index files with unregistered extensions. *Generate characterizations* specifies that character-izations, or abstracts, will be generated for each document and displayed in the results of a query.

The Directories folder under each catalog's name lists the directories indexed in the catalog. You can also add or remove directories from this list by changing the

Index this directory option in the Virtual Directory property page in Internet Service Manager.

Using Index Queries

Index Server supports HTML-based queries, and includes a sample query form. To view the sample form, select *Index Server Sample Query Form* from the Index Server menu. The sample form is shown in Figure 2-5.

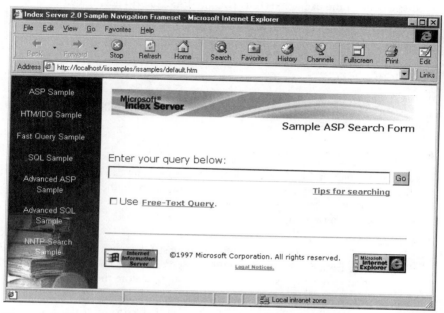

Figure 2-5: The sample query form

Queries submitted from a form like this one are sent to IDQ (Internet Data Query) files for use with Index Server. This is a simple script that lists the parameters for the query. The following are some common parameters used in IDQ files:

CiScope=path
Specifies the scope of the query. Typically \, the root directory.

CiColumns=list
Lists the columns (data items) to be listed for each document found.

CiRestriction=text
Denotes the actual text to search for in the index. The typical value here is %Restriction%, which refers to the value the user entered in the Restriction text field of the HTML form.

CiTemplate=file.htx
Specifies an HTX file for the output of the query. The HTX file is an HTML file with embedded variables to indicate the formatting of the output.

Queries can also be performed with ASP scripts or other languages. For detailed information about creating queries, see the Index Server documentation.

On the Exam

You should not need to know the exact specifications of IDQ files and other query methods for the IIS MCSE exam. However, you should view the source code of the example HTML, IDQ, and ASP files to get an idea of how they work.

Certificate Server

Microsoft Certificate Server allows you to issue, renew, and revoke digital certificates for clients or servers. Certificate Server can be installed as part of the Windows NT Option Pack installation.

Issuing Certificates

As discussed earlier in this chapter, the Key Manager utility can be used to create a certificate request file to send to a certificate authority. If the certificate will be requested from your own installation of Microsoft Certificate Server, the request can be processed in two ways:

Manual processing
> After you have obtained the certificate request file, select *Process Certificate Request File* from the Microsoft Certificate Server menu. You are prompted for the location of the request file, then the location to store the certificate.

Automated processing
> Users can submit certificate requests through a web form at the URL *http://hostname/certsrv/CertEnroll/*. The certificate is automatically processed and made available for download.

Managing Certificates

Certificate Server includes two web-based utilities for managing certificates, available from the URL *http://hostname/certsrv/*. These include the following:

Certificate Administration Log Utility
> Displays a log of certificates issued by the server with the details of the user or organization they were issued to. Select the number to the left of an entry to view its details. From this display, you can use the Revoke button to revoke the certificate.

Certificate Administration Queue Utility
> Displays the queue of certificate requests with their current status.

Transaction Server

Microsoft Transaction Server (MTS) is an Option Pack component that supports transaction-based web applications. It provides a consistent interface for applications that require transaction-based access to data.

Transactions are units of processing that encapsulate a business transaction. For example, in the sale of a product to a customer, the transaction includes billing the customer, shipping the product, and removing the product from the inventory database. Using transaction processing has four main advantages:

- The components of the transaction are either all executed, or none are executed. This prevents such problems as a product being shipped without being billed. Microsoft calls this aspect *atomicity*.

- The transactions are performed using a consistent set of rules. (For example, a product is shipped only if available in inventory.)

- Transactions are *isolated*; no two transactions that affect the same object can be executed at the same time. In our example, this would prevent the same product from being sold to two customers at the same time.

- Transactions are durable; Transaction Server tracks every stage of the transaction, and ensures that the entire transaction executes even if the server crashes.

On the Exam

Microsoft calls these four advantages of transaction processing ACID properties; this is an acronym for the four attributes (atomicity, consistency, isolation, and durability).

MTS Architecture

Transaction Server supports a three-tiered architecture for web-based applications. The three components involved in a transaction include the following:

Client
> The web client displays the graphical interface for the application, and communicates with the application server.

Application Server
> The application server is usually the same computer as the IIS server, but can be run on a separate computer. This server communicates with the client and manages transactions.

Data Source
> The data source is usually a server running Microsoft SQL Server or another database. This can be the same computer running the application, or a separate computer. The application server requests data from and sends data to the data source server.

Configuring MTS

Like other Option Pack components, MTS can be managed using MMC. An MMC snap-in called Transaction Server Explorer is included with the Option Pack. This utility is available from the Microsoft Transaction Server menu under the main NT Option Pack menu.

The hierarchy of objects in Transaction Server Explorer is organized with computers at the lowest level and the executable components and data sources at lower levels. You can add computers to this list using the *New Computer* command in the Action menu. Each computer includes the following subcontainers:

Packages installed
> Displays icons for each installed package. Open a package to display its components or add components. You can add a new package by highlighting this entry and selecting *New Package* from the Actions menu. You can then specify the location of a pre-existing package, or create a new one.

Remote components
> Displays icons for components of the application running on remote computers. You must add a computer to the list before adding components.

Trace messages
> Displays messages generated by transaction components, usually used for debugging purposes.

Transaction list
> Lists the transactions currently being processed or waiting to be processed.

Transaction statistics
> Displays statistics for the transaction server. This includes information about current transactions, historical transactions, and a measure of the server's response time.

If an application will use data on an SQL server or other remote server, you need to configure one or more data sources using the ODBC applet, available from the Windows NT control panel.

SMTP Service

SMTP (Simple Mail Transport Protocol) is an Internet standard for the transmission and forwarding of email messages. The SMTP service is a part of IIS, and can be installed as an option during the IIS installation.

SMTP Architecture

The SMTP service receives mail messages using the SMTP protocol and delivers them using one of two methods. If the addressee is in a local domain, the messages are deposited in a directory as text files. If the message is addressed to a remote domain, it is forwarded to the appropriate SMTP server.

On the Exam

The SMTP service is not a full-featured mail server; for example, it cannot manage individual mailboxes for users. Rather, it is intended to receive messages from other Internet nodes and forward them to the appropriate location to be processed by a domain's mail server (such as Microsoft Exchange Server, described in Part 5, *Exchange Server 5.5*). It can also be used as a mail handler for HTML forms.

The SMTP service uses a Mailroot directory, created during IIS installation. Several subdirectories are used to manage mail messages:

Drop
> Stores the delivered messages as text files. If you are using the SMTP service to deliver mail to multiple domains, they each have a separate Drop directory.

Queue
> Incoming messages are stored here before being sorted and delivered. They are then delivered to the appropriate Drop directory or to a remote server.

Pickup
> This directory can be used to manually queue messages. Any text file found here is processed and moved to the Queue folder for delivery.

Badmail
> Undeliverable messages (those that are no longer in the queue, but were not successfully delivered) are stored here.

Basic SMTP Configuration

You can configure SMTP using the Internet Service Manager utility. A Default SMTP Site entry is created under the computer name at installation; you cannot create additional SMTP sites.

To configure the SMTP site, right-click on the Default SMTP Site entry and select *Properties*. The Properties dialog is divided into a number of pages. The first of these, SMTP Site, includes the following options:

SMTP Site Identification
> Specify a description and IP address for the SMTP service. The Advanced button allows you to configure multiple addresses and ports for the service.

Incoming Connections

Specify a TCP/IP port number for incoming SMTP connections. The standard port for SMTP services is 25. You can also limit the number of concurrent incoming connections and specify a timeout.

Outgoing Connections

Specify a port number, connection limitation, and timeout for outgoing SMTP transactions. Additionally, the *Limit Connections per Domain* option allows you to limit the number of simultaneous connections for a single remote domain.

Enable Logging

Enable this option and choose a log file format to log SMTP transactions. The available log formats are described in "Working with Log Files," later in this chapter.

The second property page, Operators, stores a list of users who are allowed access to the SMTP properties. By default, the Administrators group is the only member of this list.

On the Exam

You should have experience in setting up and configuring an SMTP server for the IIS MCSE exam. Be sure you are familiar with the property dialogs described here and in the following sections.

Message Configuration

The Messages property page includes the following options related to mail messages:

Limit messages

If enabled, the lengths of messages are restricted. The *Maximum message size* field is a recommended limit, while the *Maximum session size* field is enforced: an SMTP session is aborted if the message reaches this size.

Maximum number of outbound messages per connection

Specify the number of messages that can be sent in a single SMTP connection.

Maximum number of recipients per message

This option limits the number of addresses in the To and CC fields of the message. The default is 100; values higher than this may cause problems with other SMTP servers.

Send a copy of non-delivery report to

Specify an address (typically an administrator) to receive a copy of the report sent in response to undeliverable messages.

Badmail directory

Specify the directory for undeliverable messages. The default is the Badmail directory under the Mailroot directory.

Delivery Configuration

The Delivery property page includes options relating to outgoing messages:

Local Queue
Specify the maximum number of retries and the time between them for the delivery of messages to local domains.

Remote Queue
Specify the maximum number of retries and the time between them for delivery to remote domains.

Maximum hop count
This value specifies the number of servers a message can pass through before being discarded; by default, the value is 15. Each server adds a Received header to the message's headers; when the number of headers exceeds this value, the message is discarded.

Masquerade domain
If a domain name is specified here, it is used in From headers of outgoing messages. Otherwise, the actual domain name is used.

Fully qualified domain name
Specifies the Fully Qualified Domain Name (FQDN) of the mail server.

Smart host
If a host is specified here, all outbound SMTP messages will be sent to that host. If this option is not specified, an SMTP connection is made to the host specified in the message address.

Attempt direct delivery before sending to smart host
If this option is selected, SMTP will attempt to connect to the host specified in the message address; if this fails, the smart host will be used.

Perform reverse DNS lookup on incoming messages
If selected, IP addresses of incoming SMTP servers will be translated to domain names with reverse DNS, and the domain name will be included in the Received header; otherwise, the IP address will be included.

Outbound Security
Specifies security options for outbound SMTP connections. The Basic Authentication method is the Internet standard; Windows NT Challenge/Response is also supported.

In the Real World

Many of IIS's services support the Windows NT Challenge/Response protocol in addition to basic (clear text) authentication. If an exam question asks which is the most secure, NT Challenge/Response is usually the answer; however, this option is supported only by Windows NT servers, and is only useful for NT-only networks such as local Intranets.

SMTP Security

The Directory Security property page includes the following security options, each of which opens a separate dialog:

Anonymous Access and Authentication Control
Specifies whether anonymous SMTP connections are allowed. For non-anonymous connections, specify the method of authentication: Basic or Windows NT Challenge/Response.

Secure Communications
Supports SSL-encrypted SMTP connections, a new standard for SMTP security.

IP Address and Domain Name Restrictions
Allows the exclusion (or inclusion) of one or more IP addresses or network addresses.

Relay Restrictions
Allows you to restrict the use of the SMTP server as a relay (used by remote clients to send mail to addresses outside the local network). Since SMTP relay servers are often abused and can create traffic problems, all relaying is disabled by default.

NNTP Service

Newsgroups, more recently known as discussion groups, allow non-realtime public discussions between users on different servers. NNTP (network news transfer protocol) is used to transfer messages between news servers, and to provide services to clients.

On the Exam

The NNTP server included with IIS is somewhat limited: it cannot receive a newsfeed from another server. Exchange Server 5.5, described in Part 5, includes a full-featured NNTP server.

NNTP Architecture

Newsgroups allow for distributed discussions. Each message, or *article*, is posted by a user with access to an NNTP server. The server then forwards the article to other servers that carry the same newsgroup.

The NNTP service is a component of IIS, and can be selected during the IIS installation process. The NNTP service uses a directory specified during installation, typically \Inetpub\Nntproot, to store articles. The NNTP service can be used without other servers to allow discussions on a local network.

The USENET newsgroups are the most widely distributed groups. These are named based on a hierarchy, with larger categories listed first. For example, Windows NT discussions are held in several groups, such as *comp.os.ms-windows.nt.admin.misc*.

Under the Nntproot directory, directories are created to correspond with the newsgroup hierarchy. The newsgroup mentioned above would be stored in the \Inetpub\Nntproot\comp\os\ms-windows\nt\admin\misc directory. Within each directory, messages are stored as text files.

On the Exam

To prepare for the IIS MCSE exam, you should configure the NNTP service and access it from a client to post and read messages. Any NNTP client will work; Microsoft Mail and News, included with Internet Explorer 3, and Outlook Express, included with IE4, are two such clients.

Basic NNTP Configuration

The NNTP service is configured using Internet Service Manager. A site called Default NNTP Site is created under the IIS computer. To configure the NNTP service, modify the properties of this site. The properties are displayed in several pages. The News Site property page includes the following options:

News Site Identification
> Specify a description, IP address, and port number for the service. The Path header option allows you to specify the value added to the Path headers of messages passing through the server (usually the server domain name).

Connections
> Specify unlimited connections, or a limited number of simultaneous connections to the server. You can also specify a timeout for idle connections.

Enable Logging
> If enabled, NNTP transactions are logged to a file. The log formats are described in "Working with Log Files," later in this chapter.

Configuring News Directories

The Home Directory property page for the NNTP site allows you to specify the location of the NNTP root directory. In addition, you can specify whether the posting of messages is allowed.

You can also create one or more additional directories in the Directories folder under the NNTP site. This allows you to distribute the newsgroup storage among multiple disks or remote computers; for example, newsgroups under the comp hierarchy could be stored in a separate location.

NNTP Protocol Options

The NNTP Settings property page includes the following options for the NNTP protocol:

Allow client posting
> If selected, clients can post (create new) articles.

Limit post size
Limits the allowable size of individual articles.

Limit connection size
Limits the total size of articles posted by a single client during a single session.

Allow servers to pull news articles from this server
If enabled, other NNTP servers can receive news articles from this server, including both locally posted articles and those received from other servers.

Allow control messages
Enables automatic processing of control messages. Control messages are sent in a special newsgroup called control, and perform administrative functions: for example, cancel a message, add a group, or remove a group. If this option is disabled you can still read the messages in the control group and process them manually if desired.

SMTP server for moderated groups
Moderated newsgroups are administered by a person (or sometimes an automated program) called the moderator. Articles posted to these groups are sent to the moderator's address via email rather than posted. Specify an SMTP server address to receive this outgoing mail.

Default moderator domain
If specified, postings to moderated newsgroups without a designated moderator are sent to this domain.

Administrator email account
Specify the email address to receive a copy of reports when newsgroup postings fail.

Managing Newsgroups

The Groups property page allows you to add, delete, or modify entries in the list of newsgroups. Use the *Create new newsgroup* option to create a new group (either a local group, or one that corresponds to a group on other servers).

Articles in newsgroups are never deleted by default; this can quickly consume disk storage. You can modify this behavior in the Expiration policies folder under the NNTP site. You can define a policy for all groups or for specific sets of groups.

Policies limit the number of articles in two ways: by specifying a number of days for expiration (articles older than this many days are deleted) or by specifying a maximum size for the group (when this size is reached, the oldest articles are deleted to make room for new ones).

NNTP Security

The Directory Security property page includes the following security options:

Password Authentication Method
Specify whether anonymous access to the NNTP server is allowed. For non-anonymous access, you can specify Basic Authentication (the Internet standard) or Windows NT Challenge/Response.

Allows you to restrict access to the server based on IP address or domain name.

In the Real World

NNTP servers are frequently abused by users who wish to conceal their identities or simply to access a group not available on the local network. If your network is connected to the Internet and you do not restrict access to the NNTP service, these users may create unnecessary network traffic.

IIS 4.0

Optimization and Troubleshooting

IIS and its related components add a significant load to a Windows NT server, and can be slowed down by disk and CPU bottlenecks, network speed, and other factors. The following sections describe techniques for monitoring the performance of the IIS components using log files and Performance Monitor, optimizing IIS performance, optimizing web documents themselves, and troubleshooting common problems.

Working with Log Files

IIS can be configured to create a log file listing accesses to a web or FTP site. Each site can be configured separately, and has a separate log file. In addition, IIS includes utilities that can be used to analyze and create reports based on log files.

Setting Logging Options

The properties of web, FTP, NNTP, and SMTP sites include an *Enable Logging* option, and allow you to choose a log file format. The following formats are available:

Microsoft IIS Log File Format
An IIS-specific format. This format is an ASCII file with a fixed number of fields.

NCSA Common Log File Format
The standard format used on NCSA (National Center for Supercomputing Applications) web servers, and the Internet's de facto standard. This is an ASCII file with a fixed number of fields.

ODBC Logging
Specifies that log entries will be added to a database server (such as Microsoft SQL Server) connected via the ODBC (open database connect) protocol.

W3C Extended Log File Format
A format developed by the World Wide Web Consortium. This format allows you to select from a number of fields to be included.

The Properties button next to the *Enable Logging* option allows you to modify the log location and the logged items. This dialog includes one or more pages, depending on the log format:

General Properties
> Specify a location for the log files, and indicate when new log files are created. New files can be created daily, weekly, or monthly, or when the current log file reaches a certain size.

Extended Properties
> This page, available only for the W3C Extended log format, lists a variety of items that can be included in the log. Select the items you wish included. The more items are selected here, the faster the log file's size will increase.

ODBC
> This page is included for the *ODBC Logging* option. Specify the data source, table name, user name, and password for the ODBC database.

Creating Reports

Site Server Express, included with the NT Option Pack, includes a feature to import and analyze log files. To use this utility, first import one or more log files using the Usage Import utility, found under the Site Server Express 2.0 menu.

When running this utility, you are first prompted for the log file format. Site Server supports only the fixed formats (IIS and NCSA). The utility then prompts you for information about the web or FTP site, including the IP address, domain name, and home page URL. This information is used in analyzing the log files.

Once the information is entered, the Log File Manager window is displayed. Use the Browse button to specify one or more log files, then choose *Start Import* from the File menu. The files are imported into the Site Server database; this may take several minutes.

Once you have imported one or more log files, you can create reports using the Report Writer utility, available from the Site Server Express 2.0 menu. This utility includes a number of predefined reports, and allows you to create your own reports.

On the Exam

You should have experience importing log files and creating reports with these utilities for the IIS MCSE exam. You should not need to know the details of creating custom reports.

Monitoring IIS Performance

The Performance Monitor utility, introduced in Part 1 of this book, displays statistical information about Windows NT's operation. The installation of IIS adds a number of counters to this utility, which can be used to monitor IIS. The following categories of counters are included:

Active Server Pages
  Counters related to ASP scripts

Content Index and Content Index Filter
  Counters for the content index process, used by Index Server

FTP Service
  Counters that track the performance of the FTP service

HTTP Content Index
  Counters for HTTP queries using Index Server

Internet Information Services Global
  A set of global counters that track the performance of IIS

NNTP Commands and NNTP Server
  Counters related to the NNTP server and its current usage

SMTP Server
  Counters related to the SMTP server

Web Service
  Counters for the web (HTTP) service

Optimizing IIS

A busy web site can slow down even the fastest server, but there are some adjustments that can improve the performance of IIS. These are described in the following sections.

Allocating Bandwidth

You can select the *Enable Bandwidth Throttling* option in a computer's properties in Internet Service Manager to limit the total bandwidth used by IIS services. This is useful if you are running other services that may require network bandwidth, or if the IIS server is also used for file and print sharing.

Bandwidth throttling can also be specified separately for each web or FTP site in the Performance property page. This allows you to prioritize sites or services; for example, if web services are used by customers and FTP is used only by employees, you may want to allocate a greater bandwidth to web services.

Limiting Concurrent Connections

Each site's properties allow you to specify a maximum number of concurrent connections. This feature can be used to limit the bandwidth used by these services, or to restrict the use of one service to allow more bandwidth for another.

A timeout value is also available; this specifies the number of seconds a session must remain idle before being disconnected. If the maximum number of connections is reached quickly, reducing this timeout will allow more connections; values too low will disconnect active users.

Optimizing Memory Use

The Performance property page for a web site allows you to specify the approximate number of hits per day the site receives; IIS optimizes its memory usage accordingly. There are only three options (*Fewer than 10,000, Fewer than 100,000,* and *More than 100,000*).

Increasing the amount of memory in the server is often an economical way to increase speed without reducing functionality. Use the Memory counters in Performance Monitor to determine if memory is causing a bottleneck.

Analyzing Web Content

In a complex set of web documents, it is easy to lose track of a document, neglect to provide a link to a document, or link to documents that no longer exist. Content Analyzer, part of Site Server Express 2.0, analyzes the HTML documents in a web site and creates maps and reports that are useful in locating these problems.

Web Maps

Content Analyzer is available from the Site Server Express 2.0 menu. To map a web site, select *New web Map* from the menu. Maps can be created based on a URL or directly from an HTML file. After you specify the URL and other information, the map is created; this may take several minutes, especially over a modem link.

A typical web map is shown in Figure 2-6. The left portion of the screen displays the names of the pages on the site in a hierarchical view, called the tree view. The right portion displays the cyberbolic view, a map that provides a graphical overview of the site.

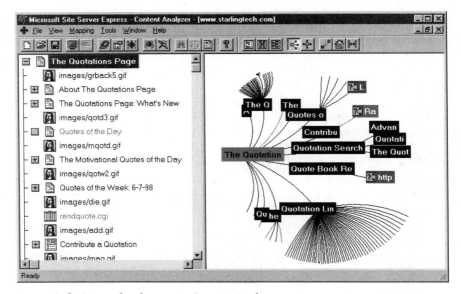

Figure 2-6: A typical web map in Content Analyzer

Site Report

Content Analyzer also produces a site report, which lists the total size used in pages and images, the number of links that resulted in an error during the search, and other information. To display the report, select *Generate Site Reports* from the Tools menu.

On the Exam

Site Server Express 2.0 includes only a single report, a summary of all documents on the site. The full version of Site Server, available from Microsoft, includes a variety of report options. For the IIS MCSE exam, you only need to be familiar with the report and map features of Site Server Express.

Troubleshooting Common Problems

Along with the performance problems described in the previous sections, IIS occasionally requires troubleshooting. The following sections describe some of the most common IIS problems and their solutions.

Installation Problems

The Option Pack setup program is usually reliable, but it is possible for the installation to fail. If the setup program does not finish, or if IIS fails to function after installation, follow these guidelines:

- Check the error logs in Event Viewer for a log entry that may explain the problem.

- Verify that the computer meets the hardware requirements for IIS, and that the required software (IE 4.01 and SP3) was installed.

- Verify that there is enough available disk storage for the IIS files.

- If you are upgrading a previous version of IIS, you may want to try removing the old version before installation. This is especially true of beta versions of IIS.

WWW and FTP Service Problems

If users on the Internet or your local network are unable to access the web or FTP services, follow these guidelines:

- Check the IIS log files for an entry that may explain the problem.

- Verify that the user has the correct access rights. For anonymous users, verify that the IUSR_*servername* account exists, is not disabled, and has the appropriate permissions.

- For anonymous users, verify that the *Allow Anonymous Access* option in the Directory Security property sheet for the site, directory, or file is enabled.

- Verify that the appropriate IIS services (web and FTP services) are running, and that the site has not been disabled or stopped.

- If some users can access the site but others cannot, try increasing the number of available concurrent connections.

Content-Related Problems

In addition to server problems, problems with web content can affect clients' ability to view documents. Follow these guidelines:

- Use the Content Analyzer utility to scan the documents in the site for broken links and missing files.

- Verify that the correct HTML syntax was used in the documents.

- If server-side scripts are being used, verify that the appropriate script handling engine is installed. Engines are built into IIS for JScript and VBscript.

- Verify that the client browser is compatible with the HTML and scripting languages used in the documents. For Internet sites, be sure to test new documents on several browsers.

Suggested Exercises

To study for the IIS exam you will need at least one computer, capable of running Windows NT Server, to use as a testbed for IIS. You can use the same computer as a client for most purposes, but it will be helpful to have a second computer.

The IIS software is available for download from Microsoft, but may test the limits of your Internet connection: the full Windows NT Option Pack installation for NT Server is a total of 76 MB in size. As an alternative, you can order an evaluation CD from Microsoft for a small fee.

The IIS exam includes a number of simulation questions that test your knowledge of the various MMC snap-ins. You should have as much experience as possible managing a site with these utilities before taking the exam.

Performing the following exercises will help you prepare for the IIS MCSE exam. In addition, you should study the "IP Addressing" and "Subnet Masking" sections of Part 1, *Internetworking with TCP/IP*, of this book.

1. Install the Windows NT 4.0 Option Pack, including IIS, on a Windows NT Server computer. Be sure to use the Custom installation method and select all of the components.

2. Configure the IIS installation by following these steps:

   a. Create a new web site using port 8000. Place several documents in the site's root directory (these can be copied from the IIS sample files or documentation).

   b. Using Internet Explorer, verify that the new site is accessible from the local machine and from another machine on the network.

   c. Create a virtual directory under the new site's directory that points to the original WWWROOT directory.

   d. Verify that the WWWROOT directory is accessible both from the Default web site and from the new site you created.

e. Create a new FTP site using port 2100. Place several files in the site's root directory, and verify that they are accessible from an FTP client (use Internet Explorer or the command-line FTP client included with Windows NT).

3. Configure two web sites as virtual servers:

   a. Create two web sites with the same IP address, the same port number, and different host header identifiers.

   b. Copy some files into the root directory for each site.

   c. Assign two domains corresponding to the host headers to the IP address. This can be done using a DNS server if you are running one yourself; otherwise, add the two entries to a client's HOSTS file.

   d. Using IE4 or another HTTP 1.1-compatible browser, access both of the domain names and verify that you are shown content from the two different sites.

4. Create a new web site and create several simple HTML documents for the site from scratch. This will require some study of HTML (which is not covered on the exam) but is a good way to become familiar with all of the issues involved in creating and managing a site.

5. Configure Index Server to index the site you created. Copy the sample query form and IDQ file to your site and modify them to work on your content.

6. Configure the SMTP service. To verify that it is running, configure Internet Explorer to use the SMTP server and attempt to send an email message (the message will not be sent over the Internet, but should show up as a text file in the Queue directory).

7. Install the NNTP service and create a new non-moderated newsgroup. Configure Internet Explorer or another newsreader to access the server, and verify that you can post messages to the newsgroup.

8. Enable logging on one of your web sites using the NCSA log format. Access the site several times to create log entries, then import the log file using Site Server's Usage Import utility. Run the Report Writer utility and experiment with the available reports.

9. Using Content Analyzer, create a web map and report for a web site. You can use a site you created, a site that came with IIS (such as the IIS documentation), or an online site.

Practice Test

Test Questions

1. Which of the following is the protocol used for web documents?

    a. HTML

    b. HTTP

    c. SMTP

    d. NNTP

2. Which of the following is a valid URL for a web document?

    a. http:/www.oreilly.com/

    b. ftp://www.oreilly.com/

    c. http://www.oreilly.com/

    d. http:oreilly.com

3. Which of the following protocols are related to email? (select all that apply)

    a. HTTP

    b. SMTP

    c. POP

    d. SNMP

4. Which of the following languages uses script commands embedded within an HTML document? (select all that apply)

    a. JavaScript

    b. VBScript

c. ASP

d. Java

5. Which of the following languages execute within a web browser? (select all that apply)

   a. JavaScript

   b. VBScript

   c. ASP

   d. Java

6. The command <%NumPages=1%> is an example of which language?

   a. JavaScript

   b. Active Server Pages

   c. VBScript

   d. HTML

7. <APPLET> is an example of which language?

   a. JavaScript

   b. Active Server Pages

   c. HTML

   d. Java

8. Which of the following IIS components includes a tool for creating reports from log files?

   a. Index Server

   b. Certificate Server

   c. Site Server Express

   d. NNTP Service

9. Which version of IIS is included with Windows NT Server 4.0?

   a. IIS 4.0

   b. Personal Web Server

   c. IIS 2.0

   d. IIS 3.0

10. Which of the following is *not* a feature new to IIS 4.0?

   a. Index Server 1.0

   b. HTTP Post

   c. HTTP 1.1

   d. HTTP redirection

11. You are installing IIS on a computer with a 486 processor, 32 MB of RAM, and 200 MB of free disk space. Which of the computer's specifications is below the minimum for IIS?

    a.   RAM

    b.   Disk space

    c.   Processor

    d.   None of the above

12. Which of the following software must be installed in Windows NT Server before installing IIS 4.0? (select all that apply)

    a.   Service Pack 3

    b.   Internet Explorer 4.01

    c.   TCP/IP protocol

    d.   IIS 2.0

13. To install all of the IIS components, which installation method should be used?

    a.   Typical

    b.   Custom

    c.   Full

    d.   Minimum

14. Which of the following is *not* included in the Minimum installation of IIS?

    a.   Web Server

    b.   FTP Server

    c.   Index Server

    d.   Management Console (MMC)

15. Which of the following utilities can be used to manage both Internet Information Server and Index Server?

    a.   Internet Service Manager

    b.   Internet Service Manager (HTML)

    c.   Microsoft Management Console

    d.   Index Server Manager

16. Which of the following set of web site properties affects sites you create in the future?

    a.   Master properties

    b.   Default properties

    c.   File properties

    d.   New site properties

IIS 4.0

17. Which web site property sheet includes an option to limit the number of connections to the site?

    a.   Bandwidth

    b.   Connections

    c.   Web Site

    d.   Performance

18. You have configured a web site and notice that users can view a list of files in a directory by entering a URL without specifying a filename. You want to disable this feature.

Required Result: The directory listing should no longer be available.

Optional Result: The change should affect all directories in the web site.

Optional Result: Index Server should also be prevented from indexing the directory.

Solution: Deselect the Directory Browsing Allowed option on the Home Directory property sheet within the web site's properties.

    a.   The solution meets the required result and both of the optional results.

    b.   The solution meets the required result and only one of the optional results.

    c.   The solution meets the required result only.

    d.   The solution does not meet the required result.

19. User TOM has the Read and Change NTFS permissions for the Inetpub\ Wwwroot\Data directory. The directory's properties have been changed in Internet Service Manager to disallow Write access. What are Tom's effective permissions for the directory?

    a.   Read only

    b.   Read and Change

    c.   No access

    d.   Read, Write, and Change

20. Which is the minimum web site permission that must be set for a directory in order to run an ASP script on a page in the directory?

    a.   Read

    b.   Browse

    c.   Script

    d.   Execute

21. How many IP addresses are required to configure a set of four virtual servers using the host headers method?

    a.   1

    b.   2

    c.   3

    d.   4

22. Assuming IIS has been installed with the default options on the server WEST1, which user account should be modified to control anonymous access to the default web site?

    a.   Guest

    b.   Anonymous

    c.   IUSR_DEFAULT

    d.   IUSR_WEST1

23. Which of the following authentication methods represents the greatest security risk?

    a.   Windows NT Challenge/Response

    b.   Basic Authentication

24. Which utility is used to create a certificate request file?

    a.   Certificate Manager

    b.   Internet Service Manager

    c.   Key Manager

    d.   Certificate Server

25. You are using Index Server to index a group of web documents. The total size of the web documents is 100 MB. What is the total amount of disk storage required for the documents and index files?

    a.   100 MB

    b.   40 MB

    c.   140 MB

    d.   160 MB

26. Which of the following utilities can be used to start or stop the Index Manager background indexing process? (select all that apply)

    a.   Internet Service Manager

    b.   Index Server Manager

    c.   Services control panel

    d.   User Manager for Domains

27. Which of the following are scripting languages that can be used for Index Server queries? (select all that apply)

    a.   ASP

    b.   IDQ

    c.   HTX

    d.   INX

28. Which of the following utilities can be used to revoke a certificate issued by Certificate Server?

    a.   Certificate Administration Log Utility

    b.   Certificate Administration Queue Utility

    c.   Certificate Server Manager

    d.   Key Manager

29. Which of the following SMTP directories can be used to manually submit messages as text files?

    a.   Drop

    b.   Queue

    c.   Pickup

    d.   Submit

30. The NNTP protocol is used to transfer articles from (select all that apply):

    a.   Server to Server

    b.   Client to Server

    c.   Server to Client

31. The NNTP service is configured using which utility?

    a.   NNTP Manager

    b.   Internet Service Manager

    c.   Key Manager

    d.   Server Manager

32. Which of the following types of sites can be created with Internet Service Manager? (select all that apply)

    a.   New Web site

    b.   New FTP site

    c.   New NNTP site

    d.   New SMTP site

33. Which of the following log file formats can be used with the Report Writer utility? (select all that apply)

    a.   NCSA Common Log File Format

    b.   Microsoft IIS Log File Format

    c.   ODBC Logging

    d.   W3C Extended Log File Format

34. Which of the following log file formats allows you to specify the fields included in the log file?

    a.   NCSA Common Log File Format

    b.   Microsoft IIS Log File Format

    c.   ODBC Logging

    d.   W3C Extended Log File Format

35. The Bandwidth Throttling option can be set for which of the following? (select all that apply)

    a.   Computer

    b.   Web site

    c.   Web virtual directory

    d.   FTP site

36. You have a network of web sites running IIS 4.0 and need to make changes to the authentication method for each of them. Which of the following tools would allow this change to be made as quickly as possible?

    a.   Internet Service Manager

    b.   Internet Service Manager (HTML)

    c.   Windows Scripting Host

    d.   Microsoft Management Console

37. For an FTP site, which of the following levels of properties can be set? (select all that apply)

    a.   File properties

    b.   Directory properties

    c.   Site properties

    d.   Master properties

38. Which of the following utilities can be used to find broken links in a set of web documents?

    a.   Internet Service Manager

    b.   Site Server Express

    c.   FrontPage Express

    d.   Windows Scripting Host

IIS 4.0

39. If IIS is installed using the default options on a Windows NT server called WEST2, what user name will be used for anonymous web access?

    a. IUSR_WEST2

    b. IUSR_GUEST

    c. Guest

    d. Anonymous

40. Which languages are supported by Windows Scripting Host by default under IIS 4.0? (select all that apply)

    a. JScript

    b. Perl

    c. VBScript

    d. IDQ

Answers to Questions

1. B. The HTTP (Hypertext Transfer Protocol) protocol is used with web documents.

2. C. The valid URL is http://www.oreilly.com/. Choices A and D use invalid syntax. Choice B is a valid URL, but uses FTP rather than HTTP.

3. B, C. The SMTP (Simple Mail Transport Protocol) and POP (Post Office Protocol) protocols are used with email.

4. A, B, C. The JavaScript, VBScript, and ASP languages use script commands within HTML documents.

5. A, B, D. The JavaScript, VBScript, and Java languages execute within a web browser. ASP (choice C) executes on the web server.

6. B. The command is an ASP command; the delimiters <% and %> are used only by ASP.

7. C. The <APPLET> command is an HTML command, although it is used to embed a Java program.

8. C. Site Server Express includes a tool for creating reports from log files.

9. C. IIS 2.0 is included with Windows NT Server 4.0.

10. A. Index Server 1.0 was included with IIS 3.0.

11. D. All of the components listed meet the minimum values for IIS.

12. A, B, C. Service Pack 3, Internet Explorer 4.01, and the TCP/IP protocol must be installed befor installing IIS 4.0. IIS 2.0 (choice D) should not be installed.

13. B. The Custom option is required to install all components of IIS.

14. B. The FTP server is not included in the Minimum installation of IIS.

15. C. Microsoft Management Console (MMC) can be used for administration of both IIS and Index Server.

16. A. Master properties affect sites you create in the future. The Default properties (choice B) are merely the properties for the Default web site, and do not affect new sites.

17. C. The Web Site property sheet includes the Connections option, which allows you to limit the number of concurrent connections to the site.

18. B. The solution meets the required result (restrict the directory listing) and only one of the optional results (affect all directories in the web site). This change does not affect Index Server; the Index this Directory option would be used to prevent Index Server from indexing a directory.

19. A. Since the most restrictive permissions are used, all but the Read permission are lost.

20. C. The Script permission is required to execute an ASP script. The Execute permission (choice D) also includes the Script permission, but is not the minimum permission needed.

21. A. Since the host headers method uses headers to distinguish between server names, only one IP address is required.

22. D. IUSR_WEST1 is the correct username. IIS creates the user at installation using the name of the server.

23. B. Since it transmits ASCII passwords over the network connection, Basic Authentication represents the greatest security risk.

24. C. The Key Manager utility allows you to create a certificate request file.

25. C. Since the index files use about 40% of the total space used by the web documents, the total space for web documents and index files is 140 MB.

26. B, C. The Index Server Manager utility and the Services control panel can be used to start or stop the Index Manager service.

27. A, B. ASP (Active Server Pages) and IDQ (Internet Data Query) are scripting languages that can be used for Index Server queries.

28. A. The Certificate Administration Log Utility can be used to revoke an issued certificate.

29. C. Files placed in the Pickup directory are processed and delivered as new messages.

30. A, B, C. The NNTP protocol can transfer articles between servers, from a client to a server (posting) or from a server to a client (reading).

31. B. The NNTP service is managed using the Internet Service Manager utility.

32. A, B. New FTP and web sites can be created from Internet Service Manager. NNTP and SMTP (choices C and D) can be managed from this utility, but only one of each service is allowed.

33. A, B. The NCSA and Microsoft IIS formats are fixed ASCII text and can be used by the Report Writer utility.

34. D. The W3C Extended log format allows you to specify the fields included in the log file.

35. A, B, D. The Bandwidth Throttling option can be set for a computer, a web site, or an FTP site. It cannot be set for individual virtual directories.

36. C. Windows Scripting Host could be used to make the change to all servers quickly using a script.

37. B, C, D. For an FTP site, you can set directory, site, and master properties. FTP sites do not allow file properties (choice A).

38. B. Content Analyzer, a component of Site Server Express, can be used to find broken links.

39. A. The anonymous access user would be IUSR_WEST2.

40. A, C. VBScript and JScript are supported by Windows Scripting Host by default.

Highlighter's Index

IIS and Internet Basics

Web (HTTP)

Server uses Hypertext Transfer Protocol (HTTP)

Clients are called browsers

Documents typically in HTML (Hypertext Markup Language)

FTP

File Transfer Protocol

Transfers files between clients and servers

Cross-platform

Email

SMTP (Simple Mail Transport Protocol):Transports messages

POP (Post Office Protocol) delivers messages to clients

SMTP is supported by IIS

Newsgroups

Also called discussion groups

NNTP (Network News Transfer Protocol) used for clients and servers

Messages (articles) are forwarded between servers

IIS NNTP Service does not support pulling newsgroups from other servers

Web Content Types

HTML: Text with links, formatting

Java: Compiled Client-side language; platform independent

JavaScript: Client-side scripting, based on Java syntax

VBScript: Client-side scripting, based on Visual Basic syntax
ActiveX: Compiled client-side language; Windows only
CGI: Executes on server; any language; responds to forms
ASP: Executes on server; embedded within HTML document

IIS Components

WWW service: Supports HTTP protocol
FTP service: Supports FTP protocol
Index Server: Indexes web documents; allows queries
Certificate Server: Issues, renews, revokes digital certificates
Transaction Server: Manages transaction-based applications
Message Queue Server (MSMQ): Allows messaging between applications
Site Server Express: Adds management features to IIS

Installation and Configuration

Hardware Requirements

RAM: 32 MB required, 64 MB recommended
Processor: 486 required, Pentium recommended
Disk storage: 50 MB required, 200 MB recommended

Software Requirements

Windows NT Service Pack 3
Internet Explorer 4.0
Windows NT Server
Personal Web Server: NT Workstation or Windows 95/98

Installation Methods

Minimum: Basic requirement for web server; does not include FTP
Typical: Typical components (all not included)
Custom: Allows you to select all components

Administration Tools

MMC (Microsoft Management Console): Snap-ins support various services (IIS, Index, etc.)
Internet Service Manager: MMC snap-in for Web, FTP, SMTP, NNTP services
Internet Service Manager (HTML): HTML version; available remotely
Windows Scripting Host: Batch administration using scripts
Metabase: Stores configuration information in RAM; similar to registry

Virtual Servers

Multiple IP addresses: Standard method
Host headers: Requires HTTP 1.1; uses only one IP address
Servers correspond to Internet Service Manager sites
Web and FTP can use virtual sites (web only with host headers)

Authentication

Basic Authentication: Internet standard, uses clear text; insecure
Windows NT Challenge/Response: NT only; uses encryption; more secure
Anonymous authentication: Uses IUSR_*servername* account

Address Restrictions

All addresses can be granted or denied access by default
Exceptions for single addresses; network addresses and subnets; domain names
Available for web, FTP, other services

Other Services

Index Server

Indexes HTML, text, Microsoft Office documents
Uses Content Indexer background process
Manage with Index Server Manager (MMC snap-in)
Indexes are about 40% of size of all web documents

Certificate Server

Issues, revokes, renews digital certificates
Process Certificate Request file: Creates certificate based on request
Log utility: Displays issued certificates, allows revoke
Queue utility: Displays queued certificates and status

Transaction Server

Supports transaction-based applications
ACID: Atomicity, consistency, isolation, durability
Components: Client, application server, data source
Manage with Transaction Server Explorer (MMC)

SMTP Service

Simple Mail Transport Protocol; delivers mail from server to server or client to server
Manage using Internet Service Manager
Drop directory: Stores delivered messages; one directory per domain
Queue directory: Stores incoming messages
Pickup directory: Text files stored here are added to queue
Badmail directory: Stores undeliverable mail messages

NNTP Service

Network news transport protocol
Transfers articles from server to server, client to server, or server to client
Manage using Internet Service Manager
Stores messages under Nntproot directory; one directory per group

Monitoring and Optimization

Log File Formats

Microsoft IIS Log File Format: IIS-specific format; fixed ASCII file
NCSA Common Log File Format: NCSA standard format; fixed ASCII file
ODBC Logging: Stores records in database (SQL, etc.)
W3C Extended Log File Format: Allows choice of fields in file

Log Reports

Part of Site Server Express
Supports IIS or NCSA log formats
Usage Import:Import log files, specify format
Report Writer: Generate reports

Optimizations

Bandwidth throttling: Set for computer or site
Concurrent connections: Specify for each site
Memory use: Specify number of hits

Content Analyzer

Part of Site Server Express
Web map: Tree view, cyberbolic view
Site report: Summary including link information

PART 3

Internet Explorer 4.0 Administration

Need to Know	Reference
IE4 hardware requirements	"Hardware Requirements" on page 162
IE4 installation methods	"The Installation Process" on page 163
IEA K administrative roles	"Administration Roles" on page 185
Settings available in the IEAK Wizard	"Creating a Customized Version of IE4" on page 187
Capabilities of advanced IE4 options	"Advanced Options" on page 180

Need to Apply	Reference
Install Internet Explorer 4.0 and other components.	"The Installation Process" on page 163
Configure IE4 options.	"Browser Options" on page 164
Configure advanced IE4 features.	"Advanced Options" on page 167
Uninstall IE4 and other components.	"Adding and Removing Components" on page 172
Configure the Active Desktop and other Desktop Update features.	"Windows Desktop Update" on page 173
Configure and use Outlook Express.	"Outlook Express" on page 176
Configure and use NetMeeting.	"NetMeeting" on page 180
Install the Internet Explorer Administration Kit (IEAK).	"Configuring the Administration Kit" on page 186
Customize IE4 using the IEAK.	"Creating a Customized Version of IE4" on page 187
Install or distribute a customized version of IE4.	"Using the Customized Package" on page 193
Modify settings with IEAK Profile Manage.	"Using Automatic Configuration" on page 193

Study Guide

This chapter includes the following sections, which address various topics covered on the Internet Explorer 4.0 Administration Kit exam:

Internet Explorer Basics
Describes the basic features of Internet Explorer 4.0, the other components included in the IE4 suite, and the IE4 Administration Kit.

Installing and Configuring IE4
Describes the process of installing and configuring the IE4 browser and the other components in the suite.

Working with IE4 Components
Discusses the operation and configuration of the Desktop Update, Outlook Express, and NetMeeting components.

Using the Administration Kit
Describes the Internet Explorer Administration Kit (IEAK) and the process of installing and using it to create customized versions of Internet Explorer 4.0.

Internet Explorer Basics

Internet Explorer is Microsoft's web client, or *browser*. The current version, 4.0, includes a variety of features beyond web browsing, including mail and news clients, an update to the Windows desktop, and a variety of other tools. The basic Internet services and their corresponding IE4 components are described in the following sections.

Internet Services

The Internet is a large network of interconnected machines, ranging from corporate networks and universities to individual computers. A wide variety of services can be made available over the Internet; the most common (and those supported by IE4 and its related components) are described in the following sections.

On the Exam

You should have experience using all of the services described below for the IE4 MCSE exam, at least from a client point of view. IIS, covered in Part 2, *Internet Information Server 4.0*, acts as a server for these services.

World Wide Web

The World Wide Web (WWW) is the best known Internet service. Web servers act as a repository for web documents, and distribute the documents to clients using the HTTP (Hypertext Transfer Protocol) protocol. Web clients are called *browsers*.

The most popular current browsers are Microsoft Internet Explorer (IE) 4.0, the subject of this chapter, and Netscape Navigator 4.0. Web documents include text, HTML (Hypertext Markup Language), and multimedia formats. Web documents (and documents using other protocols) can be referred to with a URL, or Uniform Resource Locator. A URL has this form:

http://site/directory/filename

The first portion of the URL, *http://*, refers to the HTTP protocol. FTP, News, and other protocols can also be specified. The remainder of the URL specifies a site name (a fully qualified IP host name, such as *www.oreilly.com*) and a directory and file under the site.

FTP (File Transfer Protocol)

FTP allows file transfers (uploads and downloads) between hosts on a TCP/IP network (such as the Internet). This protocol predates the Web, and is still widely used. FTP clients can run on virtually any platform.

Internet Explorer 4 and other browsers include an integrated FTP download client, which can be used by specifying a URL beginning with the *ftp://* method. Windows 95 and Windows NT also include a command-line FTP client; to use it, type ftp *sitename* at the command prompt.

Email

Email (electronic mail) allows person-to-person messaging over the Internet or other networks. Users can choose from a wide variety of email clients to send text-based messages to other users. Internet email is largely distributed by two protocols:

SMTP (Simple Mail Transfer Protocol)
> Used by clients to send and receive messages, as well as between hosts to route messages to their destinations.

POP (Post Office Protocol)
    A more recent protocol, typically used by graphic email clients to transfer messages from a server for reading offline.

IE4 includes Outlook Express, a mail client with support for both of these protocols.

Newsgroups

Newsgroups, also known as discussion groups, are linked databases of messages (called *articles*) that allow non-realtime discussions, similar to email but in a public forum. A large number of newsgroups are available, including the standard USENET groups.

The Outlook Express client also supports newsgroup reading and posting. News articles are transferred using NNTP (Network News Transfer Protocol).

On the Exam

IIS, described in Part 2 of this book, includes server components for NNTP as well as the email-related protocols described in the previous section. A more sophisticated NNTP server is included in Exchange Server, covered in Part 5, *Exchange Server 5.5.*

IE 4.0 Admin

IE4 Components

IE4 began its life as a simple web browser, but now includes a variety of other components. All of these can be selected or deselected during the IE4 installation. Currently, versions of IE4 and its related components are available for Windows 95/98 and Windows NT.

Internet Explorer

Web browsers act as clients for the HTTP protocol to display HTML (Hypertext Markup Language) and text documents. IE4's display of a simple HTML document is shown in Figure 3-1.

IE4 supports version 3.2 of the HTML specification and many features of the new HTML 4.0 standard. IE4 also supports the following types of content:

Java
    A platform-independent, object-oriented language developed by Sun Micro-systems. Java programs, or *applets*, are created in a simple C-like language, compiled into platform-independent bytecodes, and executed by a web browser as an embedded object within an HTML document. IE4 uses Microsoft's proprietary version of the Java virtual machine.

ActiveX
    Microsoft's specification for embedded executable programs. ActiveX programs are compiled Windows programs that can be downloaded and

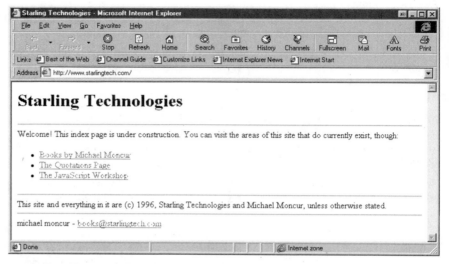

Figure 3-1: The Internet Explorer 4.0 web browser

executed. ActiveX is proprietary to IE4, and to the Microsoft Windows operating systems.

JScript

A client-side scripting language. JScript is Microsoft's implementation of Netscape's JavaScript language. JavaScript uses simple statements, based on Java syntax, embedded within the actual text of an HTML document.

VBScript

Microsoft's proprietary client-side scripting language, also called Visual Basic Scripting Edition. VBScript statements are included within HTML, and the syntax is based on Visual Basic.

Dynamic HTML

A recently proposed extension to HTML which allows all or part of a document's content to be modified without reloading the entire document. Microsoft and Netscape have both introduced versions of Dynamic HTML, not entirely compatible with each other.

On the Exam

For the IE4 MCSE exam, you should be familiar with all of the types of content that can be displayed by IE4. You should also be aware that other types of files (such as Adobe's PDF format) can be displayed in the browser, but require the use of a third-party plug-in.

Desktop Update

New to version 4.0 of Internet Explorer is an update to the Windows 95 desktop and Explorer user interface. This update includes *Desktop Integration*, which allows HTML documents (either from files or from web sites) to be displayed on the desktop or in Explorer windows.

Additionally, the *Active Desktop* feature allows web content on the desktop to be updated periodically, either using a schedule or using channels, which automatically update when new content is available. Several minor user-interface changes are also included, making the Explorer interface similar to (and in many cases, interchangeable with) Internet Explorer. Many of these changes are also included in Windows 98.

Desktop Integration can be selected or deselected during the IE4 installation, and can be added or removed at any time.

In the Real World

If you do install the Desktop Integration features, you can turn them off from the Desktop control panel to retain the standard Windows 95 interface. However, even if turned off, Desktop Integration uses a significant amount of RAM. This memory can be reclaimed by uninstalling the desktop update as described in "Adding and Removing Components," later in this chapter.

Outlook Express

Outlook Express, new to IE 4.0, is an integrated utility for reading and posting email and newsgroup messages. Outlook Express uses an Explorer-like interface to display messages.

While email messages are usually ASCII text, Outlook Express includes the ability to send and receive HTML messages, and can attach files to messages in a variety of formats. Outlook Express uses POP (Post Office Protocol) version 3 to receive email messages, SMTP (Simple Mail Transport Protocol) to send email messages, and NNTP to read and post newsgroup articles.

In the Real World

While Outlook Express and several other email clients support the use of HTML for messages, this format is still not standard for Internet mail, and is unsupported by many browsers and email clients.

FrontPage Express

Microsoft FrontPage is a visually-oriented HTML editor. The current version, FrontPage 97, is available separately from Microsoft. The IE4 suite includes FrontPage Express, a feature-limited version. This version includes the basic

FrontPage features for working with single pages, but lacks FrontPage's features for managing large-scale sites.

NetMeeting

Microsoft NetMeeting, new to the IE4 suite, is a utility that allows real-time conferencing over the Internet. NetMeeting allows audio and video conferencing, provided the network has sufficient bandwidth. In addition, it offers *collaboration*, allowing users to concurrently view or edit a document in a Windows program.

The IE4 Administration Kit

The Internet Explorer Administration Kit (IEAK) is a tool that allows you to create customized versions of IE4 and its associated components. This allows Internet service providers and corporate administrators to distribute pre-configured versions for easy installation, and also allows several aspects of the browser to be modified. The IEAK is explained in detail later in this chapter.

Installing and Configuring IE4

The following sections discuss the hardware and software requirements for running IE4 and its related components, the process of installing the software and upgrading from previous versions, and the options available after installation.

Hardware Requirements

IE4 requires the Windows 95, Windows 98, or Windows NT operating systems. It requires a 486 or faster processor, 8 MB of RAM under Windows 95 or 98, and 16 MB of RAM under Windows NT. In addition, the Windows NT version requires that Windows NT Service Pack 3 (SP3) be installed before IE4.

Versions of Internet Explorer 4.0 are also available for Windows 3.1, Macintosh, and UNIX, but do not include the Desktop Integration feature. The instructions here are for the 32-bit Windows version, but the installation under other systems is similar.

On the Exam

For the IE4 MCSE exam, remember that 8 MB of RAM is the official requirement for IE4 under Windows 95. In practice, Windows 95 and IE4 will be significantly slow with less than 16 MB.

IE4 also requires a significant amount of disk storage. This amount depends on the selected options, and ranges from 67 MB to 86 MB. The disk storage requirements for specific installation options are discussed later in this section.

The Installation Process

IE4 can be obtained from Microsoft on CD-ROM, or downloaded from the Web. To download a copy of IE4, use the URL *http://www.microsoft.com/ie4/*. The downloadable version uses the Active Setup wizard, which downloads first, then runs and allows you to select components to install.

On the Exam

The IE4 installation overrides any previously installed version of IE4; it is not necessary to uninstall these versions. If you want to replace another browser, such as Netscape Navigator, it should be manually uninstalled; however, IE4 can coexist with other browsers.

There are three basic installation options for IE4 and its related components:

Minimal Installation
   Includes only the IE4 browser and support components. This option may not be available with all installation packages.

Standard Installation
   Includes the browser, Outlook Express, VDOLive Player, and Microsoft Wallet.

Full Installation
   Includes the browser, Outlook Express, NetMeeting, Microsoft Chat, NetShow, VDOLive Player, RealAudio Player, FrontPage Express, the Web Publishing Wizard, and Microsoft Wallet.

On the Exam

For the IE4 MCSE exam, you should know these options, the components they include, and be familiar with the installation process.

To start the installation, run IE4SETUP.EXE from the distribution directory. The wizard prompts for the following information to complete the installation:

1. The license agreement for IE4 is displayed. You must select the *I accept the agreement* option to continue the installation.

2. Choose one of the installation options described above.

3. Select the country you are in; this is used to determine the default list of channels.

4. Choose a destination directory for the IE4 files.

5. The files are now installed. IE4 icons are added to the desktop and the Start menu.

IE 4.0 Admin

IE4 does not include a custom installation option. However, you can customize the available options with the Administration Kit, described later in this chapter.

Browser Options

In most cases, IE4 can be used immediately after installation without further configuration. However, a wide variety of options are available to customize IE4. To set these options, select *Internet Options* from the View menu in IE4. These options are also available from the Internet icon in the Control Panel.

The IE4 options dialog is divided into several tabbed categories. These are described in the following sections.

General

This dialog includes the following basic options:

Home Page
Specify a URL for a home page. This is the default page displayed when IE4 is launched. An online or local URL can be specified. The Use Blank button inserts the special URL *about:blank*, which displays a blank window.

Temporary Internet Files
IE4 keeps a cache of documents, graphics, and other content to allow pages to be revisited without downloading all of their content. The Settings button allows you to change the size of the cache. By default, the cache uses 5% of the storage available on a drive.

History
The History folder under the Windows directory stores links to URLs recently visited by IE4. These entries are used to display visited and unvisited links in different colors, and to allow quick access to the URLs. You can specify the number of days of history IE4 will keep in this section; the Clear History button clears the current history entries.

Colors
Allows you to modify the default foreground and background text colors, and the colors used for visited and unvisited links.

Fonts
Allows you to select the fixed and proportional fonts used to view Web documents. You cannot specify an exact point size for fonts, but can select a relative size (smallest to largest).

Languages
Allows you to specify the default language (such as English) for web documents. This setting is used only when a document includes versions for multiple languages.

Accessibility

This dialog includes several options to improve the readability of web documents. You can choose to ignore font colors, sizes, and font faces specified by HTML tags in a web document. In addition, you can specify a style sheet (a list of specifications for different HTML tags) to be used rather than style sheets included with web documents.

Security

This dialog allows you to configure Internet Explorer's security options. IE4 handles security by dividing sites into *zones*. You can select *High*, *Medium*, *Low*, or *Custom* security for each zone. The following zones are included:

Internet Zone

For Internet sites; all sites not defined as part of another site are considered to be in this zone. This zone is set to Medium security by default.

Local Intranet Zone

For sites on the local network. You can use the Add Sites button to automatically add all local sites, or all sites that bypass the proxy server, to this zone. The Local Intranet Zone defaults to Medium security.

Trusted Sites Zone

This zone is for sites you explicitly trust. Use the Add Sites button to add sites to the list. You can also specify that only sites using secure communication can be included in this zone. This zone defaults to Low security.

Restricted Sites Zone

Use the Add Sites button to add any sites that you wish to explicitly secure to this zone. This zone defaults to High security.

The *Low*, *Medium*, and *High* options provide preset levels of security. The *Custom* option allows you to individually control each of the following categories of content. Each can be set to enabled, disabled, or to prompt the user.

ActiveX controls and plug-ins

Specify whether signed or unsigned ActiveX controls and plug-ins should be downloaded, whether they should be run, and whether they can be controlled by scripting.

Java

Choose the safety level for Java applets, or disable Java entirely. The *Custom* option allows you to individually specify permissions for signed and unsigned applets.

Scripting

Choose whether scripting is enabled for ActiveX controls and for Java applets.

Downloads

Choose whether files or fonts can be downloaded.

User Authentication

For sites that require name and password authentication, specify whether to prompt for this information or to attempt to use the user's current username and password.

Miscellaneous
Includes options to control form submissions, application launching, desktop items, drag and drop, and channels.

On the Exam

Most of these options can be preconfigured using the Administration Kit, described later in this chapter. They can also be disabled or restricted.

Content

This dialog includes options related to web page ratings, authentication, and personal information. The following options are included:

Content Advisor
Allows you to use the RSAC (Recreational Software Advisory Council) rating system to control which pages can be displayed on the computer. Once ratings are enabled with a password, you can set the levels of various types of rated content that can be accessed. This only affects pages which contain RSAC rating information.

Certificates
Allows you to configure digital certificates: personal certificates, used to authenticate the client with web servers; certificate authorities, used to authenticate web content; and trusted software publishers. Software from these publishers can be installed automatically without prompting the user.

Personal Information
This section allows you to configure Microsoft Profile Assistant, a system for sending personal information (such as name and address) to web sites. If this feature is enabled, web sites can request the user profile; you are prompted whether to send the information to the site.

On the Exam

You can disable the Profile Assistant with the *Enable Profile Assistant* option in the Security category of the Advanced IE4 settings dialog, described later in this section.

Connection

This dialog includes options related to the Internet or network connection used by Internet Explorer. The first section of this dialog allows you to choose whether to use dial-up networking to connect to the Internet, or use an existing network connection. If dial-up networking is selected, IE4 will attempt to dial the specified connection when you load a web page.

The second section of the dialog includes proxy settings. Choose whether to use a proxy server, and specify its IP and port address. The Advanced button allows you to define specific servers for HTTP, security, FTP, Gopher, and the SOCKS protocol. You can also specify a list of addresses that can be accessed without using the proxy.

The final section of the dialog allows you to specify a server address for automatic configuration. The address refers to an INS file; you can create these files using the IEAK Profile Manager utility, described later in this chapter.

Programs

This dialog allows you to define external programs used with Internet Explorer. The available options include the following:

Mail
    This program is used to send an email message when the user clicks on a *mailto:* link. Outlook Express is the default option, if installed.

News
    This program is used to read or post newsgroup messages when the user follows a *news:* link. Outlook Express is the default, if installed.

Internet Call
    This program is used for voice communications or videoconferencing; NetMeeting is the default if installed.

Calendar
    An optional calendar program. Microsoft Outlook (not the limited Express version) can be used for this purpose.

Contact List
    An optional contact list program. The default address book is built into Internet Explorer.

Internet Explorer should check to see whether it is the default browser
    If this option is enabled, IE4 will check the registry each time it is run to verify that it is the default program for Internet shortcuts. This program is used when you click on a URL shortcut or type a URL into the Run dialog or Windows Explorer address bar. If this option is enabled and IE4 is not the default browser, you will be prompted to choose whether to change the registry.

Advanced Options

The Advanced tab of the IE4 properties dialog includes a number of options to control IE4's behavior. These should rarely need to be changed by most users. The options are divided into several categories, described in the sections below.

On the Exam

All of the Advanced options are described here for your reference. For the exam, you should have a general idea of the available options, but you should not need to know the exact option names and functions.

Accessibility

The Accessibility category of Advanced options includes two options that may make IE4 more useful for disabled users:

Move system caret with focus/selection changes
> If selected, the caret (text cursor) is moved to the appropriate part of the screen when a form element or link is clicked with the mouse; this is needed for some text reading programs for the visually impaired.

Always expand alt text for images
> Images in HTML documents can include the ALT tag, which specifies a description of the image. If graphics are disabled in IE4, these text messages are displayed, but may be truncated to fit in the space the image would have occupied. If this option is selected, the entire text is always displayed.

On the Exam

Other accessibility options can be modified using the Accessibility button in the General tab of the IE4 Properties dialog.

Browsing

The Browsing category of advanced options includes options to customize the browser's behavior:

Disable script debugging
> If this option is selected, errors in JavaScript or VBScript programs will not result in the display of a debugging dialog.

Show channel bar at startup
> If enabled, the channel bar (described later in this chapter) is displayed on the desktop at startup.

Launch channels in full screen window
> If enabled, information from channels is always displayed in full screen mode.

Launch browser in full screen window
> If enabled, IE4 always opens a full screen window when started.

Use AutoComplete
> The AutoComplete feature attempts to complete URLs as you type them in the browser's Address field using URLs in the History folder. As you type each letter of the URL, the closest match from history is displayed (if any); press Enter to select that URL. AutoComplete is enabled by default.

Show friendly URLs
> If selected, the status line of the browser display will display only the document name for the link under the mouse pointer. Otherwise, the entire URL is displayed.

Use smooth scrolling

If enabled, scrolling in the IE4 window is performed one pixel at a time instead of one line of text at a time. Disabling this option may improve performance on slower computers.

Enable page transitions

If enabled, IE4 uses a fade in/out effect when moving from one page to another, if the site being viewed has pages that use this feature.

Browse in a new process

If the Desktop Update is installed, IE4 is basically loaded into memory at startup, and can be quickly launched when a URL is selected. If this option is enabled, a separate copy of IE4 will be launched instead; this is slower, but may improve system stability.

Enable scheduled subscription updates

If enabled, subscribed web pages or channels will be automatically updated at the selected interval.

Show welcome message each time I log on

If enabled, the initial IE4 welcome dialog (usually displayed the first time IE4 runs) is displayed each time IE4 starts.

Show Internet Explorer on the desktop

If enabled, an Internet Explorer is included on the desktop. This is enabled by default.

Underline links

Specify whether links within web documents are indicated with an underline, in addition to the appropriate color. Underlining can be always on, always off, or only on while the cursor is over a link.

Multimedia

This category of options allows you to disable certain types of multimedia content within web pages; all options are enabled by default. The following options are included:

Show pictures

If disabled, pictures included in web documents using the <IMG> tag are not displayed. The ALT text, if included, is displayed instead.

Play animations

Enables the animation feature included in the GIF89A specification. Animated GIF images are displayed only if this option and the *Show Pictures* option are selected.

Play videos

Enables the display of video clips embedded in web documents in the MPEG or AVI formats.

Play sounds

Enables WAV sounds and MIDI music files to be played when included in a web document.

Smart image dithering

If enabled, IE4 modifies displayed images to improve their appearance in the number of colors available on the screen. This may cause undesirable effects on high-color displays.

Security

The Security category of the Advanced dialog includes a number of advanced security options not available in the Security dialog. These include the following:

Enable Profile Assistant

If selected, requests for personal information using the Profile Assistant (described earlier in this section) will be denied.

PCT 1.0

Enables the PCT (Private Communications Technology) protocol, a proprietary Microsoft protocol for secure HTTP communications. This and other secure protocols are used only when the server supports them.

SSL 2.0

Enables SSL (Secure Sockets Layer) 2.0, an Internet standard for secure HTTP communication.

SSL 3.0

Enables SSL 3.0, a more recent and more secure version of SSL.

Delete saved pages when browser closed

If enabled, the contents of the cache (temporary Internet files) directory are erased each time you exit IE4.

Do not save encrypted pages to disk

If enabled, pages received in an encrypted protocol (PCT or SSL) are not written to the cache directory.

Warn if form submit is being redirected

If enabled, a warning dialog is displayed when data you enter into a form is submitted to a site other than the site hosting the form.

Warn if changing between secure and not secure mode

If enabled, a warning message is displayed when IE4 switches between secure protocols (PCT or SSL) and standard HTTP.

Check for certificate revocation

If enabled, an extra check is performed to check the validity of digital site certificates.

Warn about invalid site certificates

If enabled, a warning message is displayed when a site attempts to authenticate itself using an invalid digital certificate.

Cookies

Cookies are items of information stored on the local machine by a web site, and can be subsequently received by the same site; these are frequently used to store personal information or track your movement through a site. All cookies are accepted by default; you can choose to disable them entirely or prompt when a site attempts to store a cookie.

Java VM

This section of the Advanced Properties includes options relating to the Java virtual machine and the execution of Java applets:

Java console enabled
> If enabled, a Java console window is displayed when Java applets are in use, providing access to debugging functions. This option is disabled by default.

Java JIT compiler enabled
> Java applet bytecodes are traditionally interpreted by the browser one at a time. If this option is enabled, a just-in-time (JIT) compiler is used to compile the bytecodes into native code before running the applet. This causes a delay when loading the applet, but improves execution speed.

Java logging enabled
> If enabled, Java applet execution and debugging information is logged to a file. This file is available as \WINDOWS\Java\Javalog.txt.

Printing

This section includes a single option, *Print background colors and images*. If enabled, printed copies of web documents will include background colors and background images, if included on the page. This may use excessive amounts of ink or produce unreadable printouts; this option is disabled by default.

Searching

This section of the Advanced Properties dialog includes two options related to web searching:

Autoscan common root domains
> If this feature is enabled, IE attempts to complete URLs entered into the Location field by adding common domain suffixes. For example, if you enter "oreilly" into the field, the domains *oreilly.com* and *oreilly.org* will be tried.

Search when URL fails
> IE4 can also query a web search engine when you enter an invalid URL in the Location field. This option can be set to *Never search*, *Always ask*, or *Always search*.

Toolbar

This section of the Advanced Properties dialog includes two options related to the IE4 toolbar:

Show font button
> If enabled, a Font button is included in the toolbar. This allows you to change font sizes and language settings.

Small icons
> If selected, small toolbar buttons are displayed.

HTTP 1.1 Settings

This section of the Advanced dialog includes two options related to the HTTP 1.1 protocol:

Use HTTP 1.1
> If enabled, IE4 will attempt to use HTTP 1.1 instead of 1.0 if a site supports it. This option is enabled by default.

Use HTTP 1.1 through proxy connections
> If this option and the previous option are enabled, IE4 will also attempt to use HTTP 1.1 with sites reached through a proxy server. This option is disabled by default, as many proxy servers do not yet support HTTP 1.1.

Adding and Removing Components

The Add/Remove Components dialog in the Control Panel can be used to uninstall Internet Explorer 4.0, add components, or remove components. To access this feature, select *Microsoft Internet Explorer 4.0* from the list and press the Add/Remove button. The Active Setup dialog, shown in Figure 3-2, is displayed.

Figure 3-2: The IE4 Add/Remove components dialog

The following options are available:

Uninstall Internet Explorer 4.0 and all its components
> Removes IE4 and its related components entirely. The Advanced button displays a dialog that allows you to select the components to be uninstalled. Additionally, this dialog includes an option to delete the IE4 backup (uninstall) information.

In the Real World

Removing the IE4 backup information saves about 4 MB of disk storage. However, after doing this IE4 cannot be uninstalled; in addition, you may be unable to remove subsequently installed versions of IE without reinstalling Windows entirely.

Add a component to Internet Explorer

If this option is selected, IE4 is launched and loads a page on Microsoft's server listing available components. Any components you select can be downloaded and installed.

Remove the Windows Desktop Update component

This option removes the Desktop Update, if installed with IE4. The browser and other components remain installed. This frees up a significant amount of memory and disk storage.

On the Exam

Since Internet Explorer 4.0 is integrated with Windows 98, this version does not list IE in the Add/Remove Programs control panel. Instead, you can use the Windows Setup page of this control panel to remove IE4 and related components.

Working with IE4 Components

As discussed earlier in this chapter, Internet Explorer includes a variety of components along with the basic web browser. The major components include the Windows Desktop Update, Outlook Express, and NetMeeting. These are described in the following sections.

On the Exam

All of the IE4 components described here may be covered on the IE4 MCSE exam. You should install, configure, and familiarize yourself with each of these components in preparation for the exam.

Windows Desktop Update

The Desktop Update can be installed as part of the IE4 installation or added using the *Add/Remove components* option in the Control Panel. The update adds a number of features to the desktop:

- The Start menu includes a *Log off* option, replacing the *Close all programs and log in as a different user* option in the Shut down dialog. A new Favorites menu provides access to IE4 bookmarks, and Internet-related options are added to the Find menu. The Start menu also supports drag-and-drop editing.

- Toolbars can be created on the taskbar or anywhere on the desktop; a default toolbar is included on the left portion of the taskbar. To add, hide, or modify toolbars, right-click the taskbar and select the *Toolbars* option.

- Explorer windows include a *View as Web Page* option, which displays an HTML background. Additionally, desktop icons and Explorer entries can be activated with a single click.

In addition to these features, the Active Desktop feature allows HTML content, channels, and automatic updates on the desktop. The following sections describe how to configure the desktop and folders.

Configuring the Active Desktop

The Desktop Update adds a new option to the Display control panel to control Active Desktop features. To access these features, select the Display icon in the Control panel (or right-click the desktop and select *Properties*) and choose the Web tab. This dialog is shown in Figure 3-3.

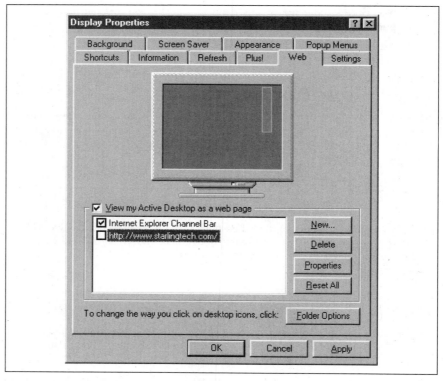

Figure 3-3: The Active Desktop Properties dialog

This dialog allows you to configure the HTML content of the Active Desktop. The desktop can include subscribed web sites and channels and local HTML documents. By default, the Internet Explorer Channel Bar is the only HTML component on the desktop; this is a default menu of available channels.

Both ordinary web sites and channels can be added to the desktop and subscribed to for regular updates. The main difference between the two is that channels are designed for this purpose. A channel's CDF (channel definition file) file describes the channel and includes information about how often the content is updated.

To add a web site subscription, use the New button. You are first prompted for the URL or file location of the site. After this is entered, a confirmation dialog is displayed. Select OK to complete the subscription. The Customize Subscription button starts the Subscription Wizard, which allows you to change subscription options. Follow these steps to customize a subscription:

1. Select whether the site should be loaded on a scheduled basis, or manually. If the *Scheduled* option is selected, you can choose Daily, Weekly, or Monthly updates. Additionally, you can use the New button to create a custom schedule (for example, every two weeks).

2. Select whether the site requires authentication, and enter the username and password if required.

3. Select Finish and then OK to complete the subscription.

Once a component is added, IE4 attempts to load the contents of the page to initialize the subscription. The page or channel is displayed on the desktop, and can be moved, resized, or hidden. You can also hide or delete items from the Web tab of the Display control panel.

On the Exam

HTML components will not be displayed on the desktop unless the *View as Web Page* option is enabled for the Active Desktop. To access this option, select *Active Desktop* from the Settings menu under the Start menu.

Configuring Folders

You can customize the appearance of Explorer dialogs and icons with the Options dialog, available from the View menu in Explorer. The General tab of this dialog includes options to switch to web style (single click access) or Classic style (normal Windows 95 behavior). The *Custom* option allows you to individually configure the following options:

Active Desktop
> Choose to enable or disable web-related content; this is equivalent to the *View as Web Page* option in the Web tab of the Display settings dialog. The Customize button opens the Display settings dialog.

Browse folders as follows
> Choose whether clicking on a folder name in an Explorer window opens a new window or loads the folder into the existing window.

View web contents in folders
> Choose whether to view folders as web pages. The *For all folders with HTML content* option enables this feature for all folders (all Explorer windows have default HTML content). The other option displays HTML only when you select the *As Web Page* option from Explorer's View menu.

Click items as follows
> Choose whether a single or double click is required to launch items; this applies to Explorer windows and to icons on the desktop. You can also select whether icon titles are always underlined or underlined when the mouse cursor is over them.

Outlook Express

Outlook Express, introduced earlier in this chapter, is an Internet mail and news-group client. It can be installed as part of the IE4 suite, or added separately using the Add/Remove Programs control panel.

Outlook Express can be launched from the Start menu, the desktop, or from the Go menu in Internet Explorer 4 (if Outlook Express is configured as the Mail or News program). The following sections describe how to configure and use Outlook Express.

Configuring an Email Account

When Outlook Express is first launched, it runs the Internet Connection Wizard, prompting you to create an email account. Follow these steps to create an account:

1. Choose whether to create a new account or import an existing account. Outlook Express can import settings from the Netscape Navigator and Eudora mail clients.

2. If you are creating a new account, enter a name for the account. This name is used to form the From field of outgoing messages.

3. Enter your email address. This will be used to retrieve mail and will be included in the From field of outgoing messages.

4. Specify names for incoming and outgoing mail servers. Outlook Express supports SMTP for outgoing mail and POP3 or IMAP for incoming mail.

5. Specify the email account name and password for the POP3 or IMAP incoming mail server. You can also choose to use SPA (secure password authentication), a Microsoft-specific protocol that transmits encrypted pass-words, if supported by the mail server.

6. Specify a friendly name for the email account. This name is displayed in the Outlook Express Inbox dialog.

7. Choose the network connection that will be used to reach the mail servers. This can be a dialup or LAN connection.

After you have configured an email account, the main Outlook Express window is displayed, as shown in Figure 3-4. The left portion of the screen displays Inbox, Outbox, and other folders. The right portion is divided into an upper portion that displays message headers and a lower portion that displays the current message.

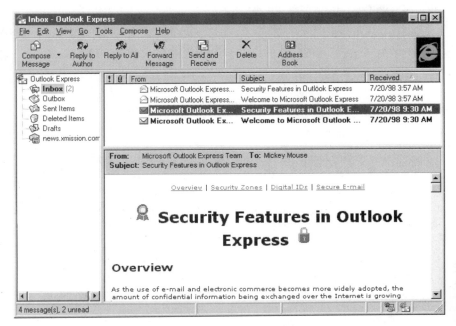

Figure 3-4: The main Outlook Express email window

Configuring Newsgroup Access

To read and post to newsgroups with Outlook Express, select *News* from the Go menu. When you start the newsreader for the first time, you are required to create a news account using the Internet Connection Wizard. Follow these steps:

1. Select a name for the newsgroup account. This will be used in the From field of posted messages.

2. Specify your email address. This is also used in the From field of messages.

3. Specify the name of the NNTP server. This can be a server at an Internet provider, or a local server. If the server requires a username and password, select the *My news server requires me to log on* option.

On the Exam

Internet Information Server, described in Part 2 of this book, includes an NNTP server that can be used to set up local newsgroups.

---

4. Choose a friendly name for the account. This name is used only in the Outlook Express window.

5. Choose a network connection to access the news server (LAN or modem).

After configuring the newsgroup account, the main Outlook Express window is displayed. You must subscribe to one or more newsgroups before using the news-reader. To do this, use the Newsgroups button in the toolbar. This downloads and displays a list of groups and allows you to subscribe or unsubscribe.

On the Exam

If you need to configure a Mail or News account after the initial configuration, select *Accounts* from the Tools menu.

General Options

To modify Outlook Express options, select *Options* from the Tools menu. The Options dialog includes a number of tabbed categories, described here and in the following sections.

The General tab of the Options dialog includes the following options:

Check for new messages
> Specify how often, in minutes, the news server should be polled for new messages.

Play sound when new messages arrive
> If enabled, a sound is played when new messages are received; the sound can be set using the Sounds control panel.

Empty messages from the Deleted Items folder on exit
> When you delete mail messages, they are moved to the Deleted Items folder. If this option is selected, this folder is cleared when you exit Outlook Express.

Automatically put people I reply to in my address book
> If enabled, addresses used in email replies are automatically added to the address book.

Make Outlook Express my default email program
> Sets Internet Explorer's email program to Outlook Express.

Make Outlook Express my default Simple MAPI client
> Registers Outlook Express as the default MAPI (Mail Application Programming Interface) client. This allows Outlook Express to be used as the email program for other browsers or programs that support MAPI.

Make Outlook Express my default news reader
> Sets Internet Explorer's news program option to Outlook Express.

When starting, go directly to my Inbox folder
> If selected, the Inbox folder is opened at startup (otherwise, a menu is displayed).

Notify me if there are any new newsgroups
> Queries the NNTP server for new newsgroups each time it is connected, and prompts you to download the new list of groups.

Automatically display folders with unread messages
> If enabled, the hierarchical folder display expands items containing folders with new messages.

Message Sending Options

The Send tab of the Options dialog includes the following options related to sending messages:

Mail sending format
> Specify whether mail messages are sent in plain text or HTML format. The default is plain text.

News sending format
> Specify the format for news messages.

Save copy of sent messages
> If selected, a copy of each message sent is saved in the Sent Items folder.

Include message in reply
> If selected, the news or email message you reply to is copied into the text of the reply message.

Send messages immediately
> If selected, the SMTP or NNTP server is contacted to send a message as soon as you are finished composing it. Otherwise, messages are queued until the server is polled.

Reply to messages using the format in which they were sent
> If selected, the HTML or ASCII format will be selected depending on the format of the message being replied to.

Automatically complete email addresses when composing
> If enabled, Outlook Express attempts to complete email addresses as you type them, using the addresses in the Address Book.

Message Reading Options

The Read tab of the Options dialog includes the following options related to reading messages:

Message is read after being previewed for
> If enabled, the current message is marked as read after being previewed for the specified number of seconds.

Download headers
> Specify the maximum number of message headers that can be downloaded at one time.

Automatically expand conversation threads
> Newsgroup messages are displayed in threads, or groups of messages that share the same subject. If this option is enabled, the list of messages in the thread is displayed.

Automatically show news messages in the Preview pane
> If selected, the bottom pane of the Outlook Express window displays the currently selected news message.

Mark all messages as read when exiting a newsgroup
> If selected, all messages are marked as read when you close a newsgroup.

Automatically show picture attachments in messages
> If enabled, message attachments with GIF or other image extensions are displayed within the Outlook Express window.

Font Settings
> Allows you to configure the fonts used to display messages and headers.

Security Options

The Security tab of the Options dialog includes the following security-related settings:

Security Zones
> Choose whether to use the settings specified in Internet Explorer's Internet Zone or Restricted Sites Zone to control the use of programs and scripts within HTML messages.

Secure Mail
> Includes options to digitally sign outgoing mail messages, and to encrypt messages and attachments. This requires that the receiving email client also support encryption.

Digital IDs
> Allows you to connect to the Internet and register for a digital ID to be used in signing messages.

Advanced Options

The Advanced tab of the Options dialog includes a number of advanced options:

Local Message Files
> Outlook Express keeps local copies of newsgroup messages to avoid repeated downloads. Here you can specify the number of days to retain these copies, and specify whether read messages should be kept. The Clean Up Now button erases all of the current local copies of messages.

Logging Options
> Specify which actions are logged to a file. Three categories of actions can be logged: News Transport, Mail Transport, and IMAP transport. No logging is enabled by default.

NetMeeting

NetMeeting is a versatile application for chatting, audio and video conferencing, and document sharing over the Internet or a local network. NetMeeting can be installed as part of the IE4 suite, or added on separately. The following sections describe the process of configuring and using NetMeeting and setting its options.

NetMeeting Configuration

The first time NetMeeting runs, it displays a configuration wizard. Follow these steps to configure NetMeeting:

1. Choose whether to log onto a directory server, and specify the name of the server. These servers use the ILS (Internet Locator Service) protocol. Using a directory server allows you to display a list of other users online, and makes your status visible to other users.

2. Specify first name, last name, email address, and other personal information.

3. Specify whether your personal information should be made available to other individuals or businesses.

4. Select your modem or network connection speed. This allows NetMeeting to optimize its communications.

5. The Audio Tuning Wizard runs and prompts you to test your speakers and microphone, if installed.

Using NetMeeting

After the configuration information has been entered, the main NetMeeting window is displayed, as shown in Figure 3-5. This shows a directory of users on the current ILS server. Highlight a user and press the Call button to initiate a call. You can also initiate a call by specifying a user's email address or other information.

IE 4.0 Admin

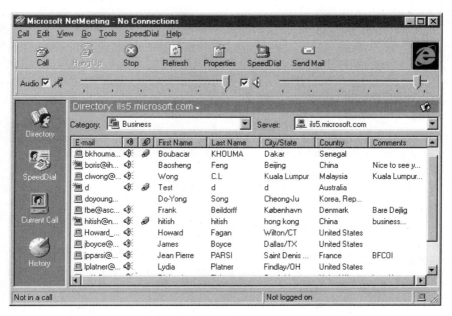

Figure 3-5: The main NetMeeting dialog

Once a call has been started, the Current Call window opens to show the status of the current call. Audio and video connections are made automatically, depending on the equipment supported by both parties. NetMeeting also supports multiple parties through the meeting option; select *Host Meeting* from the Call menu to start a meeting.

Once a call has been initiated, the following options are available from the toolbar:

Hang Up
> Disconnects the current call.

Switch
> Switches the audio and video connection to a different user; these features can only be used between two users at a time.

Collaborate
> Allows one or more users to work at the same time in a shared application. The application should first be started on one user's computer and shared with the *Share Application* option in the Tools menu.

Chat
> Opens a text-based chat window for discussions.

Whiteboard
> Opens the whiteboard (similar to a paint program). One or more users can draw in this space, which is visible to all users in the meeting.

On the Exam

You should have experience making calls, sharing documents, and using the whiteboard with NetMeeting for the IE4 MCSE exam.

General Options

To configure NetMeeting options, select *Options* from the Tools menu. The Options dialog is divided into several tabbed categories, described here and in the following sections.

The General category of the Options dialog includes the following basic options:

Show Microsoft NetMeeting icon on the taskbar
> If enabled, an icon to run NetMeeting and show its status is included in the tray portion of the taskbar.

Run when Windows starts and notify me of incoming calls
> If selected, NetMeeting runs automatically. This option is most useful if you have a fixed network connection rather than a dial-up connection.

Automatically accept incoming calls
> If selected, calls are opened automatically when received; otherwise, you are prompted that an incoming call has been requested.

Show the SpeedDial tab when NetMeeting starts
> If enabled, the SpeedDial tab is shown rather than the Directory tab when NetMeeting is launched.

Show Intel Connection Advisor icon on the taskbar
> If enabled, the Connection Advisor utility is run and displayed in the taskbar. This utility monitors network use and determines potential bandwidth problems.

Network Bandwidth
> Specify the speed of the modem or network connection in use.

File Transfer
> Specify the directory for files transferred from remote parties.

Personal Information

The My Information tab of the Options dialog includes the options for first name, last name, and other personal information that you were prompted for during the initial setup.

Calling Options

The Calling tab of the Options dialog includes the following options related to the directory and speed dial options:

Directory
> Specify whether to log onto a directory server at startup, and specify the server name. Additionally, you can choose not to display your name in the directory.

Automatically add SpeedDials
> Specify whether entries are added to the SpeedDial list when you make or receive a call.

SpeedDial defaults
> Specify how frequently the SpeedDial list should be refreshed, and how many entries can be added to the list automatically.

Audio Options

The Audio tab of the Options dialog includes the following options:

Enable full-duplex audio
> If selected, audio can be transmitted and received at the same time. This requires a sound card and drivers that support full duplex.

Enable auto gain control
> If enabled, NetMeeting will attempt to amplify received audio signals for maximum volume.

Tuning Wizard
> Press this button to run the Audio Tuning Wizard to reconfigure the settings made when you first ran NetMeeting.

Advanced

Displays a dialog that allows you to configure the audio compression protocols used by NetMeeting.

Microphone Sensitivity

Adjust the input gain for the signal from your microphone. By default, this is adjusted automatically.

Calling a Telephone Using NetMeeting

Allows the use of the H.323 protocol to connect NetMeeting with the telephone system. This requires a working H.323 gateway machine.

Video Options

The Video tab of the Options dialog includes the following options related to videoconferencing:

Sending and receiving video

Choose whether video should be automatically sent or received. The send option is only available if a video camera is attached to the computer.

Send image size

Specify the size of the sent video image (small, medium, or large).

Video Quality

This setting adjusts video compression settings based on your preference: faster video, better quality, or a compromise between the two.

Video Camera Properties

Specify the video camera or capture device to be used for sending video.

Protocol Options

The Protocol tab of the Options dialog allows you to configure protocols for use with NetMeeting. By default, the TCP/IP protocol is supported. A *Null Modem* option is also available for computers connected directly with a cable.

Using the Administration Kit

The Internet Explorer Administration Kit (IEAK) allows you to create customized versions of Internet Explorer 4.0. Customizations allow you to preconfigure IE4 settings, to add specific logos, links, or bookmarks, and to restrict certain functions.

On the Exam

A large number of the questions on the IE4 MCSE exam will be based on the Administration Kit. You should have experience installing the kit, using its customization features, and installing customized versions of IE4.

Administration Roles

IEAK prompts you for a role when you begin the customization process. The main difference between these roles is in the license agreements they require with Microsoft; in addition, some customization features are limited based on the role you choose. The available roles are described in the following sections.

On the Exam

You should understand the differences between these roles for the exam. The Corporate Administrator role is emphasized on the exam, but you should experiment with all three roles.

Corporate Administrator

The Corporate Administrator role is for company-specific distributions of IE4, allowing installation to be simplified with preconfigured settings. Selecting this role enables almost all of the optional settings in the IEAK wizard.

Additionally, this role supports the Auto-configuration feature. Clients with this feature enabled periodically poll a server location for new configuration files, and update their configuration accordingly. You can customize the configuration files using the IEAK Profile Manager utility, described later in this section.

Service Provider

The Service Provider role is for Internet Service Providers (ISPs). This allows you to create a preconfigured version of IE4 that allows easy installation. This role supports an online signup process, allowing some settings to be specified by the server; additionally, an option is available to create a single floppy disk distribution of IE4.

On the Exam

The single floppy disk distribution contains the Active Setup program and allows components to be downloaded from a server. It does not include a fully self-contained version of IE4.

Content Provider

The Content Provider role is for companies that create web content. IE4 can be customized with bookmarks and other settings to allow easy access to content. In addition, this role allows users to sign up for an ISP using Microsoft's referral server.

Configuring the Administration Kit

In order to use the IEAK, you must apply for a license and customization code from Microsoft. The following sections describe this process and the process of installing the Administration Kit.

Licensing IEAK

Before using the IE4 Administration Kit, you must obtain a customization code from Microsoft. This code will be required each time you create a customized IE4 package. You can obtain a code and download the IEAK files from this URL:

http://ieak.microsoft.com/

On the Exam

You must separately apply for a license for each administrative role you plan to use (corporate administrator, service provider, or content provider). For testing purposes, however, any customization code should allow you to experiment with all three roles.

Installing IEAK

The Administration Kit runs under Windows 95, Windows 98, or Windows NT 4.0, and should run on any computer that meets the requirements of these operating systems. IE4 must be installed before you install the Administration Kit.

The IEAK files require approximately 50 MB of disk storage. In addition, you will need between 45 and 70 MB of storage for the customized distribution of Internet Explorer, depending on the options you include.

On the Exam

A separate version of the IEAK is available for Macintosh computers. This version runs on a Macintosh, and creates a customized version of IE for Macintosh computers.

To install the Administration Kit, run the SETUP.EXE program on the CD or downloaded distribution. The setup program does not prompt you for any information, but immediately begins the installation; this process takes several minutes.

The IEAK setup program places all of its files in the C:\Program Files\IEAK directory, and creates a Microsoft IEAK entry in the Programs menu under the Start menu.

Creating a Customized Version of IE4

The IEAK Wizard is the basic tool for creating customized IE4 versions. This utility
is available in the Microsoft IEAK menu under the Start menu. The wizard prompts
you for information in five stages; these are described in order in the following
sections.

Basic Information

Stage 1 of the IEAK Wizard prompts you for basic information about your
company and the version of IE4 you are creating. The first dialog prompts you for
a company name, customization code, and a role (as described above). In addition, you can enable or disable Automatic Version Synchronization (AVS); this
feature attempts to download the latest versions of components, and requires an
active Internet connection.

Press Next to proceed to the next dialog, which allows you to choose the operating system for the customized version of IE4. If the version of the IEAK you are
using supports only 32-bit Windows, this dialog is not displayed. The IEAK can
create versions of IE4 for Windows 95/98 and NT, Windows 3.1 and Windows NT
3.51, or UNIX. You can create a package for only one operating system at a time.

The next dialog allows you to choose the target language for the IE4 distribution.
The languages available in your version of the Administration Kit are listed. If you
need to support multiple languages, you will need to run the wizard once for each
language.

The final dialog in this stage prompts you for a destination folder for the IE4 distribution files. This folder should be on a drive with the appropriate amount of free
space, either on the local computer or a network share. The basic distribution is
intended to be downloaded; you can also choose to create versions for CD-ROM

or floppy disk distribution. In Service Provider mode, an option to use a single floppy disk is included.

Active Setup Settings

Stage 2 of the wizard prompts you for the information normally gathered by the IE4 setup program. If you have enabled AVS, the first dialog prompts you for a download site for the IE4 components; choose the closest available site. If AVS is disabled, this list is blank.

The second dialog, shown in Figure 3-6, displays a list of components of the IE4 suite, and indicates the components for which a new version is available online. If you disabled AVS, all of the components are labeled as older versions. No components are downloaded by default; to download a component, highlight it and select the Synchronize button, or the Synchronize All button to download all newer components.

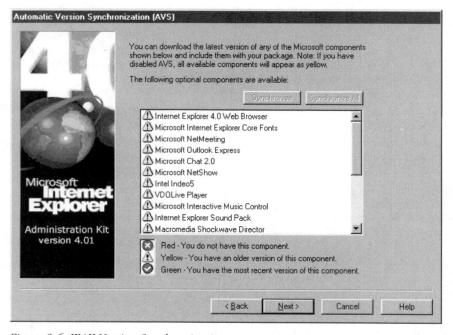

Figure 3-6: IEAK Version Synchronization

The third dialog in this stage allows you to specify one or more custom components. Any program that uses an EXE or CAB file for distribution can be included here. For each component, specify the following information:

Component
    The component's name. This name will be included in the list of optional components when the user installs the custom version of IE4.

Location

The path to the EXE or CAB file that installs the application.

Command

The command that will be executed to extract or install the application.

GUID

GUID is short for globally unique identifier, a numeric code unique to each program. Windows uses these codes as the names of registry keys. If the component you selected does not have a GUID, use the Generate button to generate a random code.

Parameter

Specify command-line switches to be used with the installation program, if any.

Version

Specify the version number of the component. This will be used to determine if a newer version of the component is available.

Size

Specify the size of the installed files for the component in KB. This number is used to calculate the total disk storage required in the installation program.

Uninstall Key

Specify a registry key that contains uninstall information for the component. Registry keys are stored under the following registry key:

```
HKEY_LOCAL_MACHINE\Software\Microsoft\Windows\
CurrentVersion\Uninstall
```

Customizing the Setup Program

Stage 3 allows you to customize the setup program itself. The first dialog in this stage prompts for basic information:

Active Setup wizard title bar text

Specify the text to be included in the title bar of the Setup dialogs.

Active Setup wizard bitmap path

Specify the path and filename of a bitmap (BMP) picture to be displayed by the setup program. The dimensions of the bitmap must be 120 x 239.

The next dialog includes a single option: *Install Package Silently*. If this option is selected, the setup program will install the default list of components without prompting the user for any information. This is similar to the behavior of the IEAK setup program.

The next dialog, shown in Figure 3-7, allows you to construct one or more installation options for IE4. By default, the *Standard*, *Minimal*, and *Full* options are defined.

You can delete the existing options or create new options. For each option, you can specify the components to be included; the potential list of components includes the IE4 components and any additional components you specified in Stage 2.

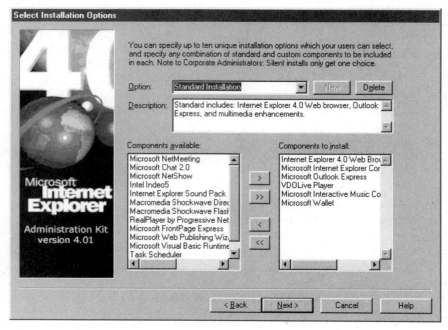

Figure 3-7: The IEAK Installation Options dialog

On the Exam

If you chose the silent installation option, you can only create one installation option. This option will be used without prompting the user for additional information.

The next dialog prompts you for download sites for the installation package. These sites are used if the user runs a version of the Active Setup wizard that does not include local versions of all components. You can specify between one and ten sites. For each, specify a site name, URL, and graphical location.

The next dialog prompts for information about the customized version of IE4:

Version Number

Specify a number to identify the version of your customized package. The IEAK increments this number each time you create a new package. The version number is used to determine whether the user has already installed the latest version or a newer version.

Configuration Identifier

This is an optional 8-digit code that is also used to ensure that the user does not install an earlier version of the package over a later version. If you are creating multiple versions of a package (with different components or languages) each should have a different configuration identifier.

URL of Add-on Component Page

This is an optional URL for a page containing add-on components for the browser. This URL is loaded when the user selects *Product Update* from the Help menu. If you leave this field blank, the URL of the download site you specified earlier will be combined with the filename addon95.htm or addonnt.htm, depending on the user's operating system.

The next dialog prompts you for the location on the user's computer where IE4 and the other components will be installed; by default, this is C:\Program Files\Internet Explorer. You can choose a directory under the Program Files or Windows folders, or specify a full path.

The final dialog in this stage prompts whether to include the Desktop Update in the installation package. Choose *Yes* or *No*, or select *User Choice* to allow the user to choose whether to install the update.

On the Exam

The *User Choice* option is not available if you selected the silent installation option.

Browser Settings

Stage 4 prompts you for various IE4 settings. Some of these customize the browsers, and others provide default values that can be changed by the user in the Internet Options dialog. You are prompted for information in a number of dialogs:

1. Choose whether to customize the browser's title bar, and specify a value. You can also specify a bitmap picture to be used as the background of the IE4 toolbar.

2. Specify a home page URL and Search page URL. The Search page is loaded in a frame when the user presses the Search button on the toolbar.

3. Specify the URL for an online support page. This page is loaded when the user selects *Online Support* from the Help menu.

4. Choose the contents of the Favorites (bookmarks) menu. The items in this list are used for the Favorites menu. Items in the Links folder are included on the IE4 links toolbar. Rather than create the list here, you can use the Import button to use the list from the local computer's installation of IE4.

5. Specify the URL of a Welcome page, if desired. This page is loaded instead of the home page the first time the user runs IE4. This dialog also allows you to disable the welcome dialog displayed the first time IE4 runs, and specify a bitmap file to be used as the default desktop wallpaper if the Active Desktop is enabled.

6. You are now allowed to customize the channel bar. To modify the channels, add or delete channels from the channel bar on the local computer and select the *Import* option.

7. Customize the software distribution channels, if desired, by modifying the list on the local computer and selecting the *Import* option. Software distribution channels are described earlier in this chapter.

8. Choose whether to customize components in the Active Desktop. To customize components, use the *Import* option to import the setup from the local computer.

9. Choose whether to customize desktop toolbars (such as the toolbar to the right of the Start button). Again, the settings from the local computer will be used.

10. Select HTML files to be used as the backgrounds of the Control Panel and My Computer windows, if desired. The filenames should be mycomp.htt and controlp.htt.

11. Customize the user agent string, if desired. This text is sent to HTTP servers with each URL request, and appears in server log files. Any text you specify is appended to the usual IE4 user agent string.

12. Choose whether to enable the Auto-configure feature. This allows settings to be changed after installation; the user's machine will automatically poll a server location for new settings. If you enable this option, specify URLs for the auto-configure (INS) file and an optional proxy configuration file. You can also specify the interval for updating settings. For information about creating and modifying these files, see "Using Automatic Configuration," later in this section.

13. Specify proxy settings for the customized browser, if needed. The options in the IE4 proxy configuration dialog are included here.

14. If desired, certificate authority settings can be imported from the local computer's settings. If one or more authorities are specified, the customized browser will disallow non-authenticated documents. You can also specify trusted Authenticode software publishers for executable content.

15. Specify security zone settings and content rating settings. These correspond to settings in the Security tab of the IE4 Properties dialog.

Optional Components and Policies

Stage 5 prompts you for customization information for the optional components included with IE4. The dialogs presented in this stage depend on the components selected for installation.

The System Policies and Restrictions dialog is presented as the last step in this stage. This dialog includes a variety of settings that allow you to enforce settings and disable features for the browser and other components. The following categories of policies are typically included; this list may vary depending on the selected components.

Internet Restrictions

The settings in this category correspond with the settings available in the IE4 Properties dialog, and allow you to disable user modification of most of the settings.

Internet Settings

This category includes a variety of settings in the IE4 Properties dialog that were not prompted for in previous IEAK wizard dialogs. The subcategories of settings include Colors, Fonts, Languages, Modem settings, Programs, and Advanced settings.

Microsoft Chat

Includes settings related to the Microsoft Chat application if included in the IE4 installation. You can specify server names, room restrictions, and other settings.

Microsoft NetMeeting

Includes settings related to NetMeeting, if included in the installation package. You can specify values for most NetMeeting preferences and restrict the use of various features and protocols.

Outlook Express

Includes settings related to Outlook Express, if included. You can set defaults for some mail and news settings, and change the default appearance of the Outlook window.

Subscriptions

Includes settings related to web site subscriptions and channels. Restrictions are available to prevent excessive use of network bandwidth and disk storage.

Web Desktop

Includes settings for the Active Desktop. These include restrictions for most Active Desktop features, the Start menu, and the Windows shell.

Using the Customized Package

Once you have entered all of the required information in the IEAK wizard dialogs, press Finish to create the installation files. The files can then be transferred to a shared directory on a local or Internet server from the directory you specified.

The DOWNLOAD directory under the destination directory stores the IE4 setup program, and the IE4SITE directory includes all of the distribution files. If you chose to create CD-ROM or floppy disk versions, these are stored in the CD and MFLOPPY directories.

In the Real World

Remember not to distribute any customized versions of IE4 you create unless you follow the license agreement (displayed when you obtained a customization code).

Using Automatic Configuration

If you enabled the Auto-configure feature for your customized IE4 package, you can modify settings after the installation by using the IEAK Profile Manager utility to create an INS file and store it in the location you specified when creating the package.

To start the Profile Manager utility, select *IEAK Profile Manager* from the Microsoft IEAK menu under the Start menu. This utility is shown in Figure 3-8.

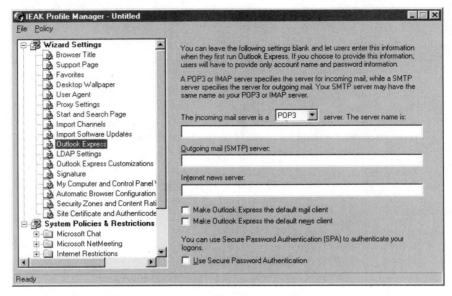

Figure 3-8: The Administration Kit Profile Manager utility

To begin using the Profile Manager utility, you must specify an INS file. You can either create a new file or load the file created when you ran the IEAK wizard, stored in the distribution directory.

On the Exam

For the IE4 Administration Kit MCSE exam, you should have experience creating and modifying INS files using Profile Manager. You should also configure at least one client with the Auto-configure feature to verify that settings can be changed after installation.

Profile Manager includes two main categories of options: *Wizard Settings* includes all of the options set from the dialogs in the IEAK wizard, and *System Policies and Restrictions* includes the policy settings from the wizard's final dialog.

When you have modified the settings, use the *Save* option in the File menu to save the INS file. If you replace the INS file used for automatic configuration, each client's settings will be changed at the next update interval (set in the IEAK wizard).

Suggested Exercises

The IE4 Administration exam covers the operation and configuration of Internet Explorer and the other components of the IE4 suite, and the use of the Internet Explorer Administration Kit is emphasized.

This is one of the easier exams to prepare for, since all of the components you need to study can be run under Windows 95/98 or Windows NT. In most cases a single computer should be sufficient, although two computers may be helpful.

Performing the following exercises will help you prepare for the IE4 Administration MCSE exam. In addition, you should have a basic understanding of TCP/IP, covered in Part 1, *Internetworking with TCP/IP.*

1. Install IE4 on a Windows 95 or Windows NT computer. Use the Minimal or Standard installation, and include the Desktop Update.

2. Use the Add/Remove Programs control panel to remove IE4 and its related components, as described in the *Study Guide.*

3. Reinstall IE4 using the *Full* option (you will need some of the components, such as NetMeeting, that are included only in the full package).

4. Study the Options dialog in Internet Explorer, and verify that you have configured the browser correctly to access web documents.

5. Activate the Active Desktop. Customize the HTML background document and subscribe to one or more web documents.

6. Configure Outlook Express to access an email account, and to read and post newsgroup messages. Verify that it works correctly.

7. Install and configure Microsoft NetMeeting. Connect to one of the Microsoft ILS servers and try to find a user who is available to talk to you; depending on your machine's capabilities, try audio or video conferencing. Try the whiteboard and document sharing options.

8. Install the IEAK. Using Corporate Administrator mode, view all of the dialogs in the IEAK wizard, customizing as many features as possible. Be sure to enable the Auto-configure option.

9. After you create the customized package, install it on a computer.

10. Use the IEAK Profile Manager utility to modify the INS file in your customized package. Verify that the client computer automatically loads the modified configuration.

Practice Test

Test Questions

1. Which of the following is the file format used for web documents?

    a.   HTTP

    b.   FTP

    c.   HTML

    d.   SGML

2. Which of the following protocols are supported by Internet Explorer 4.0 as a client? (select all that apply)

    a.   HTTP

    b.   FTP

    c.   POP3

    d.   NNTP

3. Which of the following protocols is used to send email?

    a.   HTTP

    b.   POP3

    c.   SMTP

    d.   ILS

4. Which of the following is a valid URL for a file on the FTP server ftp.starlingtech.com in the directory /pub/documents?

    a.   http://starlingtech.com/pub/documents

    b.   ftp://ftp.starlingtech.com/pub/documents

c.   http://ftp.starlingtech.com/pub/documents

d.   ftp:/ftp.starlingtech.com//pub/documents

5. Which of the following protocols is used to send and receive newsgroup articles?

   a.   HTTP

   b.   NNTP

   c.   FTP

   d.   POP3

6. Which of the following is the language used for typical web documents?

   a.   HTML

   b.   JavaScript

   c.   HTTP

   d.   XML

7. Which of the following languages use commands embedded directly within an HTML file? (select all that apply)

   a.   JavaScript

   b.   Java

   c.   VBScript

   d.   ActiveX

8. Which of the following web languages can be used on both Windows and Macintosh platforms, and both Netscape and Microsoft browsers? (select all that apply)

   a.   HTML

   b.   Java

   c.   ActiveX

   d.   VBScript

9. Which of the following IE4 suite components can be used to create HTML documents?

   a.   Internet Explorer

   b.   Outlook Express

   c.   NetMeeting

   d.   FrontPage Express

10. Which of the following IE4 suite components can be used to send email? (select all that apply)

   a.   FrontPage Express

   b.   Outlook Express

     c.   Internet Explorer

     d.   NetMeeting

11. Which of the following operating systems can be used to install Internet Explorer 4.0's Desktop Integration feature? (select all that apply)

     a.   Windows 3.1

     b.   Windows 95

     c.   Windows 98

     d.   Windows NT

12. How much RAM is required under Windows 95 to install Internet Explorer 4.0?

     a.   4 MB

     b.   8 MB

     c.   16 MB

     d.   32 MB

13. What is the approximate amount of disk storage required for a minimal installation of Internet Explorer 4.0?

     a.   20 MB

     b.   40 MB

     c.   60 MB

     d.   80 MB

14. Which of the following IE4 installation options include Outlook Express? (select all that apply)

     a.   Minimal

     b.   Standard

     c.   Full

     d.   Custom

15. Which of the following IE4 installation options includes FrontPage Express? (select all that apply)

     a.   Minimal

     b.   Standard

     c.   Full

     d.   Custom

16. Which tab of the IE4 Properties dialog includes an option to reduce the size of the disk cache?

     a.   General

     b.   Disk

IE 4.0 Admin

      c.   Security

      d.   Advanced

17. By default, all non-local sites are located in which Internet Explorer zone?

      a.   Local Intranet zone

      b.   Trusted Sites zone

      c.   Internet zone

      d.   Restricted Sites zone

18. You are configuring an Internet Explorer 4.0 client and need to disable the execution of Java applets completely. Which security level should you select to accomplish this?

      a.   High

      b.   Medium

      c.   Low

      d.   Custom

19. Which of the following are secure protocols for transmissions of Web pages? (select all that apply)

      a.   HTTP

      b.   SSL

      c.   PCT

      d.   FTP

20. Which of the following IE4 suite components can be removed without removing the Internet Explorer browser?

      a.   Outlook Express

      b.   NetMeeting

      c.   FrontPage Express

      d.   Desktop Update

21. Which of the following file extensions refers to web content that is updated regularly and can be subscribed to?

      a.   HTML

      b.   CDF

      c.   HTTP

      d.   CGI

22. Which control panel dialog should be used to add HTML content to the desktop?

      a.   Desktop

      b.   Network

c. Display

d. Active Desktop

23. Which of the following protocols are supported for incoming mail in Outlook Express? (select all that apply)

    a. POP3

    b. SMTP

    c. ILS

    d. IMAP

24. Which of the following capabilities is *not* included in Outlook Express?

    a. Post messages to a newsgroup

    b. Read newsgroup messages

    c. Host a local newsgroup

    d. Post email messages

25. Which of the following protocols is used by NetMeeting to display a directory of available users?

    a. IMAP

    b. ILS

    c. NNTP

    d. POP3

26. Which IEAK administrative role allows you to create a single floppy disk distribution of IE4?

    a. Corporate Administrator

    b. Service Provider

    c. Content Provider

27. Which administrative role allows you to modify IE4 settings after a client is already installed?

    a. Corporate Administrator

    b. Service Provider

    c. Content Provider

28. What is the approximate amount of disk storage required by the IEAK files (not including the distribution files you create)?

    a. 20 MB

    b. 40 MB

    c. 50 MB

    d. 80 MB

29. Which of the following capabilities is *not* included in the Administration Kit?

    a.   Modify the appearance of the Setup program

    b.   Modify the Favorites list

    c.   Modify the Help files

    d.   Modify the default channels list

30. Which utility can be used to change settings on clients already installed using a customized version of IE4?

    a.   IEAK Wizard

    b.   IEAK Control Panel

    c.   Internet Options

    d.   IEAK Profile Manager

Answers to Questions

1. C. HTML (Hypertext Markup Language) is the file format used by web documents. HTTP (choice A) is the protocol used to transmit web documents.

2. A, B. Internet Explorer 4.0 supports HTTP (Hypertext Transfer Protocol) and FTP (File Ttransfer Protocol). POP3 and NNTP (choices C and D) are supported by Outlook Express.

3. C. SMTP (Simple Mail Transport Protocol) is used to send mail messages. POP3 (choice B) is used to receive messages.

4. B. The correct URL is ftp://ftp.starlingtech.com/pub/documents. The other choices use the http:// method, invalid for an FTP server, or have incorrect punctuation.

5. B. The NNTP protocol is used to send and receive newsgroup articles.

6. A. HTML (Hypertext Markup Language) is the language typically used by web documents.

7. A, C. The JavaScript and VBScript languages can be embedded directly within an HTML file.

8. A, B. The HTML and Java languages are supported by browsers under the Windows and Macintosh platforms. ActiveX and VBScript (choices C and D) are supported only by Internet Explorer under Windows platforms.

9. D. FrontPage Express can be used to create HTML documents.

10. B. Outlook Express is the only component that can be used to send email. Internet Explorer (choice C) can follow email links, but these launch Outlook Express or another mail client.

11. B, C, D. The Desktop Integration feature works under Windows 95, Windows 98, or Windows NT.

12. B. 8 MB is required to install IE4 under Windows 95, although 16 MB or more is recommended.

13. C. Approximately 60 MB of disk storage is required for a minimal installation of IE4.

14. B, C. The Standard and Full installations include Outlook Express. The Minimal installation (choice A) includes only the browser; there is no Custom installation option (choice D).

15. C. Only the Full installation option includes FrontPage Express.

16. A. The General tab of the IE4 Properties dialog includes an option to change the cache size.

17. C. By default, non-local sites are considered to be in the Internet zone.

18. D. The option to disable Java applets entirely is available only from the Custom security level.

19. B, C. SSL (Secure Sockets Layer) and PCT (Private Communications Technology) are secure web protocols.

20. D. The Desktop Update component can be removed separately; the others can only be removed with the browser.

21. B. The CDF (Channel Definition Format) extension is used to define subscription-ready content.

22. C. The Web tab of the Display control panel allows you to add HTML items to the desktop.

23. A, D. The POP3 and IMAP protocols support incoming mail in Outlook Express. SMTP (choice B) is used for outgoing mail only.

24. C. Outlook Express can not host a newsgroup. This requires an NNTP server.

25. B. The ILS (Internet Listing Service) protocol is used by NetMeeting to display a directory of available users.

26. B. The Service Provider role allows you to create a single floppy disk version of IE4.

27. A. The Corporate Administrator role allows you to modify settings after installation.

28. C. The IEAK requires approximately 50 MB.

29. C. The IEAK does not include a provision to modify the IE4 help files.

30. D. The IEAK Profile Manager utility can be used to modify client settings.

Highlighter's Index

IE4 Basics

Web (HTTP)

Server uses Hypertext Transfer Protocol (HTTP)
Clients are called browsers (such as IE4)
Documents typically in HTML (Hypertext Markup Language)

FTP

File Transfer Protocol
Transfers files between clients and servers
Cross-platform
IE4 can act as a client

Email

SMTP (Simple Mail Transport Protocol): Transports messages
POP (Post Office Protocol) delivers messages to clients
Outlook Express supports reading and sending mail

Newsgroups

Also called discussion groups
NNTP (Network News Transfer Protocol) used for clients and servers
Messages (articles) are forwarded between servers
Outlook Express supports reading and posting messages

Web Content Types

HTML: Text with links, formatting
Java: Compiled Client-side language; platform independent

JavaScript: Client-side scripting, based on Java syntax
VBScript: client-side scripting, based on Visual Basic syntax
ActiveX: Compiled client-side language; Windows only

IE4 Suite Components

Internet Explorer: Web browser
Desktop Update: Adds Windows 98-like features to Windows 95
Outlook Express: Mail and Newsgroup client
FrontPage Express: Visual HTML composition tool
Netmeeting: Chat, audio, videoconferencing, and document sharing

Installation and Configuration

Hardware Requirements

Windows 95 RAM: 8 MB (16 MB recommended)
Windows NT RAM: 16 MB
Disk storage: 67–86 MB, depending on components
Versions also available for Windows 3.1, UNIX, Macintosh

Installation Options

Minimal Installation: IE4 browser and support components
Standard Installation: Browser, Outlook Express, VDOLive Player, Microsoft Wallet
Full Installation: Browser, Outlook Express, NetMeeting, Microsoft Chat, NetShow, VDOLive Player, RealAudio Player, FrontPage Express, Web Publishing Wizard, Microsoft Wallet.

Browser Options

General: Home page, temporary files, history, fonts, colors, accessibility
Security: Internet zone, Local Intranet zone, Trusted Sites zone, Restricted Sites zone
Content: Ratings (RSAC), digital certificates, personal information
Connection: Dial-up, proxy settings, automatic configuration
Programs: Mail, news, Internet call, and other programs
Advanced: Advanced options

IE4 Suite Components

Desktop Update

Works under Windows 95/98, NT 4.0 and later
Toolbars, new Start menu features
Web content can be included on desktop
Single-click access to files, icons
HTML backgrounds can be used in Explorer windows
To configure, use Web tab of Display control panel

Outlook Express

Email: POP or IMAP for receiving, SMTP for sending
News: NNTP for sending and receiving messages
Limited version of Outlook 97

NetMeeting

Uses ILS (Internet Locator Service) to provide directory of users
Views: Directory, SpeedDial, Current Call, History
Audio and Video conferencing (two users maximum)
Whiteboard: Shared drawing application
Shared application: One user edits, others watch
Collaboration: Multiple users can edit document

IE Administration Kit

IEAK Basics

Allows you to create customized versions of IE4
Requires a customization code and license from Microsoft
Must be run once for each language and for each operating system
Requires about 50 MB of disk storage, plus 50–100 MB for the customized package

Administrative Roles

Corporate administrator: For company-specific distributions; allows modifying client settings after installation
Service provider: For Internet providers (ISPs); includes single floppy disk option
Content provider: For creators of content; allows user to sign up for ISP

IEAK Wizard

Stage 1, Gathering Information: Company name, language, destination folder
Stage 2, Active Setup: Download and choose components
Stage 3, Customizing Setup: Title bar, bitmap, silent install, download sites, destination directory
Stage 4, Customizing Browser: IE4 properties and settings
Stage 5, Customizing Components: Component settings, IE4 policies and restrictions

IEAK Profile Manager

Modifies client settings after installation
Includes all IEAK wizard options
Creates or modifies INS (Internet settings) files
Clients re-read INS file at regular intervals, if auto-configure is turned on

PART 4

Proxy Server 2.0

Exam Overview

Proxy servers are commonly used as gateways to the Internet, and are becoming common as the Internet increases in popularity among corporations. Microsoft Proxy Server 2.0, part of the BackOffice suite, implements three types of proxy services.

Microsoft's MCSE Exam 70-088, titled *Implementing and Supporting Microsoft Proxy Server 2.0,* covers all aspects of Proxy Server 2.0: installation, configuration, management, security, and troubleshooting.

Since this exam covers a single product, it is relatively easy to study for; ideally, however, you should have experience with the use of Proxy Server in a network with Internet access and a number of clients to pass the exam.

In order to prepare for this chapter and the Proxy Server exam, you should have studied for and passed the Network Essentials and Windows NT Server MCSE exams. You should also have a basic knowledge of TCP/IP (Part 1, *Internetworking with TCP/IP*) and IIS (Part 2, *Internet Information Server 4.0*).

Proxy Server 2.0

Objectives

Need to Know	*Reference*
Understand the purposes for a proxy server	"Proxy Server Basics" on page 211
The three Proxy Server services and their features	"Proxy Server Basics" on page 211
Technical details of WinSock Proxy operation	"WinSock Proxy" on page 213
Proxy Server hardware requirements	"Hardware Requirements" on page 214
Proxy Server software requirements	"Windows NT Configuration" on page 214

Need to Know	Reference
Methods of using multiple proxy servers	"Using Multiple Proxy Servers" on page 234
Difference between reverse proxy and reverse hosting	"Web Server Security" on page 239
Performance Monitor counters useful for Proxy Server	"Monitoring Proxy Server Performance" on page 244

Need to Apply	Reference
Plan the installation of Microsoft Proxy Server.	"Planning Proxy Server Installation" on page 214
Install Proxy Server on a Windows NT computer.	"The Installation Process" on page 215
Create a local address table (LAT).	"Creating the Local Address Table (LAT)" on page 216
Configure options for client installation.	"Client Options" on page 217
Use Internet Service Manager to configure and manage Proxy Server.	"Configuring Proxy Server" on page 219
Configure the Web Proxy service.	"Configuring the Web Proxy" on page 221
Configure the WinSock Proxy service.	"Configuring the Winsock Proxy" on page 224
Configure the SOCKS Proxy service.	"Configuring the SOCKS Proxy" on page 226
Install and configure proxy client software.	"Installing Proxy Clients" on page 227
Create a custom LAT file for a client.	"Creating a Client LAT File" on page 230
Configure Proxy Server to work with dial-up networking.	"Using Proxy Server with RAS" on page 231
Use Proxy Server to support IPX clients.	"Using Proxy Server as an IPX Gateway" on page 234
Configure multiple proxy servers in an array.	"Server Arrays" on page 236
Manage routing in a proxy server array or chain.	"Managing Routing" on page 237
Configure Proxy Server to prevent unauthorized network access.	"Preventing Inbound Access" on page 239
Configure Proxy Server to allow web publishing.	"Web Server Security" on page 239
Use packet filters to increase security.	"Using Packet Filters" on page 240
Use Performance Monitor to monitor Proxy Server.	"Monitoring Proxy Server Performance" on page 244
Optimize Proxy Server's performance.	"Optimizing Proxy Server" on page 245
Troubleshoot common problems with Proxy Server.	"Troubleshooting Common Problems" on page 247

Study Guide

This chapter includes the following sections, which address various topics covered on the Proxy Server MCSE exam:

Proxy Server Basics
> Describes the purpose, features, and architecture of Microsoft Proxy Server, and the advantages and disadvantages of each of the supported services.

Installing Proxy Server
> Explains the Proxy Server hardware and software requirements and other considerations, and the installation process itself.

Configuring Proxy Server
> Describes the process of configuring each of the Proxy Server services for various purposes.

Managing Advanced Features
> Describes the use of Proxy Server with dial-up networking and the IPX protocol. The use of multiple proxy servers in a network is also explained.

Proxy Server Security
> Introduces the security features of Proxy Server, and describes how to configure them for maximum security.

Optimization and Troubleshooting
> Explains how to monitor and optimize Proxy Server's performance, and how to solve common problems.

Proxy Server Basics

Proxy servers are typically used as a gateway to the Internet, but can also be useful on local Intranets. They serve three main purposes:

- To allow multiple users to access the Internet through a single connection, with tight administrative control over the Internet addresses and services users can access.

- To reduce traffic between the local network and the Internet by caching the contents of web sites and other frequently-accessed information.

- To prevent unauthorized access to the local network from external Internet addresses, and allow limited access where appropriate.

In essence, a proxy server acts as a go-between for Internet services. A client requests a web page or other resource from the proxy, and the proxy contacts the Internet, retrieves the resource, and transmits it to the client.

A proxy server that is configured to limit the sites or services users can access and limit incoming access to the network is also referred to as a *firewall*. A proxy server that maintains a cache of web documents and returns cached documents to clients when available is called a *caching proxy*.

Microsoft Proxy Server is a full-featured proxy server that runs under Windows NT Server and provides these and other services. Proxy Server is part of the BackOffice suite, and is integrated with Internet Information Server (IIS). Proxy Server 2.0 is the current version.

Proxy Server actually consists of three separate services, each of which provides access to Internet services for clients: the web proxy, WinSock proxy, and SOCKS proxy. One or more of these services can be used, depending on the needs of the clients. The services are described in detail in the following sections.

On the Exam

You should know the features and uses of these three services for the Proxy Server MCSE exam. You should also know how to configure and maintain each of the services, as described in "Configuring Proxy Server" later in this chapter.

Web Proxy

The Web Proxy service supports the standard developed by CERN (the European Laboratory for Particle Physics, where the Web was first developed) for Internet proxies. It supports the HTTP, FTP Read, Secure HTTP, and Gopher services, the services typically supported by web browsers. This proxy is supported by most Internet browsers and on any computer platform.

The web proxy is the only Proxy Server service that supports caching. Two types of caching are included:

- *Passive caching* stores documents as they are requested by clients.

- *Active caching* attempts to determine which documents will be requested by clients (for example, those that are requested regularly) and caches them in advance, using idle time on the network connection for this purpose.

The web proxy operates as an ISAPI (Internet Service Application Programming Interface) extension to Microsoft Internet Information Server. The services of IIS are used to handle proxy requests.

WinSock Proxy

The Web Proxy service supports only HTTP, FTP, and Gopher protocols. The WinSock Proxy Service, by contrast, supports almost any available protocol or application, including TCP-based (connection-oriented) and UDP-based (connectionless) services.

The WinSock Proxy service supports only Windows 3.x, Windows 95/98, and Windows NT computers, and requires special client software. The following sections explain its operation.

The WinSock Specification

The WinSock (Windows Sockets) specification was developed by Microsoft to provide support for TCP/IP applications. This specification is based on the Berkeley Sockets standard for UNIX. This standard uses IP addresses and port numbers to establish communication between services and applications on different computers.

The WinSock specification uses an API (a standard set of procedure calls) to allow Internet applications to use a consistent interface. This standard is supported natively by Windows 95/98 and Windows NT, but requires additional software under Windows 3.x. The TCP/IP add-on for Windows for Workgroups also supports this specification.

The WinSock API functions are contained in the WINSOCK.DLL (16-bit) or WSOCK32.DLL (32-bit) file. Windows 95/98 supports both 16- and 32-bit access, and includes versions of both of these DLLs.

How the WinSock Proxy Works

The WinSock proxy client installation program replaces the 16- and 32-bit WinSOCK DLL files with a custom file designed to work with Proxy Server; the original file is renamed. The new DLL intercepts calls made to the WinSock API and uses the proxy server to satisfy requests. The renamed DLL is called if the request is for a local request.

The WinSock proxy effectively acts like a direct Internet connection; the client applications are unaware that they are using a proxy server, and do not require any configuration. This process uses a control channel opened between the client and the proxy server to act as the network interface, and additional connections to pass the requested data.

Since the WinSock proxy client acts as a network interface, it is able to offer a unique feature: support for the IPX protocol. This protocol can be used instead of TCP/IP between the client and the proxy server; the proxy server then communicates with Internet services using TCP/IP. This acts as an IPX/IP gateway for networks that do not directly support TCP/IP.

SOCKS Proxy

SOCKS is a standard proxy specification that offers many of the same features as the WinSock proxy, and is able to act as a direct connection to the Internet. It has the benefit of supporting a wide variety of non-Windows clients. However, it does not support UDP-based (connectionless) services, and does not support the IPX protocol.

The SOCKS Proxy service within Proxy Server implements version 4.3a of the SOCKS standard. This can be used by any application that supports SOCKS by specifying the server name and port number; no client installation program is required.

Installing Proxy Server

Proxy Server's installation process is relatively simple, but the installation should be planned carefully. The following sections discuss the planning required before installation and the installation process itself.

Planning Proxy Server Installation

Proxy Server can be run on any Windows NT Server computer that meets its requirements; this can be the same machine used as a file server and to run IIS and other services, or a separate machine. The following sections discuss the hardware and software requirements for Proxy Server 2.0 and other considerations you should make before the installation.

Hardware Requirements

Proxy Server runs only under Windows NT Server, and its hardware requirements are slightly steeper than those of NT Server alone. The requirements for Proxy Server are summarized in Table 4-1.

Table 4-1: Proxy Server Hardware Requirements

Item	Requirement
CPU	486/33 or higher (Pentium recommended)
RAM	24 MB (32 MB or more recommended) for Intel systems; RISC systems require 32 MB
Disk Storage	10 MB for Proxy Server components
Network Card(s)	1 per network

In addition to the 10 MB required for the installation of Proxy Server, more storage will be needed if you plan to use the caching feature. Microsoft's recommended method for estimating the required storage is 100 MB plus approximately .5 MB per client that will use the proxy services. Increasing the amount of storage available for the cache may improve performance.

Windows NT Configuration

Proxy Server 2.0 runs only under Windows NT Server 4.0. In addition, there are specific configuration requirements:

* Service Pack 3 for Windows NT 4.0 (SP3) must be installed.

* IIS 3.0 or 4.0 must be installed. (IIS 4.0, in turn, requires that Internet Explorer 4.0 and SP3 be installed.)

- The network adapter(s) should be properly configured and bound to the TCP/IP protocol. (In some cases, IPX may also be used; this is explained later in this chapter.)

- If the proxy server will be used for caching, an NTFS volume is required; Proxy Server does not support caching on FAT volumes.

Obtaining Software

Proxy Server is available as part of the Microsoft BackOffice suite, which includes Windows NT Server, IIS, SQL Server, and other components. Proxy Server is also available separately from Microsoft. For information on purchasing the software, see this URL:

http://backoffice.microsoft.com/

The Installation Process

To begin the Proxy Server installation, launch the setup program on the downloaded distribution or CD-ROM. This is typically MSP2I.EXE. Follow these steps to complete the installation of Proxy Server:

1. The license agreement for Proxy Server 2.0 is displayed. Click Yes to continue.

2. Enter the CD Key for your copy of Proxy Server; this is usually printed on the package containing the CD-ROM.

3. A product identification number is displayed; this should be written down for your records. Press OK to continue.

4. Select the destination directory for the Proxy Server files. C:\MSP is the default.

5. The Installation Options dialog is now displayed. This allows you to select whether to install three items: the Proxy Server files, the administration tool, and the documentation. Highlight the *Proxy Server* entry and use the Change Option button to deselect any client software you do not wish to install (by default, client software for Windows 95/98, Windows NT 386 and Alpha versions, and Windows 3.1 is installed).

6. Proxy Server files are now installed. At this point, the WWW service in Internet Information Server is stopped, and will be unavailable until the installation is complete.

7. The cache configuration dialog, shown in Figure 4-1, is now displayed. Choose whether to enable caching, and choose one or more NTFS volumes to store cache files. For each drive, you can select the maximum amount of space used for the cache.

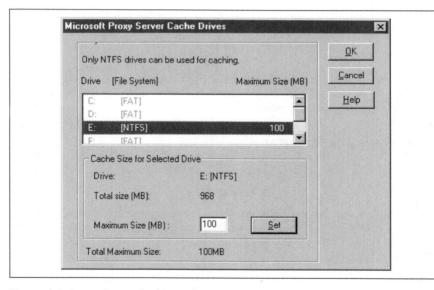

Figure 4-1: Proxy Server Cache configuration

Creating the Local Address Table (LAT)

After you have specified cache settings, the Local Address Table configuration dialog is displayed. The LAT is a text file that lists one or more ranges of IP address to be considered local addresses. Proxy Server clients use this table to determine whether to contact a host directly or to make a proxy request.

To add a range of IP addresses to the LAT, enter the starting and ending IP addresses and use the Add button. To add a single address, use the same address for the starting and ending values. Additionally, the Construct Table button provides access to a dialog with these options:

Add the private ranges 10.x.x.x, 192.168.x.x, and 172.16.x.x–172.31.x.x to the table
These ranges are defined as private ranges by the IP addressing specification. They can be used for local networks, but will be considered invalid by routers and Internet hosts; for this reason, they are often used for local networks without Internet connectivity.

Load from NT internal routing table
If the NT Server machine running Proxy Server is configured as a router, its routing table already contains a list of local addresses. You can choose to use the routing table from one network adapter or all of the installed adapters to add local addresses.

After you are satisfied with the list of local addresses, press OK to continue with the installation process.

On the Exam

After using the Construct Table options, you should examine the list of local addresses and verify that all of the local addresses are included, and that no external addresses are included. An error in this table could prevent a client from accessing certain resources.

Client Options

The next phase of the installation process prompts for information used by the client installation program, described later in this chapter. The following options are included:

Client connects to Microsoft WinSock Proxy Server by
Specify whether the computer name or IP address of the server is used by clients to access the proxy server. If you specify the IP address option, be sure the server has a fixed IP address.

Automatically configure web browser during client setup
If selected, the client installation program will configure the client's browser settings during the installation process. Specify the Proxy Server computer name and port (typically 80) for the Web Proxy service.

Configure web browsers to use Automatic Configuration
If enabled, the client installation program will configure the client's browser to use the Automatic Configuration feature. This uses a script to determine Proxy settings.

Proxy Server 2.0

The Proxy Server installation program automatically creates a script for browser configuration. The Properties button allows you to modify the values used to produce this script. The following options are included:

Use Proxy for local servers
> Normally, the client bypasses the proxy when a local address (an address with no periods, such as *http://server1*) is specified. If this option is selected, the proxy will be used for all addresses.

Do not use Proxy for the following IP addresses
> If desired, specify a list of individual IP addresses that the client can contact without using the proxy service.

Do not use Proxy for domains ending with
> If this option is selected, any address ending with one of the suffixes you list here is accessed without using the proxy. Use semicolons between the entries in the list.

Backup Route
> If this option is enabled, the client uses a backup route when the Proxy Server machine is unavailable. The *to the Internet* option connects directly to the destination address, if possible. The *to Web Proxy* option specifies an alternate proxy server address and port to be used. Use the Modify button to change the backup route settings.

On the Exam

Selecting the *to the Internet* option can be a security risk. If selected, the client will have direct access to the Internet when the Proxy Server machine is down, bypassing any access controls defined on the server.

Access Control

The next dialog in the Proxy Server installation process allows you to set the default permissions for the proxy server. You can enable or disable access control for the WinSock Proxy service and the Web Proxy service. Enable these options to immediately secure the Proxy Server.

If access control is enabled for a service, you will need to assign permissions to one or more users or groups before anyone can access the proxy. If access control is disabled, all users will be able to access the proxy by default. You can change these options and add specific permissions using the Internet Service Manager utility, described in the next section.

After completing the information in this dialog, the Proxy Server installation process is complete. The installation program copies the remaining files, restarts the web service, and terminates. The proxy services are now running; see the next section for information about managing and configuring the services.

Configuring Proxy Server

The Internet Service Manager utility, a snap-in for Microsoft Management Console (MMC), is installed when you install IIS. The Proxy Server installation adds entries to Internet Service Manager for each of the proxy services: Web Proxy, WinSock Proxy, and Socks Proxy.

After the Proxy Server installation, all three of these services are running by default. To start, pause, or stop a service, highlight its entry and use the buttons in the toolbar.

To configure a service, highlight its entry, right-click, and select *Properties*. The Properties dialog is displayed, including a number of tabbed categories. The following sections describe the available options for all three of the services.

Common Properties

The first and last properties, Service and Logging, are identical for each of the three proxy services. These are described in this section. The following sections cover the unique properties for each of the services.

Service Properties

The first category in each service's Properties dialog is the Service tab. This includes general information about the service, and provides access to a number of configuration options common to all services. The options in this dialog include the following:

Current Sessions
Displays a dialog listing current connections to the proxy service, their point of origin, and the amount of time they have been online.

Comment
An optional description of the service.

Security
Displays a dialog that allows you to set security options, including packet filtering. These are described in "Proxy Server Security" later in this chapter.

Array
Displays a dialog that allows you to configure a proxy server array (several proxy servers that work together). This is described in "Using Multiple Proxy Servers" later in this chapter.

Auto Dial
>   Displays a dialog that allows you to configure a dial-up connection using RAS (Remote Access Service) to work with Proxy Server. This allows any number of clients to share a dial-up connection. These options are described in "Using Proxy Server with RAS" later in this chapter.

Plug-ins
>   Connects to Microsoft's web page to allow you to view a list of add-on products for Proxy Server available for download.

Client Configuration
>   Displays the client configuration dialog, described earlier in this chapter.

Local Address Table
>   Displays the LAT configuration dialog, described earlier in this chapter.

Server Backup
>   Saves the Proxy Server configuration information to a file you specify.

Server Restore
>   Restores the Proxy Server configuration from a saved configuration file.

Logging Properties

The final category in each service's Properties dialog allows you to set logging options. By default, each service is enabled for logging to a file. The following options are available:

Enable logging using format
>   Check the box to enable logging, and choose Regular or Verbose format. The Verbose format writes more information to the log file, and thus uses more disk storage.

Log to file
>   Select this option to enable logging to a file.

Automatically open new log
>   If selected, a new log file will be created at the specified interval (daily, weekly, or monthly). The log files are named based on the current date.

Limit number of old log files
>   If selected, only the specified number of log files are kept in the directory. If creating a new log file exceeds this number, the oldest file is deleted.

Stop service if disk full
>   If this option is selected, when the disk containing the log files is full, the proxy service is stopped. If the option is not selected, the service continues running, but does not create log entries until disk space is available.

Log file directory
>   Specify the directory to store the log files. By default, the \WINNT\ SYSTEM32\MSPLOGS directory is used.

Log to SQL/ODBC database
>   Select this option to write log entries to a database rather than to a file. Specify the ODBC data source name and table, and the user name and password to access the database. Any ODBC database (such as Microsoft SQL Server) can be used.

Configuring the Web Proxy

Along with the standard Service and Logging property categories, the Web Proxy has four other categories of settings. These are described in the following sections.

Permissions

During installation, you chose whether to enable or disable access control for the Web Proxy service. The Permissions dialog allows you to modify this setting. If access control is enabled, you will need to add one or more permissions for the service.

You can set permissions separately for the Web, FTP Read, Secure, and Gopher services. To change the permissions for a service, press the Edit button. You can add one or more users or groups to the list. The Copy To button allows you to copy one service's permissions to one or more other services.

Proxy Server 2.0

Caching

The Caching tab in the Properties dialog includes options related to the cache. The Web Proxy service supports two types of caching:

Passive caching

This is the standard type of caching, and is similar to the behavior of a disk cache. When a client requests a document, the proxy first checks if a current copy of the document is in the cache. If a cached document is found, it is returned directly to the client. If not, the document is retrieved from the Internet and stored in the cache. Documents are kept in the cache based on their age or expiration date.

Active caching

Active caching works in conjunction with passive caching, and adds the ability to preemptively cache documents that are likely to be requested, rather than wait for a client request. The documents to be cached are selected based on their popularity with clients, and on how often the online document changes. Proxy server monitors client usage of the server, and performs active caching tasks when the load is low.

Both types of caching use a TTL (time to live) value calculated for each retrieved file. This is based on the document's age or on its expiration date, if specified. TTL values typically range from a few minutes to 24 hours. If active caching is enabled, the server automatically updates the cached copies of documents when they near the end of their time to live.

Both types of caching can be configured from the Caching dialog. The following options are available:

Enable caching
> Enables or disables caching completely. You can specifically disable caching for HTTP or FTP requests in the Advanced properties, discussed later in this section.

Cache expiration policy
> Choose an option to determine how objects in the cache are expired and removed from the cache. The *Updates are more important* option checks for expirations more often, causing more network traffic but better accuracy in updating documents for users. The *Fewer network accesses are more important* option checks expirations less frequently, resulting in less network traffic and more use of the cache. The *Equal importance* option is a compromise between these two factors.

Enable active caching
> Select this option to enable active caching; this is enabled by default. The options below this setting allow you to set the policy for active caching. The *Faster user response is more important* option pre-fetches objects frequently, resulting in better client response and more network traffic. The *Fewer network accesses are more important* option minimizes the amount of pre-fetching to reduce network traffic. The *Equal importance* option is a compromise between these two factors.

In addition to these options, the Cache Size button displays the Cache Drives dialog, which was originally shown during the Proxy Server installation process. This dialog allows you to set the cache size available for each of the available NTFS volumes.

On the Exam

For the Proxy Server MCSE exam, remember that only drives formatted with the NTFS file system can be used for caching. Additionally, remote (network) drives cannot be used.

The Advanced button displays the Advanced Cache Policy dialog, shown in Figure 4-2.

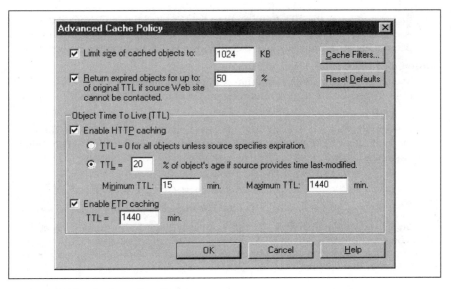

Figure 4-2: The Cache Policy dialog

The Advanced Cache Policy dialog includes the following options:

Limit size of cached objects

Select this option and specify a value in KB to limit the size of documents, graphics, or other objects. Any object larger than the specified size will be retrieved from the Internet at each request, and never cached.

Return expired objects

This option allows the TTL of documents to be extended in the event that the online version of the document is unavailable. Specify a percentage of the original TTL to make the expired object available if necessary. For example, if an object's TTL is originally set to 2 hours and this value is 50%, the cached object will be returned to clients for up to 1 hour after its expiration if the site is unavailable.

Cache Filters

This button presents a dialog that allows you to define one or more cache filters. These are entries that specify a URL; each URL can be set to *Always Cache* or *Never Cache*. The always option is useful for sites that are frequently requested. The never option is useful for problems that arise when the cache does not return the most recent copy of the document, or for sites that change constantly, such as stock quotes.

Reset Defaults

This button resets all of the options in the Cache Policy dialog to their installation defaults.

Enable HTTP caching

Select this option to enable caching of HTTP requests; this is enabled by default, and can be disabled to prevent any caching of web documents.

Additionally, choose the method of calculating the TTL for HTTP objects. The first method sets the TTL to 0 (no time limit) unless the HTTP headers include an expiration date and time. The second method calculates the TTL as a percentage of the object's age, based on the HTTP Last-modified header.

Minimum TTL and Maximum TTL

Specify minimum and maximum values in minutes for the TTL of HTTP objects. The defaults are 15 minutes and 1440 minutes (24 hours).

Enable FTP caching

If selected, FTP requests through the web proxy are also cached. The TTL is the same for all FTP objects, and is specified here. The default is 1440 minutes (24 hours).

On the Exam

You should be familiar with all of the above settings and how they effect the cache for the Proxy Server MCSE exam. Additionally, you should know how to optimize the cache performance, as discussed in "Optimizing Proxy Server" later in this chapter.

Routing

The Routing tab of the Web Proxy Properties dialog includes a variety of options related to routing between this proxy server, the Internet, and other proxies. These are explained in detail in "Using Multiple Proxy Servers," later in this chapter.

Publishing

The Publishing tab of the Web Proxy Properties dialog includes options for Web publishing. This allows the proxy to manage incoming HTTP requests. The *Enable Web publishing* option enables this feature; Web publishing is disabled by default.

To re-enable Web publishing for the local IIS server, select the *sent to the local Web server* option in this dialog. The other options in this dialog are explained in more detail in "Web Server Security" later in this chapter.

Configuring the Winsock Proxy

Along with the Service and Logging properties described above, the Winsock Proxy's properties include two tabbed categories: Protocols and Permissions. These are described in the following sections.

Protocols

The Protocols tab of the Winsock Proxy Properties dialog allows you to configure the protocols supported by the proxy. A wide variety of protocols are predefined with the installation of Proxy Server, allowing most well-known Internet services to be supported.

Use the Add button to add support for a new protocol, or the Edit button to change the properties of an existing protocol. The Protocol Definition dialog, displayed when you add or edit a protocol, includes these options:

Protocol name

Specify a name for the protocol.

Port

Specify the TCP/IP port number for the initial connection used by the application. Consult the application's documentation to determine the appropriate port number.

Type

Specify whether the initial connection uses the TCP or UDP protocol.

Direction

Specify whether the initial connection for the application is inbound or outbound. Most client-server protocols, such as HTTP, use an outbound connection. Inbound connections are used for applications that monitor a port for connections to be initiated by an outside source.

Port ranges for subsequent connections

After the initial connection, the application may need to make additional outbound requests, or receive additional incoming requests. Use the Add or Edit buttons to manage this list of additional connections. For each connection, specify a port number or range, a connection type (TCP or UDP), and a direction (inbound or outbound). Specifying port 0 in one of these entries allows the application to use any port in the range of 1024–5000.

The Load and Save buttons in the Protocols tab allow you to save or load files with the WPC extension, each containing configuration information for a protocol. This allows you to copy the protocols you define to other Proxy Server computers, and allows application vendors to provide a predefined file to configure proxy servers to support an application.

Permissions

The Permissions tab of the WinSock Proxy Properties dialog allows you to configure access control. The *Enable access control* option, initially set during installation, determines whether access controls are used. If this option is disabled, all users are allowed to access all protocols through the WinSock proxy. If this option is disabled, you must configure permissions for each protocol to allow any access.

Select one of the protocols from the list and use the Edit button to add a list of users or groups that can use the protocol. The Copy To button allows you to copy the permissions for one protocol to one or more others.

The first entry in the protocols list is Unlimited Access. This is a special entry; any user or group given access to this entry will be able to use any protocol or port, including those not explicitly defined as a protocol.

Configuring the SOCKS Proxy

Along with the common Service and Logging tabs, the Properties dialog for the SOCKS proxy includes a single tab, Permissions. This dialog allows you to configure access control for the SOCKS proxy; however, the permissions for this proxy are defined differently than for the Web and WinSock proxies.

To configure permissions for this proxy, add one or more rules to this dialog using the Add button. By default, all access to the proxy is denied. You can either allow particular types of access, or add a rule to allow all access followed by one or more exceptions.

The Socks Permission dialog, shown in Figure 4-3, is displayed when you click the Add button.

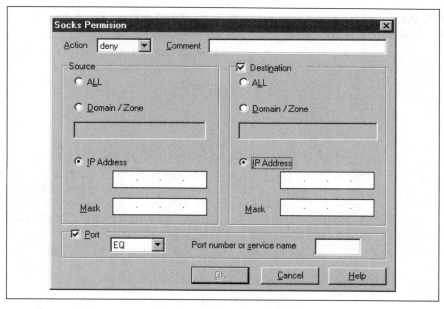

Figure 4-3: Adding a Socks Proxy Permission

Specify the following options to add a rule:

Action

Choose whether this rule will permit or deny access.

Comment

Specify an optional description for the rule.

Source

Specify the source of connections that this rule will apply to. You can specify ALL for all connections, specify a domain name, or specify an IP address and subnet mask.

Destination

Check the Destination box if the rule will be based on connections to a particular destination. The destination can be specified as ALL, a domain, or an IP address and subnet mask.

Port

Check the Port box and specify a condition if the rule will be based on access to a particular port or range of ports. Specify a port number and the condition to compare with (such as equals or is greater than). The conditions available are listed in Table 4-2.

Table 4-2: Socks Proxy Port Conditions

Condition	Meaning
EQ	Is equal to
NE	Is not equal to
GT	Is greater than
LT	Is less than
GE	Is greater than or equal to
LE	Is less than or equal to

The rules specified in this dialog are interpreted in order from top to bottom. The Move Up and Move Down buttons allow you to change the order of the rules.

Installing Proxy Clients

The Web Proxy service supports the CERN proxy standard, which simply requires a TCP/IP connection from the client to the server; thus, there is no need to install special software on the client. The SOCKS proxy also supports standard TCP/IP calls, and does not require special software.

The WinSock proxy does require custom software, since it modifies the TCP/IP stack used by Windows. Proxy Server includes a client installation program that completes this installation process, and also configures the browser for the Web Proxy.

The Client Setup Program

The Proxy Server installation creates a directory called CLIENTS under the main Proxy Server directory. Subdirectories under this directory are created for different types of clients: ALPHA, I386 (Windows 95 and NT), and WIN3X. The CLIENTS directory is shared as MSPCLNT, and should be available anywhere on the network.

The client setup program included in this directory serves two purposes. First, it
installs the custom DLL required for the WinSock proxy. Second, it attempts to
configure the browser to use the Web Proxy service. The client configuration
program is able to configure Microsoft and Netscape browsers.

Before you install the WinSock Proxy client software, you should install the TCP/
IP protocol on the client and ensure that it is working properly. Additionally, a
TCP/IP stack (such as Dial-up Networking) should be installed and configured.
This installs the WinSock DLL file that will be used in conjunction with the
WinSock proxy DLL.

To start the client installation, run SETUP.EXE in the shared MSPCLNT directory.
This program transfers control to the appropriate setup program for the operating
system. You can also start the installation from the web page *http://server/msproxy*,
where *server* is the machine running Proxy Server and IIS.

After starting the client setup program, follow these steps to complete the
installation:

1. An introductory message and copyright information is displayed. Press
   Continue to install the client.

2. Choose a folder for the installation; the default is C:\MSPCLNT. Press the
   Install button to continue.

3. The client files are now copied. After the installation is complete, restart
   Windows to begin using the WinSock Proxy.

After installing the client, the WinSock Proxy is used for all Internet accesses. MSIE
and Netscape, if installed, are configured to use the Web Proxy for the HTTP, FTP,
Gopher, and Secure services.

Changing Client Settings

After the client installation, a new item called WSP Client is installed in the Control Panel. You can use this dialog, shown in Figure 4-4, to configure settings for the WinSock proxy.

Figure 4-4: The WSP Client control panel

The following options are included in the WinSock Proxy control panel:

Server Name
Specify the proxy server to be used. The client configuration information and the LAT will be downloaded from this server.

Update Now
Press this button to update the configuration and LAT using the specified server.

Enable WinSock Proxy Client
This option enables or disables the use of the proxy client. If disabled, the local TCP/IP stack is used instead of the Proxy Server. After changing this option, you must restart the computer to make the change effective.

Force IPX/SPX Protocol
Normally, the WinSock proxy client uses the TCP/IP protocol if it is installed, and uses an IPX/SPX gateway if TCP/IP is not installed. Select this option to force the use of IPX/SPX when both protocols are installed; this is useful when the computer has a TCP/IP network interface (such as dial-up networking) but also needs to use the Proxy Server through an IPX-only network.

Maintaining Client Configuration

To modify the configuration used by clients, open the Properties dialog for one of the Proxy services. Select the Client Configuration button. This allows you to set the client options, as described in "Installing Proxy Server" earlier in this chapter.

You may also need to periodically update the LAT. Use the Local Address Table button to display the LAT configuration dialog, described in the "Installing Proxy Server" section of this chapter.

Creating a Client LAT File

The LAT file, MSPLAT.TXT, is copied to the client from the proxy server and updated periodically. In some cases, you may need to change the LAT file for a particular client to support the needs of your network.

Since the MSPLAT.TXT file is overwritten regularly, it should not be changed. However, you can create a client-side LAT file that works with the file from the server and adds local addresses to the list used by the client. Name this file LOCALLAT.TXT and place it in the proxy client directory (typically C:\MSPCLNT).

Like the main LAT file, each line of the LOCALLAT.TXT file contains a pair of IP addresses representing a range. Use the same address twice to indicate a single address.

Configuring Non-Windows Clients

The WinSock and Web proxies work together to provide full Internet access to Microsoft Windows clients. For Macintosh, UNIX, and other platforms, you must configure proxy access manually. You can use one of two services:

- To use the Web Proxy service, configure the browser to use a proxy, and specify the proxy server name and port number (typically 80). Depending on their configuration, dedicated FTP and Gopher clients can also be supported in this fashion.

- The SOCKS proxy provides similar features to the WinSock proxy, allowing many applications to be supported. To use this proxy, you must use software that supports SOCKS 4.0 or later, and specify the proxy server name and port number (typically 1080).

On the Exam

For the Proxy Server MCSE exam, you should be aware of the two main disadvantages of the SOCKS proxy compared to the WinSock proxy: it supports only TCP-based protocols (UDP is not supported), and it is less secure than the WinSock proxy.

Managing Advanced Features

Along with the basic proxy services described earlier in this chapter, Microsoft Proxy Server supports a number of advanced features: dial-up networking, an IPX to IP gateway, and the ability to use multiple proxy servers to serve busy networks. These features are described in the following sections.

Using Proxy Server with RAS

The RAS (Remote Access Service) client included with Windows NT allows you to connect to an Internet provider or other network using a modem connection. This feature is also called dial-up networking (DUN).

Proxy Server's *Auto Dial* feature allows it to work with DUN, dialing in to an Internet provider when necessary. This allows a number of users to share a dial-up Internet connection. This allows tighter security than individual dial-up connections, and ensures that the connection is used only when needed. This can provide Internet connectivity for a small company, or serve as a backup connection when a faster Internet connection goes down.

The following sections describe the process of installing and configuring RAS and configuring the Auto Dial feature.

On the Exam

This is a quick introduction to RAS, which should be sufficient for the Proxy Server MCSE exam. For more information about RAS, see the NT Workstation and NT Server sections of *MCSE: The Core Exams in a Nutshell*.

Installing and Configuring RAS

RAS can be installed during the Windows NT Server installation, or added on after installation. NT Server includes both client and server versions of RAS; only the client is needed to support the proxy's Auto Dial feature. Before installing RAS, make sure the proxy server machine meets these requirements:

- A modem should be installed and configured. (RAS also supports the use of multiple modems for greater speed, and supports ISDN connections. See the Windows NT documentation for details.)

- The TCP/IP protocol should be installed and configured.

- RAS can be installed before or after the Proxy Server installation.

To install RAS, select the *Dial-up Networking* item in the My Computer window. If RAS is not installed, you are prompted to install it; this requires the Windows NT installation files on a CD-ROM or network share.

After RAS is installed, you must create a phonebook entry for the Internet connection you will use. To do this, press the New button in the Dial-up Networking dialog. You are prompted for several categories of information about the connection, including the phone number and the protocols to support. You may also need to specify an IP address and other settings; consult the Internet provider for this information.

On the Exam

You can configure more than one phonebook entry in dial-up networking, but Proxy Server's Auto Dial feature can only use one entry at a time. However, a phonebook entry can specify alternate phone numbers.

Enabling Auto Dial

Once RAS and a phonebook entry are installed, you can configure the proxy server to use the dial-up connection. To set up the Auto Dial feature, click the Auto Dial button from the Server tab of any of the proxy service's Properties dialogs.

The Auto Dial dialog, shown in Figure 4-5, is now displayed.

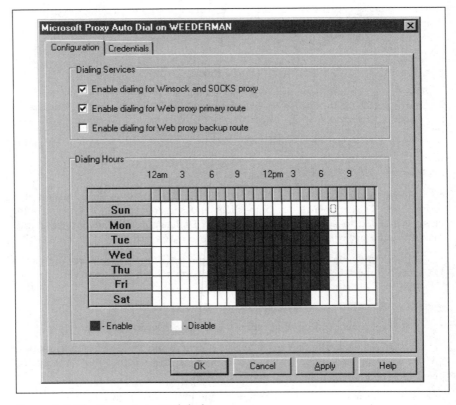

Figure 4-5: The Proxy Auto Dial dialog

The Auto Dial dialog consists of two tabbed categories. The first tab, Configuration, includes the following options

Enable dialing for WinSock and SOCKS proxy
>If enabled, the Auto Dial feature is used when needed for clients using the WinSock and SOCKS protocols.

Enable dialing for web proxy primary route
>If enabled, Auto Dial is used as the primary route to the Internet for the web proxy.

Enable dialing for web proxy backup route
>If enabled, Auto Dial is used as the backup route to the Internet for the web proxy.

Dialing hours
>Highlight the hours and days when dial-up access is permitted. This is useful for preventing use of the connection outside of business hours. When dialing is not permitted, the Internet will not be accessible if the primary route uses Auto Dial.

On the Exam

If Auto Dial is enabled for the WinSock and SOCKS proxies, the connection is dialed whenever a client makes a proxy request. For the web proxy, the connection is dialed only if the cache cannot satisfy the request. Because of this, increasing the available cache can decrease the time spent online with the Internet provider.

The second tab of the Auto Dial configuration dialog, Credentials, allows you to specify the connection to use and authentication information. The following options are included:

Entry Name
>Choose the phonebook entry to dial. The entries you defined in the Dial-up Networking dialog are included in this list.

User Name
>The user name for the Internet account.

Password
>The password for the account. The user name and password must be specified here, even though they may have already been set in Dial-up Networking.

Confirm Password
>Type the password again to confirm.

Domain
>If the system you are dialing is running Windows NT, specify the domain to log onto.

Proxy Server 2.0

Using Proxy Server as an IPX Gateway

Since the WinSock Proxy client software directly intercepts communication by TCP/IP applications, it can allow clients running only the IPX/SPX protocol to access TCP/IP services. In this configuration, the proxy server acts as an IPX gateway.

When an application on an IPX client requests a TCP/IP service, the request is forwarded via IPX to the proxy server. The proxy server satisfies the request (using TCP/IP) and returns the result to the client using IPX. This allows all TCP- and UDP-based protocols to be supported.

While this is not the most efficient arrangement, it is useful for supporting clients in an IPX network (typically used with NetWare servers) without adding the TCP/IP protocol to the network.

In the Real World

When the WinSock proxy is used in this fashion, all of the communications from IPX clients appear to come from the same IP address (the proxy server's address). This may cause incompatibilities when multiple users attempt to access the same Internet host at the same time.

Configuring the IPX Gateway

No specific configuration is required within Proxy Server to support IPX clients. Configuring the server requires only the following:

- Install the IPX/SPX protocol, if not already installed.

- Configure the IPX network number and frame type to match that in use on IPX clients, if necessary.

Setting up IPX Clients

The WinSock proxy client only supports IPX under Windows 95/98 and Windows NT; 16-bit Windows clients must have TCP/IP installed. To configure a client to use the WinSock proxy as an IPX to IP gateway, follow these steps:

1. Install the IPX/SPX protocol (NWLink).

2. Install the WinSock proxy client, as described earlier in this chapter.

3. If the client has only IPX installed, the proxy client will automatically use IPX. If both TCP/IP and IPX are installed, you can set the client to use IPX using the *Force IPX/SPX protocol* option in the WSP Client control panel.

Using Multiple Proxy Servers

As discussed earlier in this chapter, a single proxy server with sufficient processor and disk storage can support as many as 1,000 users. While this may be sufficient for your needs, large networks require the use of multiple proxy servers.

There are also benefits of using multiple servers in smaller networks: for example, separate proxies in remote WAN locations can perform caching and reduce WAN traffic. Multiple proxy servers can be configured in a number of ways, discussed in the following sections.

DNS Load Balancing

One method of dividing client traffic between multiple proxy servers is to use the *load balancing* feature of a DNS (Domain Name Service) server, such as the one included with NT Server. DNS translates between IP host names and IP addresses.

This feature allows you to define an alias that represents all of the servers. When a client sends a DNS request to look up the server's IP address, the DNS server returns a list of all IP addresses that match the alias. For each request, the list is rotated so that a different address is at the top; unless a server is down, the client will use the first address on the list.

In order to use this method, clients must refer to the proxy server by name (alias) rather than IP address. This method has the advantage of being transparent and providing a degree of fault tolerance, but relies heavily on the DNS server.

WINS Load Balancing

WINS (Windows Internet Name Service) is a service similar to DNS for Windows networks. WINS works with NetBIOS names rather than IP host names. A WINS server is included with NT Server. WINS includes a similar load-balancing capability that can divide requests among several proxy servers.

Proxy Server 2.0

Server Arrays

Microsoft Proxy Service includes the capability of configuring multiple servers as an *array*. A proxy server array appears as a single server to clients, but performs load balancing between the servers. In addition, server arrays provide three advantages:

- They provide fault tolerance: if one server goes down, one or more servers in the array can still handle the requests.

- The cache is distributed between the servers in the array, allowing for faster cache responses.

- The configuration can be automatically synchronized between array members, simplifying administration.

Microsoft Proxy Server Arrays use a protocol called CARP (Cache Array Routing Protocol) to distribute the cache between array members. This system uses a hash algorithm (a formula that converts a string of characters into a number) on each requested URL.

The result of the URL hash is added to the hashed names of each of the proxy servers; the one resulting in the highest number is used to retrieve and return the page for that URL. The result is that each URL can be matched to the same proxy server at each request, without requiring any communication between the servers. The hash algorithm is designed so that URLs are randomly and evenly distributed between the servers.

On the Exam

For the Proxy Server MCSE exam, you should understand how the CARP protocol improves array performance. Its main benefits are that it prevents the same object from being cached on two servers, it performs faster the more members are added to the array, and it automatically handles servers added to or removed from the array.

An array can be configured with a minimum of two and a maximum of approximately 20 proxy servers; all members of the array should be running the same version of Microsoft Proxy Server.

To create an array, you should already have installed Proxy Server on two computers, and configured both the same way. On one of the servers, click the Array button in the Service tab of the Properties dialog for one of the proxy services. Use the Join Array button and specify the name of the other server. You must then specify a name for the array.

After the array is in place, you can add an additional server by using the Join Array button in that server's Properties dialog. Specify the name of one of the computers in the array. The array name is automatically read.

After the array is successfully configured, each server's Array dialog lists the members of the array. You can remove a member from the list from any other array member.

Enable the *Synchronize configuration of array members* option to maintain the same configuration for the array members. Each change you make to an array member is reflected on the others. (For this reason, you should only administer one array member at a time.)

When you configure an array, the shared client installation program automatically configures clients to use the array. Clients that have already been installed should refresh their configuration automatically if the server they were installed from is now an array member.

Server Chains

Another possible configuration of multiple proxy servers is a *server chain*. Whereas only one member of an array handles proxy requests from clients, all of the members of a chain handle each request.

The chain consists of servers ranging from downstream (closest to the client) to upstream (closest to the Internet connection). A proxy request is sent to the downstream client, and the request is passed upstream until it reaches the server with the Internet connection.

This arrangement does not balance the load between servers automatically, but can be arranged to balance the load by location or department. For example, in a company with several locations and a single high-speed Internet connection, each location can have its own downstream proxy server with a large cache to minimize WAN traffic. The upstream server (or array) in the central location can also use caching to minimize traffic across the Internet connection.

Managing Routing

To create a chain of proxy servers or arrays, use the Routing tab of the Web Proxy Properties dialog to specify an upstream proxy or array for each downstream server. You can also specify a backup proxy (or a direct connection) to be used

Proxy Server 2.0

when the upstream proxy is unavailable. The Routing dialog includes these options:

Use this HTTP Via header alias for the local server
Specify an alias for the Proxy Server computer; by default, this is set to the computer name. This value is placed in an HTTP header.

Upstream routing
Choose where the proxy should request objects from for clients. The default setting, *Use direct connection*, uses an Internet or network connection available from the local computer. The *Use Web Proxy or array* option forwards the request to an upstream proxy server or array.

Enable backup route
If the Upstream Routing option is set to use an upstream proxy or array, this option can be enabled to provide a backup route. This route is used when the upstream proxy cannot be reached. The backup route can be set to use a direct connection, or to use a second upstream proxy or array.

Resolve Web Proxy requests within array before routing upstream
If this option is selected, other members of the array will be checked for a cached copy of the requested object before the request is sent to the upstream route.

When the *Use Web Proxy or array* option is selected for upstream routing or for the backup route, the Modify button in the appropriate section of the dialog allows you to specify the settings for the proxy or array. These options are included:

Proxy
Specify the network name or IP address of the upstream proxy server.

Port
Specify the port number (typically 80) for the upstream proxy server.

Auto-poll upstream proxy for array configuration
If selected, the configuration of the array of upstream proxy servers is automatically read from the upstream server.

Array URL
This is the URL to the DLL file that will be downloaded to automatically read the array configuration. The default value is *http://server:80/array.dll*, where *server* is the server name specified in the Proxy field.

Use credentials to communicate with upstream proxy/array
Select this option if the upstream proxy or array requires authentication, and specify the user name and password.

Allow basic/clear text authentication
If selected, the Internet-standard method of authentication is used when contacting the upstream server. This method sends the password as clear (unencrypted) text, and may be a security risk.

Allow encrypted authentication
If selected, the Windows NT Challenge and Response method of authentication is used to contact the upstream server. This method is more secure than clear text.

Proxy Server Security

As described earlier in this chapter, one of the reasons to install a proxy server is to increase security. The proxy can serve as a firewall, or single access point for the Internet, allowing you tight control over each client's access. In addition, inbound access is not allowed unless you specifically configure it.

Access controls, described earlier in this chapter, allow you to control access to Internet services by local network users. The following sections discuss other proxy security issues and how to manage them using Proxy Server.

Preventing Inbound Access

Since the computer running Proxy Server is typically the only computer with a connection to the Internet, it is important to ensure that Internet users cannot gain access to the network through the proxy server. The installation of Proxy Server configures Windows NT to prevent most such access. Follow these guidelines to prevent inbound access to the network:

- Be sure that IP forwarding (routing) is disabled on the proxy server computer. If enabled, this would allow outside access to any computer on the network. The installation of Proxy Server disables this feature by default, but it may be changed after installation; for example, the RAS installation activates this option. To deactivate it, open the TCP/IP Properties dialog from the Network control panel. Select the Routing tab and disable the option.

- Do not attempt to enable the Web publishing service in IIS. Instead, use the features described in the next section for secure web publishing.

- Due to security holes in Windows NT, there is a possibility that an outside user can gain access to the user list and the Administrator account on the proxy server. To minimize the damage this would cause, run Proxy Server on a member server rather than a domain controller. An even more secure strategy is to make the Proxy Server computer the PDC for its own domain and use a one-way trust to give users in your corporate domain access to the proxy.

- Use packet filtering to filter incoming network traffic, as described later in this section.

Web Server Security

When Proxy Server is installed, it disables access to the Web publishing services of IIS from non-local addresses. If you still wish to publish web documents, there are two methods of doing this securely. These are described in the following sections.

Reverse Proxy

The reverse proxy feature allows you to use the IIS Web publishing service to publish web documents on the same computer that runs the Proxy Server. This allows web documents to be served without exposing the web server directly to the Internet, and packet filtering and other Proxy Server features can prevent unauthorized access.

This feature literally acts as a proxy in reverse: clients on the Internet send an HTTP request to the proxy server. The proxy, in turn, forwards the requests to the web server running on the same machine. The web server returns the document to the proxy server, which passes it on to the client.

To enable the reverse proxy feature, select the Publishing tab in the Web Proxy Properties dialog and select the *Enable Web publishing* option. Then select the option to forward web server requests to the local web server.

Reverse Hosting

Reverse hosting is an extension of the reverse proxy feature that allows one or more computers on the local network (not including the Proxy Server computer) to publish documents, but still uses the proxy for access control. This is a more secure method, and reduces the load on the proxy server computer.

To enable reverse hosting, select the *Enable Web publishing* option as described above. Next, select the *sent to another Web server* option and specify a local server name and port number.

To use more than one computer for publishing, use the Add button to add a mapping. Specify the URL that outside clients will request and the local URL that it maps to.

Using Packet Filters

Packet filters add an extra layer of security to Proxy Server. This feature causes all incoming or outgoing packets that are not handled by the proxy to be discarded, unless specifically allowed. This feature can override any service installed on the Proxy Server computer.

For example, if you have installed a third-party web server, it will respond to incoming requests even after Proxy Server is installed. If you turn on packet filtering, this server will be inaccessible unless you explicitly allow HTTP packets to pass through the filter.

To configure packet filters, use the Security button on the Service tab of the Properties dialog for any of the proxy services. The Security dialog, shown in Figure 4-6, is displayed. This dialog includes four tabbed categories, described in the sections that follow.

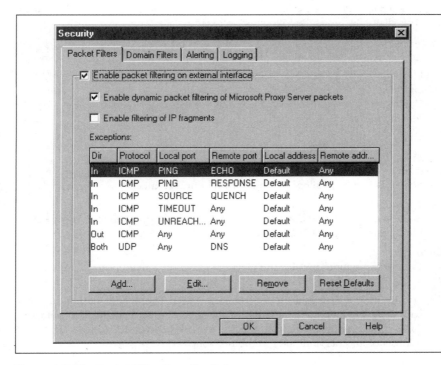

Figure 4-6: The Packet Filter Security dialog

Packet Filters

The Packet Filters tab allows you to define packet filters. The following options are included in this dialog:

Enable packet filtering on external interface
This option enables packet filtering, and enables the remaining options in the dialog. Packet filtering is only available if the computer has an external network connection (such as an Internet connection).

Enable dynamic packet filtering of Microsoft Proxy Server packets
> This enables the dynamic filtering feature, which allows the proxy services to dynamically filter all packets that are not specifically allowed by one of the services. This is the most secure setting.

Enable filtering of IP fragments
> If enabled, Proxy Server attempts to filter partial IP datagrams (caused by network errors or attempts to gain access) from incoming transmissions.

Exceptions
> Allows you to add one or more exceptions to packet filtering. This allows specific protocols to be used through the proxy.

The Packet Filter Properties dialog is displayed when you add or edit an exception. This dialog includes the following options:

Predefined filter
> Allows you to select one of the built-in filter definitions to allow a specific protocol. Predefined filters are included for a number of common protocols.

Custom filter
> To define a custom filter, select this option and specify values for the remaining options in the dialog.

Protocol ID
> Specify a protocol type (TCP, UDP, ICMP, or Any).

Direction
> Specify whether to allow inbound or outbound connections, or both.

Local port
> Specify the local port for the connection: a fixed port number, any port, or the dynamic range of 1025–5000.

Remote port
> Choose the remote port for the connection (either a fixed port, or any port).

Local host
> Specify the local IP address for the connection. The default setting automatically uses the external IP address of the proxy server (or multiple addresses, for a proxy array). You can specify a proxy server IP address or the IP address of another computer in the network.

Remote host
> Specify the remote IP address for the connection: either a specific address, or any remote host.

Domain Filters

The Domain Filters tab of the Security dialog allows you to allow or deny access to web or FTP sites based on their IP address or Internet domain name. Use the *Enable filtering* option to enable this feature and choose whether access to Internet sites is granted or denied by default.

Once you have set the default, you can add one or more exceptions with the Add button. For each exception, specify the IP address, a range of IP addresses, or a domain name.

When access is granted by default, domain filters are useful for denying access to a list of sites. When access is denied by default, you can tightly control the sites accessible by network users (perhaps limiting them to other corporate branches).

On the Exam

The domain filters in the Security dialog affect the WinSock and Web Proxies. For the SOCKS Proxy, use the Permissions dialog to add a rule that allows or denies access to a domain as specified earlier in this chapter.

Alerting

The Alerting tab of the Security dialog can be used to configure Proxy Server to monitor the packet filtering process and alert you to conditions that may indicate a security problem. The conditions include the following:

Rejected packets
> Alerts when a specified number of packets have been rejected by the packet filters.

Protocol violations
> Alerts when a specified number of illegal packets (such as fragments) have been detected. These are also included in the list of rejected packets. Protocol violations may indicate a serious network problem, or an attempt to gain access to the server.

Disk full
> Alerts when a disk is full; this may cause the proxy to stop functioning, or cause log entries to stop being written.

The remaining fields in this dialog allow you to configure the frequency and type of alerts:

Generate system event if more than
> Specify the number of events that must occur before an alert (log entry and notification). The default is twenty events for rejected packets and one event for protocol violations and disk full errors.

Send SMTP mail
> If selected, a mail message is sent using an SMTP server for each alert.

Report to Windows NT Event Log
> If selected, alerts are written to the System event log in Windows NT, and can be viewed with the Event Viewer utility. Otherwise, alerts are written to the proxy server log files.

Delay before next report
> Specify a delay between consecutive reports; this prevents excessive log entries.

Configure mail
> If the *Send SMTP mail* option is selected, use this button to specify the mail server address and email address.

Logging

The Logging tab of the Security dialog allows you to configure logging for the alerts specified in the Alerting tab. The options in this dialog are identical to those in the proxy service Logging properties. Log entries can be written to an SQL/ODBC database or to a file; the default file name is PF followed by the date.

Optimization and Troubleshooting

A variety of configuration problems and other issues can cause poor performance or unexpected behavior on Proxy Server. The following sections describe how to monitor Proxy Server's performance, optimize certain aspects of performance, and troubleshoot common problems.

Monitoring Proxy Server Performance

The installation of Proxy Server adds a number of counters to the Windows NT Performance Monitor utility. These counters can be used to monitor the proxy's performance. The following categories are included:

Packet Filtering
Includes counters related to the packet filtering process. This includes the number of dropped packets and the number of current incoming connections to the server.

Web Proxy Server Cache
Includes counters related to the Web Proxy server's passive and active caching features. These counters are useful for monitoring the efficiency of the cache.

Web Proxy Server Service
Includes a variety of general counters for the Web Proxy service. These are useful for monitoring the network bandwidth used by the proxy service.

WinSock Proxy Server
Includes counters related to the WinSock Proxy service. These can be used to monitor the network and processor use of the WinSock Proxy.

The Proxy Server installation creates a Start menu entry called *Monitor Proxy Server Performance in the Microsoft Proxy Server group*. Select this entry to start Performance Monitor with a predefined workspace containing useful Proxy Server values. The counters included are listed in Table 4-3.

Table 4-3: Default Proxy Server Counters

Object	Counter	Description
Process	%Processor Time (inetinfo)	Percentage of CPU time used by IIS processes
Process	%Processor Time (wspsrv)	Percentage of CPU time used by Proxy Server processes
WinSock Proxy Server	Active Sessions	Number of active WinSock proxy users

Table 4-3: Default Proxy Server Counters (continued)

Object	Counter	Description
Web Proxy Server Service	Cache Hit Ratio	Percentage of requests that are satisfied by the cache
Web Proxy Server Service	Requests/sec	Number of Web proxy requests per second
Web Proxy Server Service	Current Average Milliseconds/request	Average time used to satisfy each Web proxy request

These counters are the most important measures of Proxy Server performance. You may wish to use Performance Monitor's Log feature to create a file as a baseline measure of performance, so that you can compare the current results to this log when there is a performance problem.

You may also wish to monitor the performance of the Windows NT Server computer itself. The following counters may be useful in finding bottlenecks that could affect the speed of Proxy Server:

Processor: %Processor Time
> Indicates the current use of the server's CPU. If this value is frequently over 80%, a processor upgrade would improve performance.

PhysicalDisk: %Disk Time
> The percentage of time the disk drive is busy reading or writing data. If this value is over 25%, a faster drive or RAID configuration may improve performance.

Memory: Page faults/sec
> The number of times each second that the computer is unable to find a requested location in memory, and must use the swap file. Frequent page faults indicate the need for more memory.

On the Exam

If you use SNMP (Simple Network Management Protocol) on your network, it can also be used with Proxy Server. The installation includes an MIB (Management Information Base) to allow SNMP to monitor the performance of the proxy services. To use this feature you will need a SNMP management agent; Windows NT does not include this feature.

Optimizing Proxy Server

Proxy Server can add a substantial load to a Windows NT computer, since all of the Internet traffic for a company may be passing through it and being interpreted and filtered. The following sections describe common bottlenecks and methods of improving performance.

Proxy Services

The performance of the proxy server partially depends on the services you support. Follow these guidelines to optimize performance:

- When possible, use the Web Proxy rather than the WinSock or SOCKS proxies, since only the Web Proxy supports caching. Also, disabling the services you do not use will improve performance.

- Avoid running other services on the proxy server computer. If you are using the reverse hosting feature to publish web pages, you may wish to consider disabling it and hosting the pages on another server.

- If you are using the proxy server strictly for caching and other benefits and do not require security, disabling packet filtering and access control will improve performance.

Network Bandwidth

Since a proxy server can allow a number of clients to share a single Internet connection, this is one area that eventually forms a bottleneck as the number of clients increases. While the obvious solution is to use a faster connection, there are ways of improving the proxy's performance with an existing connection.

The strategy you use to optimize network bandwidth depends largely on how you are billed for the Internet connection. If the connection is available 24 hours a day at a flat rate, the best strategy is to enable active caching and increase the cache size; since the active caching tasks will be performed when the server is idle, the cache should satisfy more requests during peak periods.

On the other hand, if the Internet connection is billed based on the bandwidth you use, it may be better not to use active caching. Instead, use passive caching and as large a cache as possible.

If it is necessary to upgrade the network connection, you can add a second connection and share its traffic. While a single proxy server supports only one external connection, you can configure a proxy server array with one connection per computer.

On the Exam

Another factor that should be considered when attempting to reduce bandwidth is security. If you have considered using packet filtering to prevent access to non-work-related sites, this can provide bandwidth benefits as well as security.

Caching

As already mentioned, the caching feature of the Web Proxy can reduce the external network bandwidth used, and the larger the cache the larger the benefit. However, a large amount of caching can slow down the server. Follow these guidelines to improve the efficiency of the cache:

- Use active caching when possible; passive caching alone will use a substantial amount of disk storage for objects that will not be used again.

- Use the *Limit size of cached objects* option to prevent the caching of large objects which may consume disk space (and may not be needed again).

- Reducing the TTL settings will expire objects faster and decrease the disk storage used by the cache (at the expense of more network bandwidth).

- Consider using one or more fast disk drives strictly for caching.

- For heavily used caches, a RAID (Redundant Array of Inexpensive Disks) will improve performance. Since fault tolerance is usually not important for the items in the cache, a stripe set (RAID 0) is an effective solution. This is supported in software by NT Server.

- Consider using multiple proxy servers in an array; the cache is distributed between the servers for faster response.

On the Exam

For the Proxy Server exam, remember that the cache is only used for Web Proxy requests. The WinSock and SOCKS proxies do not support caching. If you are not using the Web Proxy, disable the cache feature to improve performance and reduce disk usage.

Troubleshooting Common Problems

Proxy Server is reasonably reliable, but may suffer from configuration problems and other issues. The first step in diagnosing a problem is to use the Event Viewer utility to read the Windows NT System log and check for any errors. You should also check the log files for the various proxy services, if enabled. The following sections discuss common Proxy Server problems and their solutions.

On the Exam

In addition to this information, you should be able to troubleshoot general TCP/IP problems for the Proxy Server exam. Part 1 of this book describes this process.

Installation Problems

If the Proxy Server installation program does not complete the installation successfully, the most likely problem is a lack of disk space or a disk problem. After checking this possibility, follow these guidelines:

- Remove any optional services that might be causing conflicts. (Do not remove IIS, which is required for the installation.)

Proxy Server 2.0

- Be sure the computer's hardware and software meet the requirements listed in the "Installing Proxy Server" section.

- Check the file C:\MSPSETUP.LOG. This is a log file created during the installation; the last entry in the log may indicate what the setup program was doing when it stopped, and may include an error message.

- Check the System event log using Event Viewer. The installation program may have caused an error that appears in this log.

- Ensure that you are logged in as a member of the Administrators group before beginning the installation.

Client Problems

If a client is unable to access the Internet through the proxy, a configuration problem is likely. Follow these guidelines to diagnose the problem:

- Check whether other computers are able to access the proxy. If not, there may be a problem with the server.

- If you are using the WinSock proxy, be sure the client installation program was run and completed successfully.

- If an application does not work correctly using the web proxy, you may wish to try using the SOCKS proxy instead, if supported by the application.

- Use the ping command at the command prompt from the client to verify communication with the Proxy Server computer.

- If access controls are enabled, be sure the user has been given permission to use the service.

- If packet filters or domain filters are in use, ensure that the service or server requested by the user is not being filtered.

The WinSock Proxy client installation program installs a utility that may be useful in troubleshooting client problems. To run the utility, start a command or MS-DOS prompt and type chkwsp32 (Windows 95 or NT) or chkwsp16 (Windows 3.x). This utility displays information about the client configuration, and checks the connection with the server.

Proxy Service Problems

The following are some common causes of problems with the three proxy services included with Proxy Server:

- Be sure the LAT is correct and is updated when the local network changes. Extra addresses in the LAT can prevent access to outside sites; missing addresses can prevent clients from using the proxy.

- The SOCKS Proxy service requires the Web Proxy for operation; do not stop or disable the Web Proxy if you need to support SOCKS.

- A client may be unable to connect to a dial-up Internet provider because the installation of the WinSock Proxy client has disabled non-proxy access. To use a dial-up provider, you must disable the proxy client using the WSP Client control panel.

Suggested Exercises

The Proxy Server exam includes questions about all aspects of Proxy Server installation and operation. You should have experience both from an administrator's point of view and from a client's point of view.

You will need a Windows NT Server 4.0 computer to run Proxy Server. While it is possible to use a proxy client on the same computer as Proxy Server, it is best to use a separate client machine. An Internet connection is also required; a dial-up connection should be sufficient for practicing with Proxy Server.

Performing the following exercises will help you prepare for the Proxy Server MCSE exam. In addition, you should have a basic understanding of TCP/IP, covered in Part 1, *Internetworking with TCP/IP*, and IIS, covered in Part 2, *Internet Information Server 4.0*.

1. Install Proxy Server under Windows NT Server 4.0. (You must first install SP3 and IIS, if necessary.)

2. Create a LAT representing the local addresses on your network using the configuration dialog.

3. From a client machine, configure the browser to use the Proxy Server machine and port 80, and verify the operation of the Web Proxy service.

4. Install the WinSock Proxy client on a client machine. Try a variety of Internet software to verify that it is operating correctly.

5. Configure logging for the Web Proxy service. Use the proxy for a while, then examine the log file.

6. Configure a client browser to use the SOCKS proxy instead of the web proxy (both IE4 and Netscape Navigator support this feature). Verify that you can access web and FTP sites.

7. Configure the Web Proxy service to support active caching. Spend some time browsing the Web from a client, then use the Network Monitor utility to test whether active caching is performed during the idle time.

8. Configure the Web and WinSock proxies to use access controls, and grant permissions to a user. Verify that that user can use the proxies from a client. Try logging in as a different user, and test whether any proxy access is available.

9. Configure access controls for the SOCKS proxy to allow one user access and prevent any others. From the client, verify that only the allowed user can access the proxy.

10. Configure RAS to use the auto-dial feature. Access the web proxy from a client, and verify that the ISP is dialed automatically.

11. Remove the TCP/IP protocol from the client and install the IPX/SPX protocol. Verify that the WinSock Proxy service still allows access to web sites.

12. If you have two NT Server machines, install Proxy Server on a second machine and configure the two machines to act as an array. Verify that a client can access the array of servers.

13. Activate packet filtering and verify that proxy server access is still available.

14. Create a domain filter to prevent access to the *microsoft.com* domain. Attempt to load *www.microsoft.com* from a client browser, and verify that access is denied.

15. Experiment with disconnecting the network connection between client and server and the Internet connection. Examine the error messages displayed by client browser under each of these conditions.

Practice Test

Test Questions

1. Which of the following is not a typical use of a proxy server?

    a.   To allow network users to share an Internet connection

    b.   To publish web documents

    c.   To prevent unauthorized outgoing access

    d.   To prevent unauthorized incoming access

2. Which of the following Proxy Server services support the HTTP protocol? (select all that apply)

    a.   Web Proxy

    b.   WinSock Proxy

    c.   SOCKS Proxy

3. Which of the following Proxy Server services requires specific client software?

    a.   Web Proxy

    b.   WinSock Proxy

    c.   SOCKS Proxy

4. Which of the following Proxy Server services support caching? (select all that apply)

    a.   Web Proxy

    b.   WinSock Proxy

    c.   SOCKS Proxy

5. Which of the following Proxy Server services support non-Windows clients? (select all that apply)

    a.   Web Proxy

    b.   WinSock Proxy

    c.   SOCKS Proxy

6. What is the name of the Proxy Server feature that pre-caches documents that are expected to be requested by clients?

    a.   Passive caching

    b.   Distributed caching

    c.   Active caching

    d.   Reverse proxying

7. Which of the following files are used to support the WinSock specification under Windows 98? (select all that apply)

    a.   WINSOCK.DLL

    b.   MSPROXY.DLL

    c.   WSOCK32.DLL

    d.   WINSOCK.EXE

8. In order to support UDP-based services such as RealAudio, which proxy service should be used?

    a.   Web Proxy

    b.   WinSock Proxy

    c.   SOCKS Proxy

9. You are installing Proxy Server on a computer. Windows NT Workstation 4.0 and Service Pack 3 are already installed. The computer has 24 MB of RAM, a 486/66 processor, and 2 GB of available disk storage. Which of the following is the most likely to cause a problem with installation on this computer?

    a.   The operating system

    b.   RAM

    c.   Disk storage

    d.   Processor

10. You are installing Proxy Server in a network with 100 clients that will use the Web proxy. Which of the following is the best estimate of the required cache size?

    a.   100 MB

    b.   150 MB

    c.   200 MB

    d.   500 MB

11. You are installing Proxy Server in a network with 20 UNIX clients, 120 Windows 95 clients, and 10 Macintosh clients, all of which will use the Web proxy. Which of the following cache sizes would provide the best performance?

    a.   150 MB

    b.   175 MB

    c.   250 MB

    d.   500 MB

12. You are installing Proxy Server 2.0 on a computer that already has Windows NT Server 4.0 installed. You plan to install IIS 4.0 before installing Proxy Server. Which of the following additional products will be required? (select all that apply)

    a.   Internet Explorer 4.0

    b.   IIS 3.0

    c.   Service Pack 2

    d.   Service Pack 3

13. Which of the following file systems can be used as a cache for Proxy Server? (select all that apply)

    a.   FAT

    b.   FAT32

    c.   NTFS

    d.   HPFS

14. Approximately how much disk storage is used by the installation of Proxy Server, not including the cache?

    a.   10 MB

    b.   20 MB

    c.   50 MB

    d.   60 MB

15. Which of the following best describes the Local Address Table (LAT)?

    a.   A list of all IP addresses in the local network, one per line

    b.   A list of IP address ranges for the local network

    c.   A list of local addresses and their corresponding remote addresses

    d.   A list of local addresses and their corresponding host names

16. If the access controls for the Web and WinSock proxies are disabled during installation, which local clients will have access to the proxies by default?

    a.   All local clients

    b.   Only members of the Administrators group

c. Clients logged into the Proxy Server computer only

d. No local clients

17. Which tab of the Web Proxy's Properties dialog includes the Array and Auto Dial options?

    a. Permissions

    b. Publishing

    c. Service

    d. General

18. Which of the following Proxy Server services can be used in a server chain?

    a. Web Proxy

    b. WinSock Proxy

    c. SOCKS Proxy

19. If you enable access controls for the SOCKS proxy, which clients are able to use the proxy by default?

    a. All local clients

    b. Members of the Administrators group only

    c. Members of the Domain Users group only

    d. No local clients

20. Which of the following is the name of the network share that stores client software for the proxy server?

    a. MSPCLIENT

    b. MSPCLNT

    c. CLIENTS

    d. MSP

21. Which of the following protocols are supported by the WinSock Proxy? (select all that apply)

    a. HTTP

    b. FTP

    c. Gopher

    d. NNTP

22. In a client with the IPX and TCP/IP protocols installed, which dialog do you use to force the use of the IPX protocol with the WinSock Proxy?

    a. WSP Client control panel

    b. Network control panel

    c. WinSock proxy client installation program

    d. NWLink control panel

23. Which filename should be used when creating a custom LAT file for a client?

    a.   MSPLAT.TXT

    b.   LAT.TXT

    c.   LOCALLAT.TXT

    d.   LAT.INI

24. Which port number should be specified when configuring a UNIX client to use the Web Proxy?

    a.   25

    b.   80

    c.   1080

    d.   1024

25. Which of the following services can be used to balance the load between multiple proxy servers?

    a.   WINS

    b.   DHCP

    c.   SNMP

    d.   DNS

26. What is the approximate limit of the number of Proxy Server computers in a single array?

    a.   10

    b.   16

    c.   20

    d.   24

27. Which of the following is not a method of preventing unauthorized inbound access via Proxy Server?

    a.   Disable IP forwarding

    b.   Use a separate domain for proxy servers

    c.   Use access controls

    d.   Use packet filtering

28. A computer running Proxy Server is configured to accept HTTP requests and pass them on to another computer running IIS for processing. This is an example of which Proxy Server feature?

    a.   Reverse proxy

    b.   Reverse hosting

    c.   Active caching

    d.   Server arrays

29. Which Proxy Server feature can be used to prevent users from accessing a particular Internet site?

    a.   Packet filters

    b.   Domain filters

    c.   Access control

    d.   Permissions

30. If only passive caching is used, which of the following changes would decrease the amount of bandwidth used on a proxy server's Internet connection?

    a.   Decrease the TTL for cached documents

    b.   Limit the size of cached objects

    c.   Increase the cache size

    d.   Disable caching

Answers to Questions

1. B. Proxy servers are not typically used to publish web documents (although Microsoft Proxy Server can allow Web publishing).

2. A, B, C. All of the Proxy Server services support the HTTP protocol.

3. B. The WinSock Proxy requires specific software.

4. A. Only the Web Proxy supports caching.

5. A, C. The Web and SOCKS proxies support both Windows and non-Windows clients.

6. C. The active caching feature pre-caches documents.

7. A, C. Windows 95 and 98 use both the WINSOCK.DLL and WSOCK32.DLL files.

8. B. The WinSock Proxy is the only service supported by Proxy Server that allows UDP communication.

9. A. The computer meets the requirements for Proxy Server except for the use of Windows NT Workstation. Proxy Server requires NT Server.

10. B. Microsoft's recommendation is to estimate 100 MB plus .5 MB per client, resulting in 150 MB in this case.

11. D. The number of clients specified totals 150, so the estimated minimum cache size required would be 175 MB (choice B); however, a larger cache would provide better performance.

12. A, D. Proxy Server requires Service Pack 3; in addition, the installation of IIS 4.0 will require Internet Explorer 4.0.

13. C. Only the NTFS file system is supported for Proxy Server caching. FAT32 and HPFS (choices A and D) are not supported by Windows NT 4.0 at all.

14. A. The Proxy Server files use approximately 10 MB of storage.

15. B. The LAT is a list of IP address ranges for the local network.

16. A. If access controls are disabled, all local clients will have access to the proxies by default.

17. C. The Service tab includes the Array and Auto Dial options.

18. A. Only the Web Proxy supports server chaining.

19. D. For the SOCKS proxy, when access controls are enabled, no clients are allowed access by default.

20. B. The share for proxy server clients is MSPCLNT. This share points to a directory called CLIENTS (choice C).

21. A, B, C, D. The WinSock proxy supports all of these protocols (and most others).

22. A. The WSP Client control panel allows you to force the use of IPX.

23. C. The LOCALLAT.TXT file is used to create a client LAT file. The MSPLAT.TXT file (choice A) also exists on the client, but is regularly over-written by the file from the server.

24. B. Use port 80 for the Web Proxy.

25. A, D. WINS and DNS can be used for proxy server load balancing.

26. C. The approximate limit of proxy servers in an array is 20.

27. C. Access controls are used to control local users' access to the proxy; the other choices can prevent unauthorized access from the Internet.

28. B. This is an example of reverse hosting. Reverse proxy (choice A) refers to using IIS on the same computer as Proxy Server.

29. B. Domain filters can be used to prevent access to particular sites.

30. C. Increasing the cache size would decrease the network bandwidth used. Choices A, B, and D would all decrease the amount of storage needed for the cache, but would not reduce bandwidth.

Proxy Server 2.0

Highlighter's Index

Proxy Server Basics

Proxy Features
Acts as an Internet gateway
Requests objects from Internet, passes on to clients
Prevents unauthorized inbound or outbound access (firewall)
Caches objects to reduce Internet connection bandwidth

Web Proxy Service
CERN standard web proxy
Supports HTTP, FTP, Gopher, and Secure services
Supports active and passive caching
Operates as an ISAPI extension to IIS

WinSock Proxy Service
Acts as a direct network interface
Requires client installation
Replaces WINSOCK.DLL or WSOCK32.DLL
Supports all TCP- and UDP-based protocols
Supports Windows platforms only
Can act as an IPX gateway

SOCKS Proxy Service
Acts as a direct network connection
Multi-platform, follows SOCKS 4.3a standard
Supports TCP-based protocols only
Does not support IPX

Installation

Hardware Requirements

CPU: 486/33 or higher (Pentium recommended)
RAM (Intel): 24 MB (32 MB or more recommended)
RAM (RISC): 32 MB
Disk Storage: 10 MB for Install; 100 MB plus .5 MB per client for cache
Network Card(s):1 per network (only one external network supported)

Configuration Requirements

Windows NT Server 4.0
NT Server 4.0 Service Pack 3
IIS 3.0 or 4.0
NTFS volume for caching

Setup Program

Installs Proxy Server software
Prompts to create LAT
Prompts for default client options
Prompts to enable or disable access control

Configuration and Management

Client Configuration

WinSock Proxy configuration program: Replaces DLLs; installs WSP Client
control panel; configures browser to use Web proxy
Web and SOCKS proxies do not require client installation
LAT (local address table): List of local IP address ranges

Auto Dial

Requires RAS (remote access service); included with NT Server
Dials an Internet provider as primary or secondary connection
Can dial within specified hours
Only one dial-up connection is supported

IPX Gateway

Requires IPX protocol at client and proxy server
Supports WinSock Proxy only
To force IPX, use WSP Client control panel
Supports Windows 95/98 and NT clients only

Multiple Proxy Servers

Load balancing: Uses DNS or WINS to distribute requests to different servers
Server array: Multiple Proxy Server computers that share configuration and
distributed cache

Server chain: Multiple servers arranged in a hierarchy (upstream to downstream)

Specify routing parameters in Routing tab of Web Proxy properties

Security

Preventing Unauthorized Access

Disable IP forwarding

Do not use IIS directly

Use a separate domain for Proxy Server computers

Web Publishing

Reverse proxy: Allows publishing from internal IIS installation

Reverse hosting: Allows publishing from any server on network

Configure from Publishing tab of Web Proxy properties

Packet and Domain Filters

Dynamic filtering: Filters all non-proxy packets

Exceptions can be specified to allow any protocol

Domain filters: Prevent access to Internet sites based on IP address or domain

Monitoring Performance

Objects Installed with Proxy Server

Packet Filtering

Web Proxy Server Cache

Web Proxy Server Service

WinSock Proxy Service

Common Counters

Process / %Processor Time (inetinfo)

Percentage of CPU time used by IIS processes

Process / %Processor Time (wspsrv)

Percentage of CPU time used by Proxy Server processes

WinSock Proxy Server / Active Sessions

Number of active WinSock proxy users

Web Proxy Server Service / Cache Hit Ratio

Percentage of requests satisfied by cache

Web Proxy Server Service / Requests/sec

Number of web proxy requests per second

Web Proxy Server Service / Current Average Milliseconds/request

Average time used to satisfy each web proxy request

PART 5

Exchange Server 5.5

Exam Overview

Electronic mail is a common feature of today's networks, and is the most heavily used service on the Internet. Microsoft Exchange Server 5.5, part of the Microsoft BackOffice suite, is a full-featured server for email, collaboration and scheduling, and discussion groups.

Microsoft's MCSE Exam 70-081, titled *Implementing and Supporting Microsoft Exchange Server 5.5*, covers all aspects of Exchange Server: architecture, installation, administration, and connectivity with other email systems.

This is one of the more difficult elective exams, although it focuses on a single product. It covers complex issues, such as the use of multiple Exchange servers and communication with legacy email systems. You should have experience with all of the Exchange Server features before taking the exam.

In order to prepare for this chapter and the Exchange Server exam, you should have studied for and passed the Network Essentials, Windows NT Server, and Windows NT Server in the Enterprise exams. Additionally, you should have a basic understanding of TCP/IP (covered in Part 1, *Internetworking with TCP/IP*).

Objectives

Need to Know	Reference
The capabilities of Exchange Server	"Exchange Features" on page 267
The protocols supported by Exchange and their purposes	"Mail Server Protocols" on page 268
Core and optional components of Exchange Server and their functions	"Exchange Server Components" on page 270
New features in version 5.5 of Exchange Server	"New Features in Version 5.5" on page 273

Need to Know	Reference
Hardware requirements for Exchange Server	"Hardware Requirements" on page 276
Software requirements for Exchange Server	"Software Requirements" on page 276
Available properties for user mailboxes	"Creating User Mailboxes" on page 284
Operating system and hardware requirements for Outlook 8.0	"Working with Client Software" on page 295
The public folder replication process	"Public Folder Replication" on page 304
Directory synchronization components used with MS Mail	"Directory Synchronization with MS Mail" on page 316
Performance monitor views installed with Exchange Server	"Using Performance Monitor" on page 318
Recommended disk configuration for Exchange Server computers	"Disk Configuration" on page 321

Need to Apply	Reference
Plan an installation of Exchange Server.	"Planning the Installation" on page 274
Install Exchange Server on a Windows NT Server computer.	"The Installation Process" on page 277
Upgrade an old version of Exchange to Exchange Server 5.5.	"Upgrading Previous Versions" on page 277
Add, modify, or remove the installed Exchange Server components	"Removing Exchange Server Components" on page 281
Use the Exchange Administrator utility to manage Exchange Server.	"The Exchange Administrator Utility" on page 281
Create and modify user mailboxes.	"Creating User Mailboxes" on page 284
Create custom recipients for other email systems.	"Adding Custom Recipients" on page 291
Create and maintain distribution lists.	"Using Distribution Lists" on page 294
Install and use the Outlook client for Exchange.	"Working with Client Software" on page 295
Create and maintain address book views.	"Managing Address Book Views" on page 300
Create and maintain public folders.	"Configuring Public Folders" on page 302
Manage replication for public folders.	"Setting Replication Options" on page 305
Create and manage Internet newsgroups.	"Configuring Newsgroups" on page 307

Need to Apply	Reference
Configure the Site Connector for communication between Exchange sites.	"Configuring the Site Connector" on page 309
Configure the X.400 Connector.	"Configuring the X.400 Connector" on page 310
Configure Exchange to work with RAS.	"Using the RAS Connector" on page 312
Configure Exchange to work with an Internet mail server.	"Configuring the Internet Mail Service" on page 314
Configure connectivity and directory synchronization with MS Mail.	"Using the MS Mail Connector" on page 315
Configure connectivity with Lotus cc:Mail.	"Using the cc:Mail Connector" on page 317
Configure directory replication between Exchange sites.	"The Directory Replication Connector" on page 313
Monitor Exchange Server performance.	"Monitoring Server Performance" on page 318
Create Server Monitors and Link Monitors.	"Monitoring Server Performance" on page 318
Optimize the performance of Exchange Server components.	"Optimizing Exchange Server" on page 321
Troubleshoot common problems with Exchange Server.	"Troubleshooting Common Problems" on page 322

Exchange
Server 5.5

Study Guide

This chapter includes the following sections, which address various topics covered on the Exchange Server 5.5 MCSE exam:

Exchange Server Basics
> Describes the basic features of Exchange Server 5.5, the protocols supported, and the components that make up the server.

Installing Exchange Server
> Discusses the hardware and software requirements for Exchange Server, and describes the installation process.

Configuring Exchange Server
> Covers the configuration tasks necessary to set up Exchange Server mailboxes and other types of recipients.

Managing Exchange Server
> Discusses the use of optional features, including address books, public folders, and Internet newsgroups.

Managing Connectivity
> Explains how Exchange sites can communicate with other sites and the Internet, and how to connect other email systems.

Optimization and Troubleshooting
> Describes methods of monitoring the performance and reliability of Exchange Server computers, and methods for improving performance.

Exchange Server Basics

Microsoft Exchange Server 5.5 is the latest version of Microsoft's email and groupware server, part of the BackOffice suite. Exchange Server runs under Windows NT Server, and can be used on the same machine as other BackOffice services.

Exchange Server is designed to support multiple servers. The hierarchy of servers begins with an *organization,* which can support one or more *sites* (usually corresponding to locations). Each site, in turn, can include one or more servers.

The following sections introduce the features of Exchange Server 5.5, the protocols it supports, and its underlying architecture.

Exchange Features

Microsoft Exchange Server is primarily a server for electronic mail (email), although it also supports discussion groups (newsgroups) and collaboration features. The most important Exchange features are described in the sections below.

Electronic Mail

Email has become ubiquitous in most companies, and, with the rising popularity of the Internet, is now used by a great many individuals. Microsoft Exchange allows you to create mailboxes for the users of a Windows NT network, supports mail clients, and supports message delivery to other servers, whether running Exchange or not.

Exchange is a client/server system. The Exchange Server runs on a Windows NT Server computer, and users run client software. Outlook 97, included with Exchange Server, is the preferred client; however, any mail client that supports the Internet-standard SMTP, POP3, and IMAP4 protocols can be used. This allows even clients on UNIX and Macintosh systems to send and receive mail through Exchange.

Connectivity

Along with the ability to accept connections from clients to read and send mail, Exchange Server can connect with other servers to transport mail. In addition to other Exchange servers, Internet-standard servers are supported.

Exchange also includes software add-ons called *connectors* to support foreign email systems. Exchange Server 5.5 includes connectors for Microsoft Mail, X.400, Lotus cc:Mail, and Lotus Notes.

Group Scheduling

Outlook, Microsoft's client for Exchange, supports scheduling features along with email. These features are integrated with email and supported by the server. Users can manage schedules for other users, schedule appointments, and send email messages that query a user and add an item to a schedule.

Public Folders

Exchange supports public folders, which are used to store messages or other files. Public folders are accessible to all Exchange users. This provides a method of distributing messages or other information to Exchange users. Public folders can be replicated to other Exchange servers or sites.

Integration with IIS

Exchange can work with IIS 3.0 (with Active Server Pages installed) or IIS 4.0 to allow Exchange client access over the Web. This feature is called Outlook Web Access. Most browsers are supported, and security features are implemented to prevent unauthorized access.

Directory Services

Exchange Server maintains a directory of users with mailboxes, with a wide variety of information fields that can be specified for each user. This information is used by the server to route messages, and can also be accessed by clients using the LDAP (Lightweight Directory Access Protocol) protocol.

Discussion Groups

Exchange also acts as a server for *newsgroups*, or discussion groups. These are public message bases shared across a number of services on the Internet; the USENET newsgroup hierarchy contains many of the most popular groups. You can also create newsgroups for local use.

News messages, called *articles*, are transferred between servers using the NNTP (Net News Transfer Protocol) protocol. This protocol is also used for communication between news clients and servers. The Outlook client included with Exchange Server also supports reading and posting articles in newsgroups.

Exchange Server uses a public folder to store newsgroups, and makes the contents available both to Outlook (which reads the public folder) and to other news clients, which access the public folder contents via NNTP.

On the Exam

Since the newsgroup articles are accessible to all users of Exchange, they are stored in a folder called Internet Newsgroups within the Public Folders storage area.

Mail Server Protocols

Exchange Server and its client software support a number of protocols, most based on Internet standards. The following sections describe the protocols commonly used with Exchange.

On the Exam

You should know the purpose and features of each of these protocols for the Exchange Server MCSE exam. You should also know how to configure them in Exchange Server, as described later in this chapter.

SMTP

SMTP (Simple Mail Transport Protocol) is an Internet-standard protocol used for transferring mail between servers and for posting messages from clients. SMTP uses a simple set of commands, and can be implemented with a relatively simple server. Exchange Server 5.5 supports SMTP with the Internet Mail Service component.

POP3

POP (Post Office Protocol) version 3 is a standard protocol for client/server email systems. A POP3-compatible client can use this protocol to download and read messages from an Exchange mailbox. POP3 does not support the sending of messages; this is accomplished with SMTP.

IMAP4

IMAP (Internet Message Access Protocol), defined in RFC 2060, is a more recent protocol for communication between mail clients and servers. IMAP4 can be used in place of POP3, and supports a number of more sophisticated features, including the ability to access public folders.

MIME

The SMTP and POP3 mail transport protocols were designed to work with messages written in plain ASCII text, and this is still the most popular format for messages. However, it is sometimes useful to use other text formats (such as HTML) or to send binary files through email.

MIME (Multipurpose Internet Mail Extensions) is a standard that specifies methods of encapsulating non-ASCII content in mail messages, while remaining compatible with the standard mail transport protocols. Documents sent using this standard are marked with a *MIME type*, such as text/html, that specifies their content.

Exchange supports the use of MIME both in supporting rich message formats (HTML and rich text) and to allow binary files to be sent as attachments with mail messages.

LDAP

LDAP (Lightweight Directory Access Protocol) is a standard protocol for servers that store directory information (users' names, addresses, and other details). Using this protocol, clients can access the information maintained by Exchange Server's directory services.

NNTP

NNTP (Net News Transfer Protocol) is an Internet-standard protocol for the transport of newsgroup articles. This protocol is used to maintain newsfeeds by transferring articles from server to server, and is used between clients and servers to read and post messages.

Although primarily used as an email server, Exchange can also receive one or more newsfeeds, send newsfeeds to other servers, and allow clients to read or post messages using NNTP. The Outlook client supplied with Exchange supports these features.

HTTP

HTTP (Hypertext Transfer Protocol) is the protocol used by World Wide Web (WWW) servers. This protocol allows clients using web browsers to view hypertext (HTML) documents, or to download and view virtually any type of document.

While Exchange Server is not a web server and does not support HTTP, it does support the use of HTTP if used in conjunction with IIS (Internet Information Server) 3.0 or 4.0. This allows you to use Web-based tools, such as the Outlook Web Access client, to read or send mail messages or newsgroup articles.

The Outlook Web Access client is implemented using Active Server Pages (ASP), a server-side scripting architecture included with IIS 4.0. IIS 3.0 requires the ASP add-on, available from Microsoft, to work with Outlook.

On the Exam

You do not need to know the exact workings of IIS for the Exchange Server MCSE exam. For information on installing and using IIS, see Part 2, *Internet Information Server 4.0*, of this book.

Exchange Server Components

Exchange Server 5.5 consists of a number of individual services and components. The core Exchange components include the information store, the system attendant, the directory service, and the message transfer agent. These and a number of optional components are described in the following sections.

On the Exam

You should be familiar with the function of each of these components, and how the components communicate with each other, for the Exchange Server MCSE exam.

The Information Store

Exchange Server handles quite a bit of data: all of the messages in user mailboxes and the messages, newsgroups, and files in public folders. All of this information is stored in a database called the *information store*.

The Exchange information store is divided into two sections: the public information store, which stores the public folders, and the private information store, which stores the user mailboxes and their contents.

System Attendant

The System Attendant service is a Windows NT service that runs continuously after the installation of Exchange Server. This service monitors the operation of Exchange Server and performs a number of maintenance tasks. These include the following:

- Creates email addresses to correspond with new user mailboxes.

- Monitors directory replication and the connection services and verifies that they are operating correctly.

- Maintains routing tables for message transfer between Exchange servers.

- Helps deliver messages by resolving custom recipient addresses and forwarding distribution list messages to the server responsible for expanding them into a list of recipients.

- Gathers information for server and link monitors (described later in this chapter).

The System Attendant service runs whenever Exchange is started, and is required for the other Exchange services. Stopping this service will also cause the other Exchange services to stop.

In the Real World

Stopping the System Attendant service manually from the Services control panel shuts down the Exchange services in much less time than a regular system shutdown. This is useful for quickly restarting the server.

The Directory Service

The Exchange Server directory service maintains a database (the directory) that stores information about each of the users, mail recipients, public folders, distribution lists, and other Exchange objects. The directory can be queried using LDAP (Lightweight Directory Access Protocol).

The directory is based on the X.500 standard, and is replicated between all of the servers in a site. The X.500 standard uses a hierarchical structure of container objects (organizations and sites) and leaf objects (servers, user mailboxes, and other items).

The directory service maintains the directory database, makes it available to LDAP queries, and manages directory replication between servers.

Message Transfer Agent (MTA)

The Message Transfer Agent (MTA) handles the routing of messages between the Exchange server and other servers. These include other Exchange servers in the same site, Exchange servers in other sites, and gateways to non-Exchange sites (such as the Internet).

The MTA communicates with MTAs on other Exchange servers, using special email messages, to exchange new messages and update public folders. It also works with connectors, described later in this section, to communicate with external email systems. The MTA also performs distribution list expansion, sending a message to each member of the list.

The MTA maintains *associations* between servers in the same site. These are connections that use RPC (Remote Procedure Calls) for communication. Associations can be one-way or two-way connections, and multiple connections can be open to the same server if there is high message traffic.

Internet Mail Service

The Internet Mail Service handles SMTP (Simple Mail Transport Protocol). This service communicates with Internet email systems and other SMTP-compatible systems to transport messages. Clients also communicate with this service to send messages.

Internet News Service (INS)

The Internet News Service (INS) handles Exchange Server's support for newsgroups. This service uses NNTP (Net News Transfer Protocol) to communicate with other news servers. Clients also communicate with this service to read or post articles.

Connectors

Connectors are special software components that handle the exchange of messages between the Exchange Server site and other sites running Exchange or foreign mail systems. The following connectors are included with Exchange Server:

Site Connector
Handles the transmission of messages between Microsoft Exchange Server sites in the same organization.

Microsoft Mail Connector
Handles communication with Microsoft's earlier email products: MS Mail for PC Networks and MS Mail for AppleTalk Networks.

X.400 Connector
Transfers messages and directory information between Exchange Server and any server that supports the X.400 standard. This connector can also be used to connect two sites running Exchange Server if the connection is too slow or unstable to support the site connector (such as a WAN link).

cc:Mail Connector
Handles messaging between Exchange and Lotus cc:Mail mail systems. Different versions of this connector are available for versions 6.0 and 8.0 of the cc:Mail database.

Dynamic RAS Connector
> Handles message transport between the Exchange system and a remote system accessible by modem, such as an Internet service provider. This uses RAS (Remote Access Service), included with NT Server.

Microsoft Schedule+ Free/Busy Connector
> This connector, installed by default with the Exchange Server installation, allows the scheduling functions of Exchange and Outlook to interface with Microsoft's earlier groupware product, Schedule+.

Web Access Components

Exchange 5.5 allows web browsers to act as mail clients. This feature is provided by the Outlook Web Access component, which can be selected for installation during the Exchange installation process. Web clients can access email messages and information in the public folders.

New Features in Version 5.5

Exchange Server 5.5, released in 1998, is a major update to the previous version, version 5.0. The major changes in the server and client components of Exchange are described in the sections below.

Server Features

The improvements in version 5.5 of Exchange Server include the following:

- A new database structure. While previous versions of Exchange were limited to a total of 16 GB for the storage of mail messages and private and public folders, the new version is limited only by the constraints of the Windows NT computer it is installed on. The new structure also allows deleted messages and other items to be recovered.

- Support for revision 1 of IMAP4 (Internet Message Access Protocol).

- Extended support for LDAP (Lightweight Directory Access Protocol); directory entries can now be changed as well as read.

- A new scripting engine, Exchange Scripting, which supports interactive applications within public folders.

- The Address Book feature now supports security measures to prevent users from viewing address books without proper access. Offline address books are also supported for dial-up users.

- Support for redundant servers with Microsoft Cluster Server.

- The Exchange Chat Service supports real-time conversations between users.

- A MIB (Management Information Base) is included to allow Exchange Server to be monitored using SNMP.

Client Features

Previous versions of Exchange included a dedicated client called the Exchange Client. In version 5.5, this client has been replaced with Outlook version 8.0, also known as Outlook 97. Outlook 97 is also part of the Microsoft Office suite, and supports email, newsgroups, scheduling, and contact management. The latest version, Outlook 98, will also work with Exchange.

Installing Exchange Server

Exchange Server 5.5 can be installed on any computer running Windows NT Server 4.0. Windows NT Workstation is not supported. The following sections describe the process of planning an installation of Exchange Server, and the installation process itself.

Planning the Installation

While the Exchange installation process is simple, you should carefully plan the way it will be used before installation. This includes planning the organization and site, setting up addressing and naming schemes, and verifying that the server meets the necessary hardware and software requirements.

Planning the Site

Before installing Exchange Server, you should document the existing network and decide how Exchange will fit into it. The following considerations are important:

- *Locations:* If the organization has multiple locations, you may wish to install a separate Exchange Server for each location. Alternately, clients at small locations can access the central Exchange Server, assuming a WAN connection is available.

- *Windows NT domains:* The arrangement of Exchange Servers in the network depends on the existing Windows NT domain structure. It is logical to use at least one Exchange Server per domain.

- *Communication between sites:* If you will be using multiple Exchange Server sites, determine whether the site connector or the X.400 connector will be used to connect the sites. These are explained in detail in "Managing Connectivity," later in this chapter.

- *Existing mail systems:* If an email system is already in operation, you should consider how it will work with Exchange before installation. You may be able to migrate to Exchange and eliminate the old system. Exchange also supports a number of systems through connectors, so you may be able to leave the existing system in place and arrange message transfer with Exchange.

- *Mail clients:* If a mail client is already installed on a number of workstations, you should verify that it will work with the new Exchange Server, or plan a strategy for upgrading clients to Outlook.

- *Security and fault tolerance:* Consider how the Exchange Server services will be secured from unauthorized access. Also plan to implement a backup system and a disaster recovery plan.

On the Exam

You should understand how to plan and organize multiple Windows NT domains for the Exchange Server MCSE exam. This information is covered in the Windows NT Server in the Enterprise section of *MCSE: The Core Exams in a Nutshell.*

Planning Addressing and Naming Schemes

As another aspect of planning, you should consider how to format the email addresses used in the company, and the naming conventions to be used when setting up user mailboxes.

If you are already using a standard naming scheme, such as first initial and last name, for Windows NT user names, this can be used for email addresses. You can set the options in the Exchange Administrator utility, described later in this chapter, to automatically format addresses based on this system.

If your naming scheme for user names is not consistent, you may want to use a different scheme for email addresses, or change the user names to fit a consistent naming scheme. A consistent scheme makes an administrator's job easier; additionally, users will be able to send email without having to look up a user's address.

In addition to the format of email addresses, you should plan how to specify names, phone numbers, and other information in the Exchange directory in a consistent form. This makes the directory feature of Exchange Server more useful.

Hardware Requirements

The basic hardware requirements for Exchange Server are slightly steeper than those of Windows NT Server. Table 5-1 summarizes the hardware requirements for Intel-based and RISC-based Windows NT systems.

Table 5-1: Exchange Server 5.5 Hardware Requirements

Item	Requirement (Intel)	Requirement (RISC)
RAM	24 MB (32 MB recommended)	32 MB (48 MB recommended)
CPU	Pentium 90 (Pentium 166 or faster recommended)	Alpha 4/275 (Alpha 5/500 or better recommended)
Disk storage	250 MB	250 MB

In addition to 250 MB of disk storage for Exchange Server components and data storage, Microsoft recommends increasing the size of the Windows NT paging file to a minimum of 50 MB more than the amount of physical RAM; this may require additional disk storage.

Software Requirements

Exchange Server 5.5 requires Windows NT Server 4.0 or later. In addition, NT Server Service Pack 3 (SP3) must be installed. The TCP/IP protocol should be installed and configured if you plan to use Internet mail features. Certain Exchange Server features have additional requirements:

Outlook Web Access
Requires Internet Information Server (IIS) 3.0 or 4.0 and the TCP/IP protocol. This feature also requires NT Service Pack 4 (SP4) or the latest hot fixes from Microsoft. If using IIS 3.0, Active Server Pages (ASP) is required.

MS Mail Connector (AppleTalk)
Requires that Services for Macintosh (SFM) be installed. SFM is included with NT Server 4.0.

Key Management Server (advanced security)
Requires Microsoft Certificate server (part of the NT 4.0 Option Pack, which includes IIS 4.0).

The Installation Process

The installation program for Exchange Server 5.5 is located in the \SERVER\SETUP\I386 directory in the installation directory or downloaded distribution. To start the installation, run the SETUP.EXE program. Follow these steps to complete the installation:

1. The license agreement for Exchange Server is displayed. Click the Accept button to continue.

2. Choose an installation option: *Typical, Complete/Custom,* or *Minimal.* Choose the *Custom* option to display all of the optional choices during the installation.

3. If you chose the *Custom* option, you are prompted to choose the components to install. These include Exchange Server, the Exchange Administrator utility, the online documentation, and the optional Outlook Web Access components. After selecting components, press the Continue button.

4. A message is displayed describing the licensing scheme for Exchange, as explained earlier in this section. Select the *I agree* option and press OK to continue.

5. Choose whether to create a new Exchange site or add the server to an existing site. For an existing site, specify the name of an Exchange server within the site that is currently online. For a new site, choose an organization name and site name.

6. If you are creating a new site, you are prompted for a user account to use for Exchange's services. This account will be granted a number of rights, and should be carefully secured; use of the Administrator account should be avoided. Specify an account name and password.

7. The Exchange Server files are now copied to the server; this process takes several minutes.

8. You are prompted to run the Exchange Optimizer utility. You can run the utility now, or later through the Start menu. This utility is described in "Optimizing Exchange Server" at the end of this chapter.

On the Exam

You should be familiar with all of the steps in the installation process for the Exchange Server MCSE exam; however, you do not need to know the exact order of steps.

Upgrading Previous Versions

The Exchange Server 5.5 setup program automatically detects a previous version of Exchange and offers upgrade options. When upgrading from Exchange 5.0, two options are available:

Standard Database Upgrade

Converts the existing database files to version 5.5 format directly.

Fault Tolerant Upgrade

Converts each database file by making a backup copy, then converting the backup copy. This prevents data loss if the installation is not completed successfully.

On the Exam

The fault tolerant option has less chance of data loss, but is no substitute for a backup. You should back up all data files before upgrading any Exchange Server installation.

When upgrading from Exchange 4.0, the fault tolerant option is not available. If you are upgrading a single Exchange Server from version 4.0, the setup program can be used to perform a standard upgrade directly. If you prefer a fault tolerant upgrade, you must first upgrade to Exchange Server 5.0, then upgrade to Exchange Server 5.5.

If you are upgrading multiple servers from Exchange 4.0, Microsoft recommends upgrading all of the servers with Exchange Server 4.0 Service Pack 2 before upgrading any servers to Exchange Server 5.5. This prevents possible conflicts in the data formats between servers. Service Pack 2 is available for download from *http://backoffice.microsoft.com/*.

An alternate method of upgrading multiple servers from Exchange 4.0 is to first upgrade the directory replication bridgehead servers (servers that are configured to replicate directory information) in each site to Exchange 5.5. After this server is upgraded and has had time to replicate the directory, the other Exchange 4.0 servers should be restarted. They can then be upgraded in any order.

Migrating to Exchange Server

If your existing email system is running software other than Microsoft Exchange, you can configure Exchange to communicate with it; you can also convert to Microsoft Exchange. This process, called *migration*, moves mailbox names, addresses, and other data to the Exchange server. For some systems, scheduling information and public folders can also be imported. Exchange Server includes support for migration from a variety of popular email systems.

Three tools for migrating other email systems are included with Exchange Server 5.5:

Source Extractors

These are custom programs that convert the existing data to a format suitable for migration. Exchange includes source extractors for some systems; others may be available from third parties. Source extractors are often designed to run on the existing system (such as a mainframe system).

Migration Wizard

This utility is available from the Microsoft Exchange menu under the Start menu after installing Exchange Server. It can directly convert files from some PC-based systems, and can read migration files created by a source extractor.

Directory Import

This feature is available from the Tools menu of the Exchange Administrator utility (described later in this chapter) and can import mailbox information formatted as a text file.

On the Exam

Exchange Server can also work together with many older email systems using connectors, described in "Managing Connectivity," later in this chapter.

Table 5-2 lists the systems supported for migration by Exchange Server 5.5, the versions supported, and the method of migration.

Table 5-2: Exchange Server Migration Support

System	Versions	Migration Method
Microsoft Mail (MS Mail) for PC Networks	Version 3.x	Migration wizard
Microsoft Mail for Apple-Talk (MacMail)	Version 3.x	Source extractor
Lotus cc:Mail	5.0 and later (Database versions DB6 and DB8)	Migration wizard
Verimation MEMO MVS	Version 3.2.1	Source extractor
IBM PROFS (Professional Office System)	all	Source extractor
Digital All-in-1	Version 2.3 or later	Source extractor
Novell GroupWise	Version 4.1x	Migration wizard
Collabra Share	Version 1.x or 2.x	Migration wizard

On the Exam

For the Exchange Server MCSE exam, you should understand the migration options available with Exchange Server 5.5 and know how to use the migration wizard with common systems, as described in the next sections.

Migrating from MS Mail

There are two basic methods for migrating from MS Mail for PC Networks to Exchange: the *one-step method*, which converts all files in one process, and the *two-step method*, which creates a user list and then allows you to migrate files later using the list.

For either of these methods, the Migration Wizard is used. To start the wizard, select *Migration Wizard* from the Microsoft Exchange menu under the Start menu. Follow these steps:

1. The wizard prompts you for the system to migrate from. Choose the *Migrate from MS Mail for PC Networks* option.

2. Specify the path for the MS Mail post office, and the mail administrator account name and password.

3. Choose one-step or two-step migration. The one-step option migrates the files immediately; the two-step option allows you to choose one of the two steps (create a user list file, or import users).

4. Choose how to migrate private files for users. These can be migrated to the Exchange server's private information store, or to .PST files that can be used by clients directly. The latter option is useful if the Exchange server will not be immediately available to clients.

5. Choose the MS Mail components to migrate. The options include information to create mailboxes, private email messages, shared (public) folders, personal address books, and schedule information. For mail messages, you can choose to migrate all messages, or those in a specified date range.

6. A list of users of the MS Mail system is displayed. Select the accounts to be migrated to Exchange, or use Select All to select all accounts.

7. Specify the name of an Exchange server to create the new mailboxes on.

8. Choose the default access permissions for shared data moved to public folders. This can be modified later using Exchange Administrator or Outlook.

9. Choose a directory container (usually Recipients) on the Exchange server to store the new mailboxes. You can also specify an existing mailbox to be used as a template; fields not included in the information from MS Mail will be copied from the template mailbox.

10. Choose whether to automatically create Windows NT accounts for the new mailboxes. If you choose to create accounts, specify the Windows NT domain and specify whether to assign random passwords or use the user's alias as a password.

11. If you chose the one-step migration option, the migration process now begins; this may take several minutes or longer depending on the amount of data.

On the Exam

If possible, you should have experience migrating an MS Mail network to Exchange for the Exchange Server MCSE exam.

Migrating from cc:Mail

Lotus cc:Mail can also be migrated using the Migration Wizard. One-step and two-step migrations are supported. For the two-step migration, a set of migration files are created in the first step. These can be used later with the Migration Wizard's *Import Migration Files* option.

The steps for migrating from cc:Mail are the same as the steps listed above for MS Mail, with minor exceptions. The main difference is that three categories of information can be migrated: information to create mailboxes, private email messages, and bulletin board information.

On the Exam

For information about migrating other email systems and using source extractors, see the documentation included with Exchange Server.

Removing Exchange Server Components

To remove Exchange Server or modify the list of installed components, run the SETUP.EXE program a second time. Choose one of the following options:

Add/Remove
> Displays the component selection dialog and allows you to add or remove components from the list.

Reinstall
> Repeats the installation process without prompting you for a choice of components. This is useful for replacing files that may be missing or corrupted.

Remove All
> Removes Exchange Server and all of its components completely. Be sure you have backed up any mail messages or public folders in use before using this option.

Configuring Exchange Server

After installing Exchange Server, a number of configuration tasks are necessary before the server can be used; at a minimum, you will need to create mailboxes for each of the users who require them, and install mail client software. The following sections discuss these and other email configuration tasks.

The Exchange Administrator Utility

After Exchange Server is installed, the Exchange Administrator utility is available in the Microsoft Exchange program group under the Start menu. This utility is shown in Figure 5-1. The left pane of the window is a hierarchical display of the

Exchange directory, with the organization name at the root. The right pane displays the contents of the currently selected object.

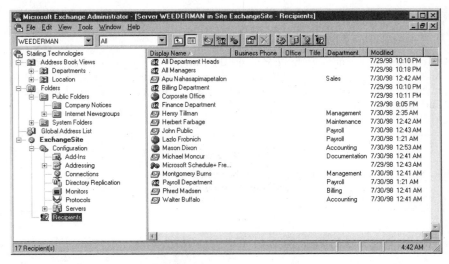

Figure 5-1: The Exchange Administrator utility

The following objects are included under the organization in the left pane:

Address Book Views
  Contains optional address book views, which allow a particular group of users to be displayed in an address book format.

Folders
  Contains two subfolders: Public Folders, used to store shared information, and System Folders, used internally by Exchange for data storage.

Global Address List
  This folder lists all of the mail addresses (mailboxes, custom recipients, and distribution lists) available in the organization, regardless of the folder they are contained in.

Configuration
  Contains a number of subfolders used to store and manage Exchange configuration information.

Recipients
  Contains mailboxes and custom recipients (links to other email systems) that can receive mail. A single Recipients folder is available by default; you can create other folders to subdivide the list of recipients.

The Options command under the Tools menu allows you to define several default options for the Exchange Administrator utility; you should examine these options, as some may need to be changed before configuring users. The Options dialog includes three tabbed categories, described in the sections below.

Auto Naming

When you create a mailbox, you specify a user's name as well as a display name, used in the Exchange client display, and an alias name, which can be used for addressing mail. The options in the Auto Naming tab allow you to configure these names to be automatically generated.

For the display name, you can select from a number of predefined formats that combine the first name, last name, and initials. The *Custom* option allows you to specify a format yourself using the codes %First, %Last, and %Initials, each of which is replaced by its corresponding field. You can also include a number to use part of a name; for example, %1Last represents the first character of the last name.

The alias name includes a number of similar options, typically with a name and initial (such as JohnS or JSmith). You can use the *Custom* option to specify the format using the same codes.

On the Exam

The Auto Naming feature provides a convenient way to make all display and alias names follow a convenient format. However, automatically generated names are not enforced; you can modify the alias or display names for a user at any time.

Permissions

Each Exchange mailbox or other object has a Permissions property, which allows you to specify one or more users or groups who can access or modify the object. The Permissions tab of the Options dialog includes the following default options for permissions:

Default Windows NT domain
Choose the Windows NT domain that will be used by default when you add users to an object's Permissions property.

Select user accounts from
When you create a user mailbox, you will be asked to specify a Windows NT user account that corresponds to the user. This option allows you to select whether the default domain (specified above) or the Exchange Server's domain is used to select this user account from.

Show Permissions page for all objects
By default, the Permissions pages of objects are hidden. Select this option to include the Permissions page in all Properties dialogs.

Display rights for roles on Permissions page
When you add a user with permissions for an object, you can select a role indicating the type of permission (for example, a full administrator, or a user who is able to send messages for another user). If this option is displayed, a

list of the specific permissions for each role is displayed, and you can create custom roles with modified permissions.

Delete primary Windows NT account when deleting mailbox
> If selected, the Windows NT account you selected to correspond with a mailbox will be deleted when you delete the mailbox. This option is disabled by default.

Try to find matching Windows NT account when creating mailbox
> If selected, the Exchange Administrator utility attempts to find the matching Windows NT account for each mailbox you create.

File Format

The Exchange Administrator utility includes a Save Window Contents command under the File menu. This saves a comma-separated ASCII list of fields for each item in the window, and is useful for exporting a list of users to a mailing list or for import into another utility. Additionally, the Directory Import and Export options under the Tools menu allow you to import or export a list of mailboxes.

The File Format tab of the Options dialog includes options that specify the file format for the Save Window Contents command, and are also used as defaults for the Directory Import and Export options. The following options are included:

Column
> Specify the character used to separate columns in the file; the default is a comma.

Quote
> Specify whether single or double quotes should be used to enclose the contents of each column.

Property
> Specify the character used to separate items in fields that support multiple entries. The default is the percent sign (%).

Character set
> Choose whether the ANSI (PC standard) or UNICODE (international standard) character set should be used in output files. ANSI is the default.

Creating User Mailboxes

To create a mailbox for a user, use the Exchange Administrator utility. Highlight the Recipients folder, and select *New Mailbox* from the File menu. The Mailbox Properties dialog, shown in Figure 5-2, is now displayed. This dialog includes a number of tabbed categories, described in the following sections.

General

The General tab includes basic information to identify the mailbox owner. The following fields are included:

Name (First, Initials, Last)
> Specify the user's first name, middle initials, and last name.

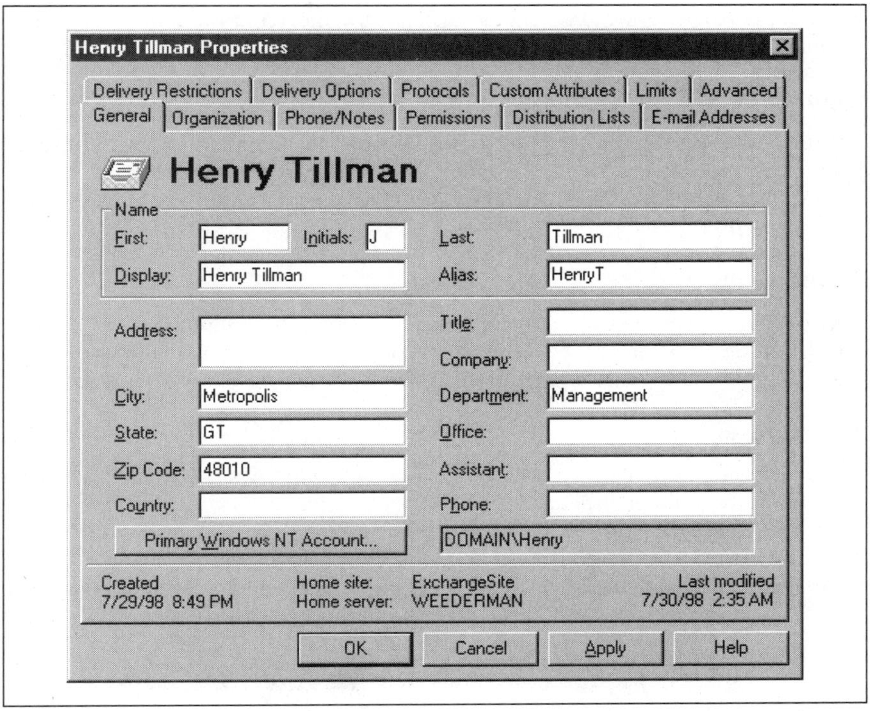

Figure 5-2: The Mailbox Properties dialog

Display

This name is used in the Exchange Administrator window and in client address books. By default, it is automatically calculated from the above name fields using the rule you specified in the Options dialog.

Alias

This is a short name that can be used to address messages or search for a user. By default, it is calculated from the name fields using the rule you specified in the Options dialog.

Address

Specify the user's postal address, city, state, zip code, and country. These fields are optional, but can be looked up by clients if specified.

Other Information

If desired, specify information for the Title, Company, Department, Office, Assistant, and Phone fields.

Primary Windows NT Account

Specify a Windows NT account to correspond with this mailbox. You can choose an existing account, or create a new account. If you create a new account, the alias name will be the default user name. The account is created automatically and given a blank password; to modify the account's properties, use the User Manager for Domains utility.

Most of the fields in this dialog are optional. The Display and Alias name fields are required. For best results, you should also specify the Windows NT account if the mailbox corresponds to a user.

Organization

The Organization tab allows you to specify optional information about how the user relates to others in the organization, for display in the address book. Specify the mailbox name of a managing user and the names of any users who report to the current user.

Phone/Notes

This tab allows you to specify a number of optional phone numbers for the user, which will be available in the address book. The Notes section at the bottom of this dialog allows you to enter a note that will also be displayed in the address book.

Permissions

The Permissions tab allows you to control which Windows NT users have rights relating to the current user mailbox. The top section displays any accounts that have inherited permissions for the object (such as the site administration account you chose during installation). The bottom section allows you to maintain a list of users with explicit permissions for this mailbox. This dialog is shown in Figure 5-3.

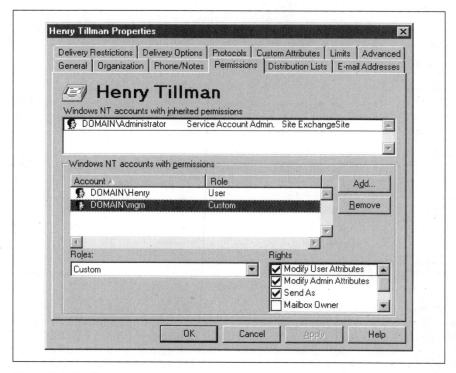

Figure 5-3: Mailbox Permissions properties

Use the Add and Remove buttons to manage the list of users with permissions, and highlight a user in the list to modify their permissions. You can select a role for each user or specify custom rights. The available rights include the following:

Modify User Attributes
> The user is allowed to modify the basic attributes of the mailbox (such as phone numbers).

Modify Admin Attributes
> The user is allowed to modify attributes of the mailbox normally accessible only by the administrator (such as the Display and Alias names).

Send As
> Allows the user to send messages using this mailbox's address as the From address.

Mailbox Owner
> Specifies that the user owns the mailbox, and is able to read and post messages using the Outlook client.

Modify Permissions
> Allows the user to modify the list of permissions for the mailbox.

Search
> Allows the user to examine this mailbox's attributes in the process of searching for a user.

These rights are organized into the following default roles:

Admin
> For administrators; includes the Modify User Attributes and Modify Admin Attributes rights.

Permissions Admin
> Includes the Modify User Attributes, Modify Admin Attributes, and Modify Permissions rights.

Search
> Includes the Search right only.

Send As
> Includes the Send As right only.

User
> Includes the Modify User Attributes, Send As, and Mailbox Owner rights. This role is assigned to the mailbox's primary user account by default.

In addition to these roles, you can select a customized list of rights if you enabled the *Display rights for roles on Permissions page* option. When you select or deselect one or more rights, the Role field is changed to Custom.

Distribution Lists

This tab allows you to make the current mailbox a member of one or more distribution lists. Distribution lists are special mail addresses that automatically send mail to all of the list members; the process of creating distribution lists is described later in this chapter.

To add the user to one or more lists, press the Modify button. A dialog displays a list of available distribution lists on the left, and the lists the current user belongs to on the right. Use the Add button to add the user to a list.

Email Addresses

This tab of the Properties dialog displays the user's email addresses for external systems (such as MS Mail and X.400). You can modify these addresses with the Edit button, or use the New button to add an additional address. These types of addresses are explained in detail in "Adding Custom Recipients" later in this chapter.

On the Exam

The Email Addresses tab of the Properties dialog are created automatically based on the name and alias information you specified in the General tab. If you modify the user's name or alias at a later time, you must manually modify these email addresses to reflect the new information.

Delivery Restrictions

The Delivery Restrictions tab of the Mailbox Properties dialog allows you to restrict the mailboxes that the current user can receive messages from. This dialog includes two sections:

Accept messages from
Choose *All*, or specify a list of addresses that the user can receive mail from. If you add a distribution list address to the list, all members of the distribution list are affected.

Reject messages from
Chose *None,* or specify a list of addresses that the user cannot receive mail from.

You can specify entries in both the Accept and Reject lists. If an address appears in both lists, messages from that address will be rejected.

Delivery Options

The Delivery Options tab of the Mailbox Properties dialog includes the following options related to message delivery:

Give send on behalf of permission to
> Allows you to specify a list of users who can send mail on behalf of the user. The mail is addressed with special headers that indicate the actual sender and the user the message was sent on behalf of.

Alternate recipient
> If desired, specify an alternate mailbox to forward this mailbox's messages to. Any address in the global address book can be specified.

Deliver messages to both recipient and alternate recipient
> If you have specified an alternate recipient, normally messages are delivered only to that recipient. Select this option to send the message to both the primary and alternate recipients.

On the Exam

The *Send On Behalf of* permission is similar to the *Send As* permission available from the Permissions tab. The difference between the two is that *Send On Behalf Of* includes a header indicating the true sender of the message. If the *Send As* permission is used, there is no indication to the recipient that the message was not sent by the actual mailbox owner.

Protocols

The Protocols tab of the Mailbox Properties dialog allows you to control the protocols that the user can use to access the mailbox. All of the protocols enabled on the server are listed here, and all are accessible by the user by default.

To prevent the user from using a protocol, double-click the protocol name and deselect the *Enable* option. The HTTP, IMAP4, LDAP, NNTP, and POP3 protocols are included in the list. The POP3, IMAP4, and NNTP protocols also allow you to specify message formatting options for the user, overriding the protocol defaults.

Custom Attributes

The Custom Attributes tab of the Mailbox Properties dialog allows you to specify values for one or more custom attributes. These can be used to specify optional information about the user for the address book. For example, you may wish to use an attribute for an employee number field.

Limits

The Limits tab of the Mailbox Properties dialog allows you to set limits on the amount of disk storage used by the user in the information store, and controls whether deleted items can be recovered. The following options are included:

Deleted item retention time
> Specifies the number of days items deleted by this user are retained, and can be recovered. Choose to use the default value, or specify a value in days. You can also choose to retain all items for this user until a backup has been performed.

Information store storage limits
> Limits the user's use of the information store. You can use the default values, or specify values in KB to perform the following actions: *Issue warning*, *Prohibit send*, and *Prohibit send and receive*.

Message sizes
> Either choose the *No Limit* option or specify a value in KB to limit the size of individual messages. Separate limits can be specified for incoming and outgoing messages.

Advanced

The Advanced tab includes a number of options that may be useful to the administrator, and may need to be changed to support some features. These include the following:

Simple display name
> A simplified version of the Display Name field. This is used by external messaging systems that cannot display the full name.

Directory name
> The name the mailbox is stored in under the directory. This value is set to the value of the Alias field by default, and cannot be changed.

Trust level

Specify a level of trust to be used in directory synchronization with other servers. If the level specified here is greater than the level specified for a server, the mailbox's information will not be sent to that server.

ILS Server

Specify an optional ILS (Internet Locator Service) server name for the user. This allows clients to determine a user's current IP address for real-time communication, such as is used with Microsoft NetMeeting.

ILS Account

If an ILS server name is specified, specify the user's account name for the server.

Home Server

Specify the server the user can log onto to receive mail. This is typically the server running Exchange server.

Hide from address book

If selected, the information for this mailbox is not displayed in the address book.

Outlook Web Access Server Name

Specify an HTTP server name for the Outlook Web Access feature.

Container Name

Displays the name of the container containing the current mailbox, typically *Recipients.* This value cannot be changed.

Downgrade high priority X.400 mail

If selected, mail sent from this user to an X.400 system will be sent at normal priority, regardless of the priority specified by the user.

Administrative note

An optional note for administrator use. This field is not included in the address book, and can be displayed only in the Exchange Administrator utility.

Adding Custom Recipients

In addition to mailboxes, you can define custom recipients under the Recipients folder. These are addresses which appear as a normal user to Exchange server clients, but actually forward mail to an address at an outside service (for example, an Internet or X.400 address).

To create a custom recipient, highlight the Recipients folder. Select *New Custom Recipient* from the File menu. You can then choose from one of the address types described in the following sections, each of which then prompts you for addressing details. After specifying the address, you are prompted for the normal Exchange mailbox properties.

The Outlook client supports *one-off addressing,* which allows users to address email to a user on an external email system without the use of a custom recipient. Therefore, you only need to create custom recipient entries for frequently-used addresses.

cc:Mail Address

Use this option for an address that delivers to a user of a connected cc:Mail post office. To create an address, specify the following fields:

Display Name
Specify a name to be used in the Exchange Administrator display and the address book.

Mailbox
Specify the mailbox name for the cc:Mail system.

Post Office
Specify the post office name for the cc:Mail system.

Microsoft Mail Address

Use this option for an address that delivers to a Microsoft Mail (PC) user. To create an address, specify the following fields:

Network name
Specify the network name for the MS Mail mailbox.

Postoffice name
Specify the post office containing the mailbox.

Mailbox name
Specify the user's mailbox name.

MacMail Address

Use this option for an address that delivers to a Microsoft Mail (Macintosh) user. To create an address, specify the following fields:

Display name
The MacMail display name for the user.

User name
The MacMail user name.

Server name
The name of the server that hosts the MacMail user.

Always send to this recipient in Microsoft Exchange rich text format
If selected, the rich text format (supported by MacMail) is used for messages to this recipient.

Internet Address

Use this option to create an address that delivers to an Internet recipient, if the server is configured to connect to the Internet. The dialog to configure an Internet address includes two tabs. The first tab, General, includes the email address field.

The Advanced tab allows you to modify the message format used for this recipient, overriding the Internet Mail Service's default settings. You can choose plain text or MIME format, and specify whether HTML messages are supported under MIME.

X.400 Address

Use this option for an address that delivers to a user of a connected X.400 system. X.400 uses a hierarchical addressing system. To create an address, specify the following fields:

Given name
> The given name (display name) of the addressee.

Common name
> The common name (username) of the recipient.

Organization
> The X.400 Organization containing the mailbox.

Organizational units
> If the X.400 directory is organized using Organizational Units, specify the container objects for the mailbox.

PRMD
> Specify the PRMD (Private Management Domain Name) if required.

ADMD
> Specify the ADMD (Administrative Management Domain Name) if required.

Country/Region
> Specify the value of the Country object, an optional container at a level above the Organization object.

In addition to these fields, the Advanced tab of this dialog allows you to define a number of optional fields. These include custom attributes, a numeric identifier, and terminal information.

On the Exam

You should not need to know the exact fields and format of X.400 addressing for the Exchange Server MCSE exam. You should be familiar with the basic fields listed above and how they can be used for communication between X.400 systems and Exchange systems.

Other Address

Use this option for email addresses that do not fit into any of the other categories. Specify an email address and the type of address. In order for messages to be delivered to this address, software that supports the address type must be installed.

Using Distribution Lists

A distribution list is a special recipient that automatically delivers messages to all of the members of the list. Distribution lists can contain mailboxes, custom recipients, and other distribution lists.

To create a distribution list, highlight the Recipients folder. Select *New Distribution List* from the File menu. The Distribution List Properties dialog, shown in Figure 5-4, is now displayed.

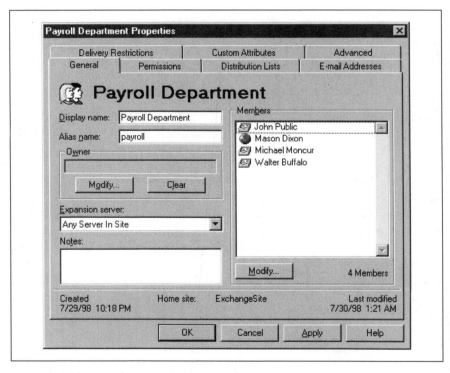

Figure 5-4: The Distribution List Properties dialog

The General tab of this dialog allows you to configure the distribution list; the remaining tabs (Permissions, Distribution Lists, E-mail Addresses, Delivery Restrictions, Custom Attributes, and Advanced) contain the same options as the corresponding tabs in the Mailbox Properties dialog. The options in the General tab include the following:

Display name
> Specify a name for the distribution list; this is the name used in the address book.

Alias name
> Specify a short name for the list.

Owner
> Select a mailbox user as the owner of the list. The owner can add or remove members from the list.

Expansion server
> If your Exchange installation includes multiple servers, specify the server that will be used to process mail sent to this list, creating separate messages for each member of the list. For large or busy lists, this process can add a significant load to the server. By default, any server in the site can be used.

Notes
> This is an optional description of the list, which is displayed in the address book.

Members
> Displays a list of the current members of the distribution list. To add to the list, press the Modify button. A dialog is displayed showing the list of available recipients on the left and the list's membership on the right. Use the Add button to add members to the list.

On the Exam

You can add also members to a distribution list using the Distribution Lists properties of a mailbox or other object; these changes are reflected in the properties of the distribution list.

Working with Client Software

The client included with Exchange Server 5.5 is Outlook 97, version 8.03. More recent versions of Outlook, such as Outlook 98, will also work as Exchange clients. The following sections describe how to install and use the Outlook client.

Hardware and Software Requirements

The full-featured client is provided for Windows 95 and Windows NT. A slightly limited version of the client is also available for Windows 3.x. Outlook should run on any machine that meets the requirements of these operating systems. Depending on the options chosen, Outlook requires between 32 and 40 MB of disk storage.

Installing Outlook

To install Outlook on a client computer, run the SETUP.EXE program on the CD-ROM or downloaded distribution. Follow these steps to complete the installation:

1. A message is displayed reminding you of Outlook's licensing requirements (note that you require a client access license for each Exchange client). Press the Continue button.

2. Enter the name and organization of the primary user of this client installation. Press OK to continue.

3. The Microsoft product identification number for the current copy of the client is displayed; keep this number for your records.

4. Choose a directory for the installation. The default is the Program Files\ Microsoft Office directory under the system drive.

5. Choose an installation option: *Typical* or *Custom*. The *Custom* option allows you to choose all components.

6. If you chose the *Custom* option, you are prompted to choose the list of components to include. Be sure the Exchange Server Support option is included.

7. The Outlook files are now copied; this may take several minutes. You do not need to restart the computer after the installation.

Reading Mail

When you run Outlook for the first time, you are prompted for the Exchange Server computer name and mailbox name. After these are specified, the main Outlook window is displayed, and shows the contents of the email Inbox. This display is shown in Figure 5-5.

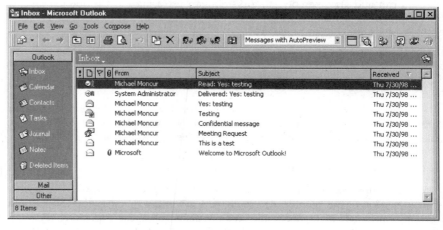

Figure 5-5: The Outlook Inbox window

The subjects of the mail messages available in the current mailbox are displayed in the right-hand portion of the window. To read a message, double-click its header. The headers are displayed in black for read messages and in blue for unread messages.

Sending Mail

To send an email message, select *New*, then *Mail Message* from the File menu. The Message tab of the mail message dialog allows you to specify the address, subject, and the body of the message. The Options tab includes a number of optional message features:

Importance
    Choose a priority level for the message: low, normal, or high. The Inbox can be configured to display high-priority messages first.

Sensitivity
    Set the message's status to Personal, Private, or Confidential, if desired.

Use voting buttons
    If selected, the message will include voting buttons, allowing the addressee to reply automatically by selecting a button. You can choose one of the predefined sets of buttons, or specify button names separated by semicolons.

Have replies sent to
    Specify a mailbox name to receive replies to this message.

Save sent message to
    Select a private folder to save a copy of the sent message. The default is the Sent Items folder.

Do not deliver before
    If desired, choose a date to allow delivery of the message. The message will be held by the server until the date arrives.

Expires after
    If desired, specify an expiration date for the message. When this date arrives, the message will be deleted if not yet read by the recipient.

Tell me when this message has been delivered
    If selected, you are sent an automatic reply when the message has been delivered to its destination mailbox. This feature is not supported by most external email systems.

Tell me when this message has been read
    If selected, you are sent an automatic reply when the recipient opens the message for reading. This feature is not supported by most external email systems. If the message was sent to multiple addresses, you will receive a separate confirmation from each address.

Categories
    If desired, specify one or more categories for the message. These can be used to filter the display of messages.

When sending a message, you can access the Address Book with the To button. The Address Book is also available from the toolbar. The Address Book dialog, shown in Figure 5-6, allows you to select addresses from the server's global address list as well as any Address Book views created on the server.

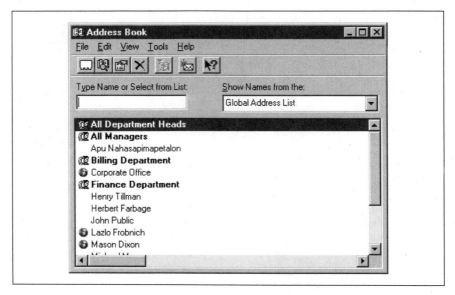

Figure 5-6: The Outlook Address Book

Public Folders and Newsgroups

Select the Public Folders icon in the left pane of the Outlook window to work with public folders. Since Exchange stores newsgroup messages in public folders, this window is also used to read and post to newsgroups.

To view a particular folder or newsgroup, click on the text, Public Folders, at the top of the window. A hierarchical view of the folders is displayed; select any folder, and its message headers are displayed in the same format as mail messages.

On the Exam

You can also create and manage public folders using Outlook. This is explained in "Configuring Public Folders," later in this chapter.

Configuring Outlook

To set options for the Outlook client, select *Options* from the Tools menu. The following categories of options are included:

General
Includes basic Outlook options, including the folder to open at startup.

Email

Allows you to configure preferences for mail messages. This includes options to alert you when new mail arrives and an option to choose whether to respond to requests to confirm delivery and reading.

Sending

Includes default settings for sent messages. These settings can be changed for an individual message in the Options tab of the message dialog, described above.

Reading

Includes settings for replying to read messages, including an option to include the original message in the reply.

Calendar

Specify preferences for the Calendar feature of Outlook.

Attachments

Choose a security method for attachments: High or None. The high-security method prevents executable content in message attachments from being automatically executed.

Delegates

Allows you to edit the list of users who have the *Send on Behalf Of* permission for your mailbox.

Manage Forms

Allows you to manage forms, which allow a more complex version of the interaction of voting buttons. You can also choose to use a web browser to read messages that contain form content not readable by Outlook.

Security

Allows you to configure options for encryption and digital signatures, if enabled at the server.

Tasks/Notes

Includes preferences for the Tasks and Notes features of Outlook.

Journal

Includes preferences for the Journal feature. You can specify that certain actions, such as email messages, are logged in the journal.

Reminders

Choose whether to display reminder dialogs for scheduled events, and whether to play a sound.

Spelling

Includes preferences for the spell-checking feature of the message editor.

AutoArchive

Allows you to specify an interval at which old items are automatically archived and deleted.

Managing Exchange Server

Exchange supports a number of features in addition to the basic email capabilities. Among these are address book management, public folders, and Internet newsgroups. The following sections describe how to manage these features.

Managing Address Book Views

The Exchange Server address book contains the names, email addresses, and other directory information for all of the users in a site. You can create one or more address book views, which allow the organization of recipients by location, department, or any other fields.

Each address book view is included in the directory under the Address Book Views container. Views, in turn, contain one or more containers. The containers are created automatically based on the values of a field you choose. For example, a view called State would automatically include containers for each of the values specified in any mailbox's State field.

Creating a View

To create an address book view, select the *Address Book Views container* in the directory display of Exchange Administrator. From the File menu, choose *New Other*, then *Address Book View*. The Properties dialog is displayed. This dialog includes four tabbed categories:

General
> Specify a Display name and Directory name for the address book view. (For example, if you were grouping users by city and state, you might call the view Locations.) You can also specify an optional administrative note (displayed only in the Exchange Administrator utility).

Group By

This page determines the grouping of recipients under the address book view, and thus determines the names of the view containers. You can select up to four fields to group by; you must choose at least one. The values of the first field will make up the first level of view containers. If you select additional fields, these will form sub-containers under the first level. The fields in the General tab of the mailbox properties dialog are included here, along with the custom properties.

Permissions

This dialog is similar to the Permissions dialog in the mailbox properties. Windows NT users with inherited permissions for the view are listed, and you can add users with specified permissions.

Advanced

The Advanced tab includes two options. *Promote entries to parent containers* lists mailboxes in both the higher-level and lower-level containers they belong to; for example, a user might be listed in the California container, and in its parent container, United States. *Show this view in the client address book* controls whether clients can see the view. This tab also includes the Remove Empty Containers button, which deletes any containers that no longer correspond to any mailbox's field value.

Creating View Containers

When you create a view that groups recipients by a field already specified in one or more mailboxes, containers are automatically created under the view corresponding to the values that have been used. (This process may take several minutes.)

You can also manually create a new view container, regardless of whether any mailboxes have the appropriate property value to appear in the container. To do this, highlight the name of the view, and open the File menu. Select *New Other*, then *Address Book View Container.*

The Properties dialog for the new view container allows you to specify a Display name and Directory name for the container. In the Group By tab, you can specify the field value that will be used to indicate members of this container; this does not have to be the same as the container name. You can also specify another field to be used to create sub-containers under this container.

Adding a Recipient to a Container

Since the address book view containers are based on mailbox property values, you can add a user mailbox or other recipient to the container by assigning the appropriate value to the appropriate field. A previously unused value in the field will create a new container.

Alternately, you can highlight one or more mailboxes and select *Add to Address Book View* from the Tools menu. The available views and containers are displayed; select the appropriate container. The field values of the mailboxes are now set to the required value for the container.

For example, suppose you have created a container called Locations that groups users by state, then by city. If you select a mailbox and choose the *Add to Address Book View* command, then select the Sacramento container under the California container, the State and City properties of the mailbox are changed to match the container.

Configuring Public Folders

As described earlier in this chapter, Public Folders are container objects under the Public Folders container in the Exchange directory. Each folder can contain one or more subfolders. Folders can also contain mail messages, newsgroup messages, or other objects.

Setting Public Folder Options

To set options for public folders, open the properties of the Information Store Site Configuration object from the Configuration folder in Exchange Administrator. This dialog allows you to configure several categories of settings for public folders.

By default, all users are allowed to create top-level folders. To modify these permissions, select the Top Level Folder Creation tab of the properties dialog. You can specify a list of users allowed to create folders, a list of users denied the right, or both.

Creating Folders

Users with the proper permissions can create top-level or lower-level public folders using the Outlook client. To create a public folder in Outlook, first open the parent folder. For a top-level folder, open the All Public Folders entry.

Next, select *New* from the File menu, then select *Folder*. The Create New Folder dialog, shown in Figure 5-7, is displayed. You are prompted for the following information about the new folder:

Name
> Choose a name for the folder. This name is included in the address book, and is visible to other users.

Folder contains
> Choose the contents of the folder: mail messages, appointments, contacts, journal entries, notes, or tasks. This value is used by Outlook to display the contents in the appropriate form.

Make this folder a subfolder of
> Verify or modify the parent folder for this folder.

Description
> Specify an optional description of the folder. This value is included in the address book, and displayed in Outlook.

Setting General Options

Once a public folder has been created in Outlook, its properties can be modified using the Exchange Administrator utility. To modify a folder, highlight it and select

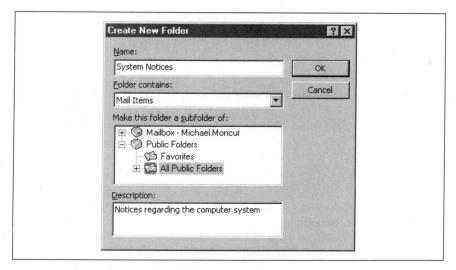

Figure 5-7: The Outlook Create New Folder dialog

Properties from the File menu. The properties dialog includes a number of tabbed categories. Some of these are the standard address book properties; the unique properties for public folders are described in this and the following sections.

The General tab of the properties dialog includes the following basic options for the folder:

Folder name
The name of the folder, originally specified when it was created.

Address book display name
Choose an optional name to identify the folder in the address book, if desired. By default, the folder name is used.

Alias name
Choose a short alias name to correspond with the folder name; by default, this is the same as the folder name.

Propagate these properties to all subfolders
If the folder contains subfolders, enable this option to copy any changes you make to the folder's properties to the subfolders.

Notes
Specify an optional description of the folder for the address book. This field contains the description entered when the folder was created.

Folder path
Displays the full path to the folder. This field cannot be modified.

Setting Client Permissions

The Client Permissions button in the General tab of the folder Properties dialog displays the Client Permissions dialog, which allows you to modify permissions for the folder. You can add mailbox users who are granted permissions with the Add button, and modify the permissions for any existing users.

You can assign permissions by selecting one of the predefined roles, or by specifying permissions manually. The following permissions are available:

Create items
> Allows the user to create mail messages or other items within the folder.

Read items
> Allows the user to view the list of messages or other items in the folder, and read them.

Create subfolders
> Allows the user to create subfolders under the current folder.

Edit items
> Specify the messages or other items that can be edited by the user: all items, only those created by the user, or none.

Folder owner
> Indicates that the user is the owner (usually, the creator) of the folder. Users with this permissions are given all other permissions by default.

Folder contact
> Specifies that the current user should be contacted for administrative needs regarding the folder (such as problems with replication).

Folder visible
> If selected, the user can see the folder in the list of public folders and in the address book.

Delete items
> Specify the messages or other items that can be deleted by the user: all items, only those created by the user, or none.

On the Exam

By default, the owner of a folder is given all permissions. Additionally, a default entry specifies permissions for any author of messages within the folder. The message author is given the Create items, Read items, and Folder visible permissions, and the right to edit and delete the author's own items, by default.

Public Folder Replication

Public folders are actually represented by two items: the folder storage area, stored on the server where the folder was created, and the public folder hierarchy, represented by objects in the directory.

Since the directory is replicated to all of the servers in a site, the hierarchy is available to all servers, and is available as a mail message destination. When a user attempts to access data in a folder, the directory is read to determine where the actual data resides, and the data is transferred.

Normally, only one copy of each public folder's contents is stored. However, this can only be accessed by servers that are directly connected with the folder's server, and support communication via remote procedure calls (RPCs).

Exchange Server supports replication for public folder contents, which must be configured manually for each replica. These replicas can be used to support servers that do not support RPC communication, to reduce the traffic on a server containing a busy folder, or to provide fault tolerance.

Setting Replication Options

Replication can be configured using several of the tabs in the public folder's Properties dialog. The first of these, Replicas, allows you to configure which servers the contents of the folder are replicated to.

To add a server for replication, highlight it in the Servers list on the left, and press the Add button to add it to the Replicate list on the right. The servers available in the current site are displayed; to display servers for another site within the organization, select the site from the pull-down menu.

The next tab of the Properties dialog is labeled Folder Replication Status. This tab displays a list of servers configured to replicate the folder contents, the time of the last synchronization with each server, and the average time used in the replication process.

The Replication Schedule tab, shown in Figure 5-8, allows you to configure the times and days when replication can occur for the folder contents. This option can also be set globally in the properties of the Information Store Site Configuration object.

For the folder, choose when to allow replication with one of these options: *Never, Always, Use Information Store Schedule,* or *Selected times.* If the last option is selected, you can specify the hours for replication in 1-hour or 15-minute increments.

Public Folder Affinity

When a client browses the folder hierarchy and attempts to open a public folder, the actual folder contents may be available from more than one server. Exchange tries the following sources in order to locate the folder contents:

- The server the client is connected to
- Any servers with RPC connections
- Any servers within the same site
- Any servers with a configured affinity

If two servers in the same category have a copy of the folder, one is chosen at random. You can configure *public folder affinity* to make folder contents accessible across site boundaries. To configure affinity, open the Configuration container in Exchange Administrator. Select the *Information Store Site Configuration* item and select *Properties* from the File menu.

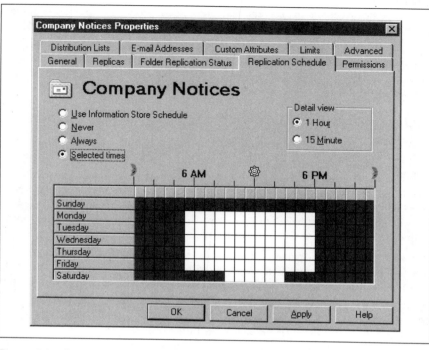

Figure 5-8: The Replication Schedule Properties dialog

This dialog allows you to add one or more sites to the list of sites with affinity. For each site, you specify a *cost* ranging from 0 to 100. Exchange uses this cost to decide which site to retrieve the folder contents from; sites with the lowest cost are tried first.

On the Exam

For the MCSE Exchange Server exam, remember that public folder contents are not replicated at all by default, that you can add replicas, and that you must configure affinity to access replicas in separate sites.

The Replication Process

The Message Transfer Agent on each server handles public folder replication. An additional service called the public folder replication agent (PFRA) monitors the replication process. The PFRA also monitors changes to objects in folders and maintains a *change number* for the folder replica.

The PFRA periodically compares the change numbers on local replicas and compares them with the change numbers for the corresponding replicas on other servers. If the numbers don't match, the PFRA sends a *backfill request* message to another server. The server responds by sending a new copy of the replica. Servers are contacted for backfill using the same rules as for client access.

Configuring Newsgroups

Exchange Server supports USENET and other Internet newsgroups as part of the Public Folders hierarchy. Newsgroups are stored in the Internet Newsgroups folder; folders are created under this folder to correspond to the hierarchy of newsgroup names. For example, the *alt.test* newsgroup would be stored in the *test* folder under the *alt* folder under the Internet Newsgroups folder.

Creating a Newsfeed

Before using Internet newsgroups, you must configure a newsfeed. This uses NNTP (Net News Transfer Protocol) to transfer newsgroup articles from another server. Articles can be received from an Exchange server or an Internet server, using a LAN or dial-up connection.

On the Exam

Before configuring a newsfeed, you will need to make arrangements with an Internet Service Provider or other site to distribute newsgroups to your site. Obtain the news server name, user name, and password if required, and other details from the newsgroup provider.

To configure an NNTP server, highlight the Connections container under the site's Configuration container. Select *New Other* from the File menu, then select *Newsfeed*. A Wizard prompts you for several categories of information during the setup process. Follow these steps to create a newsfeed:

1. Choose the computer running Exchange Server that will host the newsgroups. This computer should have enough available disk space to store the articles.

2. Choose the type of newsfeed: inbound and outbound, inbound only, or outbound only. Choose the inbound and outbound option to allow both reading and posting of newsgroups from your site. For inbound access, specify whether to wait for articles to be sent from the server, or to poll the server at a regular interval.

3. Choose whether to use an existing LAN connection or a dial-up networking connection to access the news server. For dial-up connections, specify the connection name, account name, and password.

4. If you chose to poll the server for new messages at a regular interval, choose the interval. The choices range from every 15 minutes to every 24 hours.

5. Choose the USENET site name of the news server you are connecting to. This is usually the same as the machine name portion of the IP address.

6. Specify the host name or IP address of the news server.

7. If the news server requires authentication, specify a name and password. If you chose to allow outbound newsfeeds, you can also choose a mailbox name to require authentication from other servers.

8. Choose a mailbox user to act as Internet news administrator. This user will be the owner of the folders containing newsgroup articles.

9. Specify the location of the active file, which lists all of the available news-groups on the news server. If you do not have this file, you can download it from the Internet provider.

Managing the Newsfeed

After the newsfeed has been created, you can manage it by selecting the news-feed in the Connections folder and selecting *Properties* from the File menu. The following categories of properties are included:

General
   Specify basic options for the newsfeed. The administrator you selected during the initial configuration can be changed here.

Messages
   Specify a size limit for incoming and outgoing messages in KB, if desired.

Hosts
   Allows you to modify the news server site and host names specified during the initial configuration.

Connection
   Allows you to modify LAN or dial-up connection options.

Security
   Allows you to modify the authentication settings for inbound and outbound servers.

Schedule
   If desired, specify a schedule when news articles can be sent or received.

Inbound
   This dialog displays the news server's active newsgroups in a hierarchy. Select a newsgroup and use the Include or Exclude buttons to control whether it is included in the newsfeed. By default, all groups are excluded.

Advanced
   This dialog includes a single option: *Mark all newsgroup messages as already delivered.* This option is useful when first connecting to a server with a large store of messages, to avoid downloading all messages.

Managing Connectivity

While Exchange Server can be used to support messaging in a single site, its greatest strength lies in the ability to communicate between sites. The following sections describe the process of communication between Exchange Server sites and between Exchange and other mail systems, and how to configure these connections.

Configuring the Site Connector

The Site Connector can be configured to allow communication between Exchange Server sites in the same organization. This is the easiest connector to configure and the fastest type of connection available between Exchange sites, with a speed about 20% greater than that of the X.400 connector (described in the next section).

The Site Connector only works between sites running Exchange Server. In addition, the sites must be able to communicate using an RPC (Remote Procedure Call) connection. Both LAN and WAN connections can be used, although some WAN connections may be too slow or may not support RPC communication.

Before attempting to use the site connector, you can verify that RPC communication is supported between the servers by using two utilities included with Exchange Server:

1. Run RPINGS.EXE on the target server. This program waits for an RPC communication and sends a reply.

2. Use the RPINGC32 *servername* command on the source server. A reply will be displayed if the RPC communication was successful.

You need to create a Site Connector for each site the local site will communicate with. To create a Site Connector, select *New Other* from the File menu in Exchange Administrator, then select *Site Connector.* You are prompted for the name of a server in the destination site.

If the destination site can be reached, the connector is created. You can then configure the connector by modifying its properties. The Site Connector has four property pages, described in the following sections.

General

The General property sheet for the Site Connector includes the following options:

Display name
  The name displayed for the connector in Exchange Administrator.

Directory name
  The name used in the directory.

Target site
  Choose the site that the connector will communicate with. If desired, multiple connectors can be configured for the same site.

Cost
  If you use multiple connectors to the same site, specify a cost ranging from 1 to 100 for each. The lowest-cost connector will be used by preference. This allows you to configure several routes between sites.

Messaging bridgehead in the local site

Choose a server in the local site to act as the main connection with the remote site, if desired. If you do not configure a bridgehead, all servers can communicate with the site.

Administrative note

An optional note displayed in Exchange Administrator.

Target Servers

The Target Servers page allows you to configure one or more specific servers in the remote site to communicate with. If the remote site uses a messaging bridgehead, you should specify that server's name here. You can also associate a cost from 1 to 100 with each target server. Servers with the lowest cost are tried first when communication with the site is needed.

Address Space

The Address Space page allows you to configure one or more partial email addresses that specify the destination site. If a message's address matches one of these entries, it is sent to the remote site. The X.400 address of the remote site is automatically added to this list.

Override

This page allows you to specify a username, password, and Windows NT domain name for an account on the remote server. Normally, the permissions of the service account on the local server are used; this setting can be used if the local service account does not have permissions on the remote server.

Configuring the X.400 Connector

The X.400 connector can be used for communication between an Exchange Server site and a remote site that supports the X.400 standard. It can also be used for communication between Exchange sites in situations where the Site Connector cannot be used.

Creating a Transport Stack

Before you create an X.400 connector, you must create an *MTA transport stack*. This is an Exchange service that allows communication with a particular protocol, and can be used with the X.400 connector or other connectors. Exchange supports the TCP/IP, X.25, and TP4 protocols.

On the Exam

Before you can create a transport stack for a protocol, you must have installed the right hardware and software to communicate using the protocol. The TCP/IP protocol is included with NT Server 4.0.

To create a transport stack, highlight the name of the server that supports the required protocol. Select *New Other* from the File menu, then select the appropriate protocol. After the connector is created, you can modify its three property sheets:

General
   Specify a name for the transport stack and addressing information for the remote site.

Permissions
   Allows you to specify a list of Windows NT user accounts to allow access to the transport stack.

Connectors
   Lists the connectors currently configured to use this stack. To add a connector, use the connector's properties.

Configuring the Connector

To add an X.400 connector, highlight the Connections container under the site's Configuration container. Select *New Other* from the File menu, then select *X.400 Connector*. You are prompted for the transport stack to use for the connector. After the connector is created, its properties can be modified. The following property sheets are available:

General
   Specify a name for the connector. Also specify an account name and password for the remote MTA. This page also includes an option to turn on word-wrap for messages transferred through the connector.

Schedule
   Choose when the connector can be used. The *Remote Initiated* option only communicates when the remote connector sends a request. You can also select *Always* or *Never*, or select the hours each day when the connector can be used.

Stack
   Specify the host name or IP address for the remote host. (One host on each X.400 system is used as a messaging bridgehead.)

Override
   Specify a name and password for the remote site, if required. You can also manage a variety of communication settings from this page.

Connected Sites
   This page is used only when connecting to other Exchange sites. Use the New button to add sites to communicate with.

Address Space
   Similar to the Address Space property sheet of the Site Connector, this allows you to specify email address types and formats that will be routed to the connector.

Delivery Restrictions
> This sheet includes two lists: Accept Messages From and Reject Messages From. You can add one or more address book entries to either list to control which users can send mail through the connector.

Advanced
> Includes a number of advanced options to control X.400 communication. You can also limit the message sizes transmitted through the connector.

On the Exam

If possible, you should have experience configuring communication between two Exchange sites using the X.400 Connector for the Exchange Server MCSE exam. You can configure sites in the local network to use this connector for experimentation.

Using the RAS Connector

The Dynamic RAS Connector, included with Exchange Server, allows communication between two Exchange sites using a dial-up connection. This works with the RAS (Remote Access Service) of Windows NT. The RAS Connector supports the use of RPC communication, similar to the Site Connector.

Before creating a RAS Connector, you should configure the Server to work with dial-up networking. This can be configured using the *Dial-Up Networking* option under the My Computer window. You should also configure the appropriate protocol for use with RAS (typically TCP/IP).

Creating a Transport Stack

Like the X.400 Connector, the RAS Connector requires a transport stack. To create the transport stack, highlight the computer in the Exchange Administrator utility. Select *New Other* from the File menu, then select *MTA Transport Stack*. Choose the *RAS MTA Transport Stack* option.

You are prompted for the dial-up networking phonebook entry to use for the connection. After the transport stack is configured, you can configure its properties. The RAS transport stack has two property sheets:

General
> Specify a name for the transport stack. You can also specify a callback phone number if the callback feature of RAS will be used.

Connectors
> Lists the connectors configured to use the transport stack.

Configuring the Connector

After creating the transport stack, you can create a RAS Connector. Highlight the Connections container and select *New Other* from the File menu, then select

---

Dynamic RAS Connector. You are prompted to choose the transport stack. After the connector is created, the following property sheets are available:

General
> Specify the remote server name, the transport stack, and the phonebook entry to use.

Permissions
> Specify one or more Windows NT accounts with permission to use the connector.

Schedule
> Similar to the Schedule page for the X.400 connector, choose the hours when the connector can be used.

RAS Override
> If the remote system is not in a trusted domain, specify a user account name and password to be used by the connector.

MTA Override
> Specify communications settings to be used between the message transfer agents.

Connected Sites
> Specify the Exchange sites that will be communicated with using this connector.

Address Space
> Specify the addressing format to be used for the connector.

Delivery Restrictions
> If desired, add one or more sites to the Accept Messages From and Reject Messages From lists.

The Directory Replication Connector

Exchange Server also includes a connector called the Directory Replication Connector. This is used to configure directory replication with other Exchange Server sites. (The directory is automatically replicated between servers in the same site.)

The Directory Replication Connector should be installed and used on both sites. Before configuring it, establish a connection between the sites and verify that the connection is functioning.

To create a connector, open the Directory Replication container in the site's Configuration container. Select *New Other* from the File menu in Exchange Administrator, and select *Directory Replication Connector.* You are prompted to choose a site for the connector, and to choose a *bridgehead server* for the local and remote sites. These are the servers that manage the directory replication process.

After the Directory Replication Connector is installed, you can modify its properties. The following property sheets are included:

General
> Allows you to specify a name for the connector, and to modify the bridgehead server and site settings.

Schedule

> Choose the times when directory replication can be performed. Specify the *Always* or *Never* options, or select the hours replication is allowed each day of the week.

Sites

> Along with the site specified in the General property page, you can add servers to the lists of inbound sites and outbound sites. The Request Now button allows you to request an immediate update from a site.

Configuring the Internet Mail Service

The Internet Mail Service allows communication with any system that supports SMTP (Simple Mail Transport Protocol), and is typically used as an Internet mail gateway. The Internet Mail Service can be used over a TCP/IP network connection, and can also use RAS.

Exchange includes a wizard to automate the installation of this service. Follow these steps to install the Internet Mail Service:

1. From Exchange Administrator, select *New Other* from the File menu, then select *Internet Mail Service.*

2. Choose an Exchange Server computer to run the service. This dialog also includes an option to allow RAS connections to be used.

3. Choose whether to use DNS to send mail. If this is selected, the server will attempt to establish an SMTP connection with the destination server for each message. If you are using an SMTP server, such as with an Internet Service Provider, select the *Route all mail through a single host* option and specify the host name or IP address.

4. Choose whether to use the service for all Internet email addresses, or for a specific set of addresses. For example, you could use the service only for mail to a particular Internet domain.

5. Specify your site address. This will be used to form Internet email addresses for users.

6. Choose an administrator (postmaster) mailbox. This mailbox will receive copies of reports when a message is undeliverable.

After these steps are performed, the Internet Mail Service is created and started. You can modify the service's settings by opening its Properties dialog. You can install only one Internet Mail Service per server within an Exchange site.

On the Exam

You should understand the purpose of the Internet Mail Service and have experience installing and configuring it for the Exchange Server MCSE exam.

Communicating with Non-Exchange Sites

Along with the connectors already described, Exchange includes a number of connectors for specific non-Exchange mail systems. These allow messages to be sent between Exchange and the other system, whether at the same site or at a remote site. Two of the most common connectors, the MS Mail connector and the Lotus cc:Mail connector, are described in the following sections.

Using the MS Mail Connector

The MS Mail Connector supports communication with an existing system using Microsoft Mail for PC Networks. An MS Mail Connector is created under the Connections container by default when Exchange Server is installed. This connector consists of three services:

MS Mail Connector Interchange
Receives messages from the Exchange system and routes them to the MS Mail Connector Postoffice.

MS Mail Connector Postoffice
A temporary storage area in the Information Store that holds messages to be sent to the MS Mail system.

MS Mail Connector MTA
A special message transfer agent that transfers messages between MS Mail and Exchange.

To configure the MS Mail Connector, open its Properties dialog. The following property sheets are available:

General
Choose a name for the connector. You can also limit the message size supported by the connector if desired.

Address Space
Similar to other connectors; specify the address formats for the connector.

Diagnostics Logging
Choose whether to log errors and diagnostic information to a file.

Interchange
Choose an administrator mailbox for the connection. You can also enable a compatibility option for MS Mail 3.x and enable message tracking, a diagnostic feature.

Local Postoffice
Specify the network name, postoffice name, and password for the MS Mail system.

Connections
Configure one or more connections to be used between the MS Mail system and the Exchange server. Connections can use LAN, X.25, or asynchronous serial communications.

Connector MTAs
Configure one or more MS Mail Connector MTAs. You can configure one MTA for each connection in use.

Directory Synchronization with MS Mail

In addition to messaging between Exchange and MS Mail, Exchange Server includes services to synchronize directory information (mail addresses, the public folder hierarchy, and other objects) with an MS Mail server. When directory synchronization is configured, all MS Mail users are configured as custom recipients in the directory.

The directory synchronization process uses two components: a *dirsync requestor* and a *dirsync server*. The Exchange Server computer can act as either one of these services, but not both. The MS Mail system acts as the other type of server. Exchange performs the following functions when configured as a requestor or server:

Dirsync requestor

This service monitors the Exchange directory and sends changes periodically to the dirsync server in the MS Mail system. It also requests information about any new or changed MS Mail accounts and makes the corresponding changes in the directory.

Dirsync server

This service waits to be contacted by a requestor in the MS Mail system. It receives updates sent regularly by the requestor, and sends information about new or changed recipients when requested.

To configure Exchange as a dirsync requestor, select *New Other* from the File menu, then select *Dirsync Requestor*. To configure a dirsync server, select *Dirsync Server* from the New Other menu. If you use Exchange as a server, you must also configure the requestor on the MS Mail system; to do this, select *Remote Dirsync Requestor* from the New Other menu.

Using the cc:Mail Connector

Lotus cc:Mail uses a file-based post office to store and deliver messages between clients. The cc:Mail Connector, included with Exchange Server, can be used to transfer messages between the cc:Mail and Exchange systems.

Like the MS Mail connector, this connector is installed by default. To configure the connector, open its Properties dialog. The following property sheets are available:

Post Office
> Specify the network path to the cc:Mail post office, and select an administrator's mailbox. You must also specify the version of the cc:Mail Import/Export service supported by the post office.

General
> Specify a name for the connector, and limit the message size if desired.

Dirsync Schedule
> The cc:Mail connector supports a form of directory synchronization, which automatically creates custom recipients in the directory for the cc:Mail users. Choose the hours when directory synchronization can be performed.

Address Space
> Specify the type and format of addresses that will be sent to the connector. By default, all cc:Mail addresses will use this connector.

Delivery Restrictions
> If desired, add one or more addresses to the Accept Messages From or Reject Messages From lists.

Import Container
> Choose the container in the Exchange directory to store the custom recipients from the cc:Mail user list.

Export Containers
> Choose one or more recipients containers in the Exchange directory. The addresses within these containers will be exported to the cc:Mail system.

Queues
> Allows you to view the current contents of the inbound and outbound queues used by the cc:Mail connector.

Diagnostics Logging
> Allows you to enable logging for error messages.

Optimization and Troubleshooting

Exchange Server 5.5 consumes a large amount of memory and system resources, and can cause a noticeable slowdown on a server. For companies with busy email systems, it's best to install Exchange on its own server. The following sections describe techniques for monitoring the performance of Exchange, and improving performance where possible.

Monitoring Server Performance

Exchange Server 5.5 includes a number of methods of monitoring current server performance, including Performance Monitor, SNMP, and Exchange Link Monitors and Server Monitors. These are discussed in the following sections.

Using Performance Monitor

The Windows NT Performance Monitor is a general-purpose utility for charting and logging system performance. The installation of Exchange Server 5.5 adds a number of counter objects to this utility; these all begin with MSExchange, and allow you to monitor the various Exchange services and protocols.

Additionally, the Microsoft Exchange menu under the Start menu includes links to a number of useful predefined Performance Monitor workspaces. Each of these opens Performance monitor with a list of counters displayed in Chart mode. The following workspaces are included:

Exchange Server Health
> This workspace, shown in Figure 5-9, includes general counters that indicate the processor time used for various Exchange services and the amount of memory paging. A high value of any of these counters indicates that the server is performing poorly, and may require an upgrade.

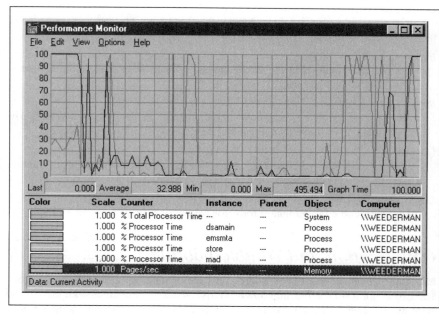

Figure 5-9: The Performance Monitor Server Health workspace

Exchange Server History
> Includes counters that measure the number of current users, the queue of jobs to be performed by the Exchange server, and the amount of memory paging.

This display updates very slowly (once every minute) so it can be used to measure long-term use of the server.

Exchange Server IMS Queues

Monitors the queues of work to be performed by the Internet Mail Service, displayed as a bar graph.

Exchange Server IMS Statistics

Measures the amount of inbound and outbound messages processed by the Internet Mail Service over time.

Exchange Server IMS Traffic

Monitors the Internet Mail Service's current connections and queues.

Exchange Server Load

Includes a variety of counters that measure the performance of Exchange, most measured in transactions per second. High values indicate heavy server usage.

Exchange Server Queues

Displays the amount of work remaining in each of Exchange Server's queues in a compact bar graph.

Exchange Server Users

Displays a single bar graph that measures the current number of connected Exchange users, scaled from 0 to 500.

On the Exam

You should be familiar with all of these workspaces for the Exchange Server MCSE exam. You should also be familiar with the individual counters used in these workspaces, and understand how to configure Performance Monitor for other options (such as creating a log file).

Using SNMP

Simple Network Management Protocol (SNMP) is an Internet standard for network and component monitoring. SNMP management agents can read information from a MIB (Management Information Base) on the computer to be monitored.

Exchange Server includes support for the MADMAN (Mail and Directory Management) MIB, a standard (specified in RFC 1566) for monitoring mail and directory servers. The same information available in the Exchange Performance Monitor counters is available through this MIB.

In the Real World

Windows NT includes a monitoring agent for SNMP, but does not include a management utility. You will need a third-party SNMP manager to monitor Windows NT or Exchange Server with SNMP.

Exchange Server 5.5

Creating a Server Monitor

Exchange Server supports monitors, special components that automatically monitor servers and connections. A Server Monitor periodically contacts one or more servers and verifies that the Exchange services are operating correctly.

To create a server monitor, highlight the Monitors container under the server's Configuration container. Select *New Other* from the File menu, then select *Server Monitor*. The Server Monitor Properties dialog includes the following tabbed categories:

General
> Specify a directory name and display name for the monitor. You can also choose a log file name, and specify the polling interval for servers.

Permissions
> Similar to other Permissions tabs, displays Windows NT users with permissions for the object.

Notification
> Allows you to specify actions to take when the monitor detects a problem. You can choose to send a mail message, launch a program, or log an error to the Windows NT Error log.

Servers
> Specify one or more servers to be monitored. Servers can be in the same site, or in another site within the organization.

Actions
> Allows the monitor to take action to attempt to resolve problems when an Exchange service is not responding. Actions include attempting to restart the service or restarting the computer. No action is taken by default.

Clock
> Allows the server monitor to check for synchronization between its clock and that of the monitored servers. If a clock is incorrect, it can be set automatically.

Creating a Link Monitor

A link monitor is similar to a server monitor, but checks for message transmission failures between servers. The link monitor sends a message periodically, and takes action if a response is not received. To create a link monitor, select New Other from the File menu, then select Link Monitor. The Properties dialog for a link monitor includes the following options:

General
> Specify a directory name and display name for the monitor. You can also choose a log file name, and specify the polling interval for servers.

Permissions
> Similar to other Permissions tabs, displays Windows NT users with permissions for the object.

Notification
>Allows you to specify actions to take when the monitor detects a problem. You can choose to send a mail message, launch a program, or log an error to the Windows NT Error log.

Servers
>Specify one or more servers to be monitored.

Recipients
>The link monitor sends mail messages to an invalid address at the servers to test their response (a bounce message should be received). Specify the address the bounce message will be sent from.

Bounce
>Specify intervals for warnings and alerts. If this interval passes without receiving a reply, notifications are sent. The defaults are 30 minutes and 60 minutes.

Optimizing Exchange Server

Exchange Server's performance largely depends on the speed and workload of the underlying Windows NT server. The following sections discuss methods of optimizing the performance of the NT server and the Exchange services.

Memory

The easiest way to improve performance in most servers is a memory upgrade. Use the Memory counters in Performance monitor to monitor memory usage. If memory is being swapped (paged) frequently, a memory upgrade would improve performance.

Disk Configuration

Since Exchange Server performs quite a bit of disk access, you can improve its performance with a faster disk configuration. You may wish to consider using a stripe set (RAID 0 or 5) to store the Exchange database, since this dramatically improves performance.

If you are setting up a computer specifically for Exchange Server, Microsoft recommends the following disk configuration:

- One drive for the Windows NT operating system and the paging file.

- One drive for the transaction log files, mirrored or regularly backed up for fault tolerance.

- A stripe set (2 or more drives) for the Exchange database and other components.

Using the Performance Optimizer

A utility called Exchange Performance Optimizer is installed with the Exchange Server 5.5 installation. This utility performs a series of checks and sets options to optimize the server. To start this utility, select *Microsoft Exchange Optimizer* from the Microsoft Exchange menu under the Start menu.

You should run the Performance Optimizer utility when the server is not in use, since it stops all Exchange services when it is run. The process of stopping services may take several minutes.

After the services are stopped, the main Exchange Performance Optimizer dialog is displayed, prompting you for information about the server. Specify these options:

Users on this server
>   Select the approximate number of users who will use this server, ranging from less than 500 to 50,000 or more.

Type of server
>   Specify the services and protocols that will be used on the server.

Users in organization
>   If you plan to install multiple servers, estimate the number of users in the entire organization, ranging from less than 100 to 500,000 or more.

Memory usage
>   If desired, select this option and specify a limit in MB to limit the memory used by Exchange Server. This may slow down the Exchange services, but will leave more memory for other services.

After you enter this information, the Performance Optimizer analyzes the disks installed in the computer and determines the best locations for the various Exchange files. You can choose to use these recommendations, or modify them.

After the changes are made, the utility finishes and restarts all of the Exchange Server services. You should verify that the server is operating correctly after running this utility.

Troubleshooting Common Problems

The following sections discuss common problems with Exchange Server installation, connectivity, client access, and mail delivery, and describe possible solutions to the problems.

Installation Problems

If the Exchange Server Setup program does not finish properly or if the Exchange server does not work after installation, check the following items:

*   Verify that the server meets the hardware and software requirements for Exchange Server 5.5.

*   If you are attempting to connect to an existing site, verify that the site is running, that you are running compatible protocols, that you have the correct rights for the remote site, and that an RPC connection is available between the sites. (Use the RPCPING utility described earlier in this chapter.)

*   Check the Event Viewer for error messages during the installation.

*   If any other applications or services are running, stop them before restarting setup. (Do not stop the IIS services, since Exchange setup looks for them.)

Connectivity Problems

If mail is not delivered properly between Exchange Server computers in the same site or different sites, or to external sites, check these items:

- For servers within a site or servers using the Site Connector, verify that RPC communication is available.

- Check for a problem with network connections or protocol settings.

- For communication between sites, verify that the Site Connector or X.400 Connector is installed and properly configured.

- Check for a problem with the Address Space configuration of a connector. An incorrect address space can prevent any messages from being delivered.

- Check the connector's scheduling options to ensure that time is available for communication.

- Use the Performance Monitor workspaces described earlier in this section to check for a network communication bottleneck.

- Use a link monitor to check the connection between the sites or servers.

Client Access Problems

If a client is unable to connect to the Exchange server and access mail or public folders, check these items:

- Verify that the correct Windows NT account has been selected for the user's mailbox.

- Check for a protocol mismatch or network communication problem.

- Verify that the client software was installed correctly.

- If using Outlook Web Access, verify that the IIS services are running and responding to requests.

Message Delivery Problems

When a message is not properly delivered to an Exchange Server computer, a non-delivery report (NDR) message is returned to the sender, and is sent to the mail administrator. This report describes the error, and usually gives you enough information to diagnose the problem.

Most Internet mail servers and non-Exchange systems also send NDRs for undelivered mail. If the NDR is not clear, the following are the most likely problems:

- The destination server is not running, or not functioning properly.

- The mail address was misspelled, or the user account no longer exists.

- A network problem exists between the source and destination servers.

Suggested Exercises

The Exchange Server exam includes questions about all aspects of Exchange Server installation and operation. You should have experience both from an administrator's point of view and from a client's point of view.

You will need at least one Windows NT Server 4.0 computer to run Exchange Server. The client can be run on the same server, although you may experience better performance installing the client on a separate computer. Ideally, you should have two Windows NT Server computers so that you can run Exchange Server on both and practice using the various Connectors.

Performing the following exercises will help you prepare for the Exchange Server MCSE exam. In addition, you should have a basic understanding of TCP/IP, covered in Part 1, *Internetworking with TCP/IP*, and an understanding of Windows NT domain administration.

1. Install Exchange Server 5.5 on a Windows NT Server computer. Be sure the computer meets the hardware and software requirements before installation.

2. Using the Exchange Administrator utility, create several user mailboxes. Create a Windows NT user account for each mailbox user.

3. Create at least one custom recipient for each address type. (Your system does not need to be configured to deliver to these systems to create addresses.)

4. Create a distribution list and add several user mailboxes to it.

5. Install the Outlook client on a Windows NT, Windows 95, or Windows 98 computer. (This can be the same computer running Exchange Server.)

6. Log on as one of the users you created a mailbox for, and run the Outlook client. Send messages to several other users and distribution lists.

7. Log on as a different user, and verify that you received the sent messages.

8. Experiment with the Calendar, Journal, Tasks, and Notes features of Outlook.

9. Create a top-level public folder using Outlook. Create several messages under the folder. Using the Exchange Administrator, modify the folder to allow all users to post messages.

10. If you have a second computer running Exchange Server, configure it to receive a replica of the public folder's contents.

11. Assign several different values to the City field for all of the mailbox users you created using Exchange Administrator. Create an Address Book View that groups users by City, and verify that several containers are created automatically.

12. Move a user to a different view container under the City view, and verify that the user's City field changes.

13. If you have access to an Internet Service Provider or other server with NNTP support, create a newsfeed. Enable two or three newsgroups from the active list, then verify that messages are downloaded. Use Outlook to read and post messages.

14. Set up two Exchange Server computers as members of different Exchange sites, and configure them to communicate using the Site Connector. Verify that messages can be sent between sites.   ·

15. Configure the computers to communicate using the X.400 connector instead. Use Performance Monitor to determine whether performance has decreased.

16. Configure directory replication between two Exchange Server computers on different sites.

17. If you have access to an Internet Service Provider or other SMTP service, install and configure the Internet Mail Service. Verify that messages can be sent to the Internet.

18. If you have access to an MS Mail or cc:Mail system, configure it to connect with Exchange.

19. Try all of the Performance Monitor views included with Exchange Server. Monitor each for a few minutes and observe the server's behavior.

20. Run the Exchange Performance Optimizer utility and follow its recommendations to optimize the server. Try several of the Performance Monitor counters again and note whether performance has improved.

Practice Test

Test Questions

1. Which of the following protocols is used by clients to send email messages?

   a. POP3

   b. IMAP4

   c. SMTP

   d. NNTP

2. Which of the following protocols are used by clients to receive email messages? (select all that apply)

   a. POP3

   b. IMAP4

   c. SMTP

   d. NNTP

3. Which protocol is used to access both mail messages and public folders?

   a. POP3

   b. IMAP4

   c. SMTP

   d. NNTP

4. Which of the following is the specification that allows HTML to be sent in email messages?

   a. POP3

   b. MIME

    c.   IMAP4

    d.   HTTP

5. Which of the following protocols is used to retrieve newsgroup articles?

    a.   HTTP

    b.   POP3

    c.   IMAP4

    d.   NNTP

6. Which of the following best describes the area used for storage of email messages?

    a.   Private information store

    b.   Public information store

    c.   Exchange database

    d.   System folder

7. Which Exchange service is required to run any other services?

    a.   Information Store

    b.   Internet Mail Service

    c.   System Attendant

    d.   Message Transfer Agent

8. Which Exchange Server component is related to the LDAP protocol?

    a.   Information Store

    b.   Directory

    c.   System Attendant

    d.   Internet News Service

9. Which of the following is not a new feature of Exchange Server 5.5?

    a.   Public Folders

    b.   Expanded database size

    c.   Exchange Scripting

    d.   Outlook client

10. What is the minimum amount of RAM required to install Exchange Server 5.5 on an Intel-based system?

    a.   16 MB

    b.   24 MB

    c.   32 MB

    d.   48 MB

*Exchange
Server 5.5*

11. You are installing Exchange Server 5.5 on a computer with a Pentium 200 processor, 32 MB of RAM, and 200 MB of free disk space. Which of the computer's specifications is below the minimum for Exchange Server?

   a. RAM

   b. Disk space

   c. Processor

   d. None of the above

12. Which of the following software must be installed in Windows NT Server before installing Exchange Server 5.5 to support Outlook Web Access and Internet connectivity? (select all that apply)

   a. Service Pack 3

   b. Internet Explorer 4.0

   c. TCP/IP protocol

   d. IIS 3.0 or 4.0

13. What is the minimum size that should be used for the paging file on a machine with 48 MB of RAM to run Exchange Server 5.5?

   a. 16 MB

   b. 48 MB

   c. 98 MB

   d. 250 MB

14. Which of the following products can be upgraded to Exchange Server 5.5 using a fault-tolerant upgrade? (select all that apply)

   a. Exchange 5.0

   b. Exchange 4.5

   c. Exchange 4.0

   d. Microsoft Mail 4.2

15. Which of the following values for the Auto Naming feature would produce an alias name of JohnS from the full name John B. Smith?

   a. %First%Initial

   b. %First%1Last

   c. %First%Last

   d. %First,%Initial(1)

16. Which of the following tabs of the mailbox properties dialog is hidden by default?

   a. General

   b. Permissions

c. Limits

d. Advanced

17. Which of the following mailbox fields are optional? (select all that apply)

　　a. Display name

　　b. Alias name

　　c. Last name

　　d. Primary Windows NT account

18. You are configuring a user to act as administrator over a mailbox and need to assign the correct permissions.

Required Result: The user should be able to modify all of the mailbox's properties.

Optional Result: The user should be able to grant permissions to other users for the mailbox.

Optional Result: The user should be able to send mail using the mailbox's address.

Solution: Assign the user the Permissions Admin role for the mailbox.

　　a. The solution meets the required result and both of the optional results.

　　b. The solution meets the required result and only one of the optional results.

　　c. The solution meets the required result only.

　　d. The solution does not meet the required result.

19. If you modify a user's Display name and Alias name properties, which of the following property categories may also require changes as a result?

　　a. Organization

　　b. Permissions

　　c. Distribution Lists

　　d. Email Addresses

20. Which of the following rights allows a user to send messages using another user's address, with no sign of the actual sender?

　　a. Send As

　　b. Send For

　　c. Send on Behalf Of

　　d. Manager

21. Which category of mailbox properties can be used to prevent a user from using the NNTP protocol?

    a.   General

    b.   Permissions

    c.   Protocols

    d.   Limits

22. Which type of external addressing uses Organizational Units?

    a.   cc:Mail

    b.   Microsoft Mail

    c.   Internet

    d.   X.400

23. In a multi-server Exchange organization, the WEST server is suffering from poor performance. After monitoring the server, you determine that much of its time is being spent dealing with distribution lists. What is the best way to alleviate this problem?

    a.   Reduce the number of members for the distribution lists

    b.   Avoid using distribution lists

    c.   Change the expansion server value for some of the lists to another server

24. What is the approximate amount of disk storage used for a full installation of Outlook?

    a.   10 MB

    b.   20 MB

    c.   40 MB

    d.   60 MB

25. Which of the following products provide full functionality as Exchange Server 5.5 clients? (select all that apply)

    a.   Outlook 8.0

    b.   Outlook Express

    c.   Exchange 5.0 Client

    d.   Microsoft Mail and News

26. Which Outlook option can be used to read messages in newsgroups?

    a.   Inbox

    b.   Newsgroups

    c.   Public Folders

    d.   Journal

27. You have created an address book view called Location, which groups addresses by the State field. The current containers under the view are AL, CA, UT, and ID. If you create a new user and specify MI for the state, which container is the new address placed in?

    a. CA

    b. No container

    c. The default container

    d. MI

28. Which of the following utilities can be used to create a top-level public folder?

    a. Exchange Administrator

    b. Outlook client

    c. Windows Explorer

    d. Services control panel

29. Which of the following servers can be used as destinations for replicating public folders? (select all that apply)

    a. Servers in the same site

    b. Servers in other sites

    c. Servers in other organizations

    d. Non-Exchange servers

30. Which of the following is the correct public folder location for articles in the comp.os.ms-windows.nt.admin.misc newsgroup?

    a. Internet Newsgroups\comp\os\ms-windows\nt\admin\misc

    b. Internet Newsgroups\comp\os.ms-windows.nt.misc

    c. Internet Newsgroups\comp.os.ms-windows.nt.misc

    d. Public Folders\comp\os\ms-windows\nt\admin\misc

31. Which of the following can be configured to send messages to a server periodically and notify an administrator if a response is not received?

    a. Performance Monitor

    b. Server Monitor

    c. Link Monitor

    d. MADMAN MIB

32. Which of the following systems requires running a source extractor to migrate to Exchange Server?

    a. Microsoft Mail for PC Networks

    b. Microsoft Mail for Macintosh Networks

    c. cc:Mail

    d. GroupWise

33. You have created a public folder called Announcements and stored several messages in the folder. Without additional configuration, which of the following are replicated to other servers within the site? (select all that apply)

    a.   The folder's name and location information

    b.   The messages in the folder

    c.   The names of subfolders under the folder

    d.   Other objects stored in the folder

34. If you are using a client connected to an Exchange Server computer that does not have a replica of a public folder's contents but is in the same site as the server containing the folder, which of the following is required to read messages in the folder?

    a.   A Directory Replication connection between servers

    b.   An RPC connection between the servers

    c.   A Site Connector connection between the servers

    d.   The messages cannot be read without a replica

35. You are trying to access the contents of a public folder, and the only replicas are stored on other sites. The WEST site is configured with an affinity score of 24, and the EAST site is configured with an affinity of 75. Which server's replica is most likely to be used?

    a.   WEST

    b.   EAST

    c.   Not enough information to determine

36. If two sites are connected by a local network, which connection method provides the best performance?

    a.   X.400 Connector

    b.   Site Connector

    c.   Internet Mail Service

    d.   RAS Connector

37. Which of the following connectors can be used with sites running software other than Exchange Server? (select all that apply)

    a.   Internet Mail Service

    b.   Site Connector

    c.   RAS Connector

    d.   X.400 Connector

38. Which of the following connectors require an MTA transport stack? (select all that apply)

    a.   Site Connector

    b.   X.400 Connector

c. RAS Connector

d. Internet Mail Service

39. Which of the following connectors uses the SMTP protocol?

    a. Internet News Service

    b. Internet Mail Service

    c. X.400 Connector

    d. Site Connector

40. To configure directory synchronization with MS Mail, which component(s) should be configured on an Exchange Server computer?

    a. Dirsync requestor

    b. Dirsync server

    c. Either requestor or server

    d. Both requestor and server

Answers to Questions

1. C. SMTP (Simple Mail Transport Protocol) is used to send messages from a client.

2. A, B. The POP3 and IMAP4 protocols support receiving messages for clients.

3. B. The IMAP4 protocol supports both mail messages and public folders.

4. B. The MIME (Multipurpose Internet Mail Extensions) specification allows HTML and other types of non-ASCII messages.

5. D. NNTP (Net News Transfer Protocol) is used to retrieve newsgroup articles.

6. A. Email messages are stored in the private information store.

7. C. The System Attendant service is required to run other Exchange services.

8. B. The Exchange Directory can be accessed using LDAP (Lightweight Directory Access Protocol).

9. A. Public Folders are not a new feature of Exchange Server 5.5.

10. B. The minimum RAM for an Intel-based system is 24 MB.

11. B. The minimum disk space required for Exchange Server is 250 MB.

12. A, C, D. This installation would require SP3, TCP/IP, and IIS. Internet Explorer (choice B) is not required.

13. C. The minimum paging file size should be the RAM amount plus 50 MB, or 98 MB.

14. A. Only Exchange 5.0 supports a fault-tolerant upgrade to Exchange 5.5.

15. B. The value should be %First%1Last, where %First represents the first name and %1Last represents the first character of the last name.

16. B. The Permissions tab of the Mailbox Properties dialog is hidden by default.

17. C, D. The Last name and Windows NT Account fields are optional; the other fields listed here are required.

18. B. The solutions meets the required result (user can modify all attributes) and only one of the optional results (user can grant permissions to other users). The Permissions Admin role includes the Modify User Attributes, Modify Admin Attributes, and Modify Permissions rights, but not the Send As right.

19. D. If you modify the Display and Alias names, the Email Addresses fields may need to be changed.

20. A. The Send As right allows messages to be sent using the mailbox's address, with no sign of the actual sender. The Send on Behalf Of right (choice C) is similar, but displays the name of the actual sender.

21. C. The Protocols property category allows you to enable or disable protocols (including NNTP) for a user.

22. D. An Organizational Unit is a component of an X.400 address.

23. C. The Expansion Server property of a distribution list specifies which server is used to deliver its mail; moving some lists to another server would alleviate the problem without loss of functionality.

24. C. A full installation of Outlook uses approximately 40 MB.

25. A. Outlook 8.0, included with Exchange Server 5.5, is the only client that provides full functionality.

26. C. Newsgroups can be accessed in Outlook through the Public Folders feature.

27. D. The new address would be placed in the MI container, which would be created automatically.

28. B. The Outlook client can be used to create a top-level (or other level) public folder.

29. A, B. Public folders can be replicated to other servers in the site, and to other sites within the organization.

30. A. The newsgroup folders are stored in a separate folder for each component of the hierarchy.

31. C. A link monitor sends messages and can notify an administrator if no response is received from the server.

32. B. Microsoft Mail for Macintosh Networks uses a source extractor for migration.

33. A, C. The folder's name and location information are replicated to all servers in the site. A subfolder is also a public folder, so its name and location are replicated. No contents of folders are replicated by default.

34. B. Reading a public folder on another server within the site requires an RPC connection.

35. A. The WEST site's replica would be used, since it has the lowest score.

36. B. The Site Connector provides the best performance.

37. A, D. The Internet Mail Service and the X.400 Connector can support sites running software other than Exchange Server.

38. B, C. The X.400 Connector and the RAS Connector require an MTA transport stack.

39. B. The SMTP protocol is supported by the Internet Mail Service.

40. C. Either the dirsync requester or dirsync server can be configured on an Exchange Server computer, but not both.

Highlighter's Index

Exchange Basics

Exchange Features
- Electronic mail
- Group scheduling
- Public folders
- Connectivity with other email systems
- Newsgroups
- LDAP directory services
- Integration with IIS
- Web Access to mail and calendar

Mail Protocols
- SMTP (Simple Mail Transport Protocol): Used to send mail
- POP3 (Post Office Protocol): Used to receive mail
- IMAP4 (Internet Message Access Protocol): Used to receive mail
- MIME (Multipurpose Internet Mail Extensions): Allows rich text and attachments
- LDAP (Lightweight Directory Access Protocol): Allows access to directory
- NNTP (Net News Transfer Protocol): Used by newsgroup clients and servers
- HTTP (Hypertext Transfer Protocol): Used for Web access to mail and schedule

Core Exchange Components
- Information Store: Stores private data (mailboxes) and public data (public folders)
- System Attendant: Monitors other services and performs maintenance tasks

Directory: Stores address book information in X.400 compatible format
Message Transfer Agent (MTA): Handles message transfers between servers

Other Components

Internet Mail Service (IMS): Supports SMTP and Internet mail transfers
Internet News Service (INS): Supports newsgroups and NNTP
Connectors: Support communication with other email systems
Web Access: Supports HTTP-based Outlook client

Version 5.5 Features

New database structure; no 16 GB limit
IMAP4 revision 1 support
Writable LDAP support
Exchange Scripting
Offline address books
Cluster Server support
Chat service
ILS Support for NetMeeting compatibility
MADMAN MIB for SNMP monitoring

Installation

Hardware Requirements

RAM (Intel): 24 MB (32 MB recommended)
RAM (RISC): 32 MB (48 MB recommended)
CPU (Intel): Pentium 90 (Pentium 166 or faster recommended)
CPU (RISC): Alpha 4/275 (Alpha 5/500 or better recommended)
Disk storage: 250 MB required; cache should be RAM + 50 MB

Software Requirements

Windows NT Server 4.0 or later
NT Server Service Pack 3 (SP3)
TCP/IP protocol for Internet features
IIS 3.0 or 4.0 for Outlook Web Access
Services for Macintosh (SFM) for MacMail
Certificate Server for advanced security

Migration

Source requestor: Converts data to migration format
Migration wizard: Migrates in one step, or reads migration files
Import/Export: Supports ASCII lists of addresses
Wizard supports MS Mail (PC), cc:Mail, GroupWise, Collabra Share

Exchange Server 5.5

Configuring Recipients

Mailbox Properties
General: Display name, alias, other details
Organization: Optional managers, direct reports
Phone/Notes: Phone numbers and notes (for address book)
Permissions: NT users with permission to modify mailbox
Distribution Lists: Lists the mailbox belongs to
Email Addresses: Addresses for non-Exchange systems
Delivery Restrictions: Restricts users who can send messages to mailbox
Delivery Options: Send on Behalf Of, Alternate recipient
Protocols: Grant user permission to use protocols
Custom Attributes: Ten administrator-defined attributes
Limits: Deleted item retention; storage and message size limits
Advanced: Advanced administrator options

Custom Recipient Types
cc:Mail Address
Microsoft Mail Address
MacMail Address
Internet Address
X.400 Address
Other Address

Distribution Lists
Forwards messages to all members of list
Can include mailboxes, folders, other lists
Properties similar to mailbox properties
Expansion server: Server that processes mail to list

Outlook Client
Runs under Windows 95/98, NT, 3.x (limited)
Requires between 32 MB and 40 MB disk storage
Includes mail, folders, calendar, journal, tasks, notes
Read newsgroups under Public Folders

Managing Exchange

Address Book Views
Grouped by one to four attributes
View containers created based on used attribute values
Moving mailbox to container changes attributes
Views available in Outlook Address Book

Public Folders

All users can create top-level folders by default
Create folders with Outlook client
Modify permissions with Exchange Administrator
Set replication options using Exchange Administrator
Hierarchy of folder names is replaced to all servers in organization
Contents can be replicated to other servers in site or other sites
Affinity: Configures replication for separate sites

Newsgroups

Stored under public folders
Create newsfeed from Exchange Administrator
Supports inbound and outbound articles
Can use LAN or dial-up connection

Connectivity

Site Connector

Allows communication between Exchange Sites
Requires RPC (Remote Procedure Call) communication
Use RPINGS and RPINGC32 utilities to verify RPC
Multiple connectors can be configured for the same site
20% faster than X.400 Connector

X.400 Connector

Used for Exchange sites or other X.400 compatible sites
Requires MTA Transport Stack (TCP/IP, X.25, or TP4)
One host on each system acts as bridgehead
Uses standard X.400 addressing

Dynamic RAS Connector

Uses RAS (Remote Access Service) dial-up connection
For other Exchange sites only
Requires RAS transport stack

Directory Replication Connector

Replicates directory between Exchange sites
Requires a connection (Site Connector, X.400, RAS)
Must be configured on both sites

Internet Mail Service

Uses SMTP (Simple Mail Transport Protocol)
Can use LAN or RAS connection
Used as Internet mail gateway or for other SMTP sites

Exchange
Server 5.5

MS Mail Connector

Supports MS Mail for PC and Macintosh
Dirsync requestor: Requests information and sends changes
Dirsync server: Receives updates and answers requests
Exchange Server can be requestor or server, not both
Other component is handled by MS Mail system

cc:Mail Connector

Supports cc:Mail database versions 6.0 and 8.0
Installed by default in Exchange Server
Imports cc:Mail users as custom recipients

Optimization

Performance Monitor Views

Exchange Server Health
Exchange Server History
Exchange Server IMS Queues
Exchange Server IMS Statistics
Exchange Server IMS Traffic
Exchange Server Load
Exchange Server Queues
Exchange Server Users

Exchange Monitors

Create under Monitors container in Exchange Administrator
Server Monitor: Monitors Exchange services
Link Monitor: Sends messages and monitors responses
Both can notify via email, launch program, or write to NT error log

Recommended Disk Configuration

One drive for Windows NT and paging file
One drive for transaction log files (mirrored if possible)
Stripe set for Exchange database and other components

Performance Optimizer

Stops all Exchange services while running
Prompts for number of users, server type
Tests disk drive speed
Recommends moving files if speed will improve

Index

<% and %> tags (HTML), 95

A
accepting email messages, 288
access restrictions (see security)
accessibility (IE4), 165, 168
accounts, email, 176
active caching (proxy servers), 212, 221
Active Desktop (Windows interface),
   161
  configuring, 174–175
Active Server Pages (ASP), 95, 98
  monitoring, 133
ActiveX components, 94, 159
  security levels for, 165
Address Resolution Protocol (see ARP)
addresses, email
  Auto Naming feature, 283
  choosing naming scheme, 275
  display for external systems, 288
  managing address book views,
    300–302
administration
  digital certificate management, 122
  Exchange Server 5.5, 281–284,
    300–308
    address book views, 300–302
    connectivity management, 267,
      308–317, 323

    creating user mailboxes, 284–291
    newsgroup configuration, 307–308
    public folder configuration,
      302–304
    public folder replication, 304–307
  FTP site operators, 113
  IIS 4.0, 98, 105–107
    file system management, 114–116
    web site operators, 109
  Index Server management, 120
  Internet Explorer (see IEAK)
  newsgroups, 130
  SMTP operators, 126
  SNMP management systems, 55
advice for taking exams, 11
affinity, public folders, 305
agents, SNMP, 55, 57
alerts for packet filter problems, 243
alias names (Exchange), 283
alternate message recipients, 289
animation feature, IE4, 169
anonymous access
  FTP connections, 113, 117
  SMTP connections, 128
  web servers, 117
<APPLET> tags (HTML), 93
applets, Java, 93, 159
  IE4 security options, 165, 171
Application layer (TCP/IP), 27

F

failing the exams, 12
fault tolerance
    Exchange Server, 278
    IIS 4.0, 101
    Proxy Server, 236
Fault Tolerant Upgrade (Exchange), 278
File properties (web server), 108
file transfer protocol (see FTP)
files
    managing file system (IIS), 114–116
    permissions (see permissions)
    saved email messages, 284
    web (see web documents)
    web documents (see documents on
        web server)
firewalls, 212
folders, configuring display of, 175
folders, public (Exchange), 267, 298
    affinity, 305
    configuring, 302–304
    PFRA (public folder replication
        agent), 306
    replicating, 304–307
        Directory Replication Connector,
           313
fonts for web documents, 164
<FORM> tags (HTML), 94
format for saved email messages, 284
forms, web-based, 94, 166
FrontPage Express, 161
FTP (file transfer protocol), 27, 90, 96,
    158
    bandwidth throttling for, 109, 133
    caching requests (web proxy), 224
    configuring services, 112–114
    file system management, 114–116
    monitoring, 133
    security, 113, 114, 117–119
    service problems, 135
    virtual servers, 116
    (see also IIS)
full-duplex protocols, 26
full installation of IE4, 163
fully qualified domain names, 41

G

gateways (IP routers), 23, 50–53
gateways (see proxy servers)
GET command (FTP), 91
GetNextRequest messages (SNMP), 56
GetRequest messages (SNMP), 56
GetResponse messages (SNMP), 56
graphics
    hiding/showing (IE4), 169
    image dithering, 170
    printing background (IE4), 171
group scheduling (Exchange), 267
guessing, 12

H

hardware
    Exchange Server requirements, 276
    IE4 requirements, 162
    IIS 4.0 requirements, 100
    Outlook client requirements
        (Exchange), 295
    Proxy Server requirements, 214
help (MCSE resources), xi
history of visited URLs, 164
H-node name resolution (NetBIOS), 43
home directory
    FTP site, settings for, 113
    NNTP service, 128, 129
    web server, settings for, 110
home page, specifying (IE4), 164
hops (intermediate nodes), 52
host headers (HTTP), 116
hostname command, 59
hosts
    DHCP (see DHCP)
    DNS for, 40–42
    host addresses, 27
        subnetting and, 28–31
        supernetting and, 31–32
        (see also IP addresses)
    name resolution, 40–50
        HOSTS file, 40
        LMHOSTS file, 49–50
        NBT for, 42–44
        WINS for, 44–49

System Attendant service, 271
system community names, 56

T

tags, HTML, 92
TCP (Transmission Control Protocol),
    26
  statistics, 58
TCP/IP exam (70-059), 6, 17–83
TCP/IP Properties dialog, 20
TCP/IP protocol suite, 20
  addresses (see IP addresses)
  DHCP, 22, 23, 25, 34–39
  installing and configuring, 20–23
  installing services, 23
  IP printing, 53–55
  IP routing, 23, 50–53
  name resolution, 40–50
    NBT for, 42–44
  optimization and troubleshooting,
    57–63
  protocols of, 24–27
  SNMP (Simple Network Management
    Protocol), 55–57
  WinSock proxy server for, 213
Telnet service, 27
TFTP (Trivial File Transfer Protocol), 27
throttling bandwidth, 109, 133
time limit for exams, 9
tips on taking exams, 11
TLDs (top-level domain names), 41
toolbar, IE4, 171
toolbars, desktop, 173
top-level domain names (TLDs), 41
tracert command (UNIX), 63
trainer (MCT) certification, 5
transaction processing with MTS, 97,
    123–124
  configuring MTS, 124
  installing MTS, 104
Transport layer (TCP/IP), 26
Trap messages (SNMP), 56
troubleshooting
  Exchange Server 5.5, 317–323
  IIS 4.0, 131–136
  Proxy Server, 244–245, 247–248
  TCP/IP performance, 57–63

Trusted Sites Zone, 165
Typical installation method (Option
    Pack), 103

U

UDP (User Datagram Protocol), 26, 58
underlining links, 169
uninstalling Internet Explorer 4.0, 172
UNIX
  print utilities, 53–55
  proxy clients, configuring, 230
upgrading Exchange Server, 277
upstream routing, 238
URLs (uniform resource locators), 90,
    158
  for add-on component page, 191
  friendly display, 168
  IE4 history of, 164
  scheduled subscription updates, 169,
    175
  searching upon failure of, 171
Usage Import and Report Writer utility,
    98
USENET (see newsgroups)
user interface, Windows
  configuring Active Desktop, 174–175
  Desktop Integration, 161
  folder display, 175
users
  accessibility (IE4), 165, 168
  authentication (see authentication)
  custom message recipients
    (Exchange), 291–294
  directory service (Exchange), 268,
    271
    consistency of information, 275
    Directory Import feature, 279
    LDAP protocol, 269
    synchronizing directories (MS
      Mail), 316
  mailboxes (see mailboxes)
  managing address book views,
    300–302
  naming (Exchange)
    Auto Naming feature, 283
    choosing scheme for, 275
    organization information, 286

About the Author

Michael Moncur is a freelance author and consultant in Salt Lake City, Utah. He is the owner of Starling Technologies, a small company specializing in network consulting and web content development. Michael is certified as both a CNE and an MCSE, and is the author of several books on NetWare, NT, and the CNE and MCSE programs, including *NT Network Security* and *CNE Study Guide for IntranetWare* (both from Sybex/Network Press), and *MCSE: The Core Exams in a Nutshell* (O'Reilly & Associates).

Colophon

Our look is the result of reader comments, our own experimentation, and feedback from distribution channels. Distinctive covers complement our distinctive approach to technical topics, breathing personality and life into potentially dry subjects.

The animal appearing on the cover of *MCSE: The Electives in a Nutshell* is an Asian elephant (*Elephas maximus*). Elephants are the world's largest terrestrial animals, striking not only for their great size (4–6 tons), but also their trunk. The trunk is used for both smell and touch, as well as for picking things up and as a snorkel when swimming. The most important use of the trunk is obtaining food and water. Another distinguishing feature is the tusks, modified incisors of durable ivory, for which man has hunted the elephant nearly to extinction. Like right- or left-handed people, elephants favor one tusk over the other.

Elephants spend most of their day—up to 17 hours—preparing and eating their food, which consists of several hundred pounds per day of bamboo, bark, grass, roots, wood, and other vegetation. They generally sleep standing up for short periods. Elephants also take frequent baths in water or mud, and, when the weather is hot, fan themselves with their ears. They can trumpet loudly, and also often make a kind of relaxed purring or rumbling noise.

The lifespan of an elephant is about 40 to 50 years, though a few live into their sixties. They have keen hearing, and can learn verbal commands, increasing their popularity as circus stars and beasts of burden. Elephants have also been used in war, mostly notably by the Carthaginian general Hannibal.

Elephant cemeteries, where old and sick elephants congregate to die, are a myth. Experiments have proved that they are not afraid of mice, but do fear rabbits and some dogs. They have no natural enemies apart from man.

Jane Ellin was the production editor for *MCSE: The Electives in a Nutshell*; Sheryl Avruch was the production manager; Nicole Gipson Arigo provided quality control; Sebastian Banker, Kimo Carter, and Amy Meterparel provided production assistance. Robert Romano created the illustrations using Adobe Photoshop 4 and Macromedia FreeHand 7. Mike Sierra provided technical support. Seth Maislin wrote the index.

Edie Freedman designed the cover of this book, using a 19th-century engraving from the Dover Pictorial Archive modified in Adobe Photoshop 4.0. The cover layout was produced with Quark XPress 3.32 using the ITC Garamond font. Whenever possible, our books use RepKover™, a durable and flexible lay-flat binding. If the page count exceeds RepKover's limit, perfect binding is used.

The inside layout was designed by Nancy Priest and implemented in FrameMaker 5.5 by Mike Sierra. The text and heading fonts are ITC Garamond Light and Garamond Book. This colophon was written by Nancy Kotary.

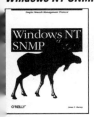
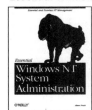

Windows NT System Administration

Windows NT Desktop Reference

By Æleen Frisch
1st Edition January 1998
64 pages, ISBN 1-56592-437-1

A hip-pocket quick reference to Windows NT commands, as well as the most useful commands from the Resource Kits. Commands are arranged in groups related to their purpose and function. Covers Windows NT 4.0.

MCSE: The Core Exams in a Nutshell

By Michael Moncur
1st Edition May 1998
424 pages, ISBN 1-56592-376-6

MCSE: The Core Exams in a Nutshell is a detailed quick reference for administrators with Windows NT experience or experience administering a different platform, such as UNIX, who want to learn what is necessary to pass the MCSE required exam portion of the MCSE certification. While no book is a substitute for real-world experience, this book will help you codify your knowledge and prepare for the exams.

Managing the Windows NT Registry

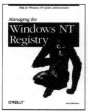

By Paul Robichaux
1st Edition April 1998
376 pages, ISBN 1-56592-378-2

The Windows NT Registry is the repository for all hardware, software, and application configuration settings. This is the system administrator's guide to maintaining, monitoring, and updating the Registry database. A "must-have" for every NT system manager or administrator, it covers what the Registry is and where it lives on disk, available tools, Registry access from programs, and Registry content.

Learning Perl on Win32 Systems

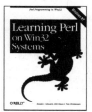

By Randal L. Schwartz,
Erik Olson & Tom Christiansen
1st Edition August 1997
306 pages, ISBN 1-56592-324-3

In this carefully paced course, leading Perl trainers and a Windows NT practitioner teach you to program in the language that promises to emerge as the scripting language of choice on NT. Based on the "llama" book, this book features tips for PC users and new, NT-specific examples, along with a foreword by Larry Wall, the creator of Perl, and Dick Hardt, the creator of Perl for Win32.

How to stay in touch with O'Reilly

1. Visit Our Award-Winning Site

http://www.oreilly.com/

★ "Top 100 Sites on the Web" —*PC Magazine*
★ "Top 5% Web sites" —*Point Communications*
★ "3-Star site" —*The McKinley Group*

Our web site contains a library of comprehensive product information (including book excerpts and tables of contents), downloadable software, background articles, interviews with technology leaders, links to relevant sites, book cover art, and more. File us in your Bookmarks or Hotlist!

2. Join Our Email Mailing Lists

New Product Releases
To receive automatic email with brief descriptions of all new O'Reilly products as they are released, send email to:
listproc@online.oreilly.com
Put the following information in the first line of your message (*not* in the Subject field):
subscribe oreilly-news

O'Reilly Events
If you'd also like us to send information about trade show events, special promotions, and other O'Reilly events, send email to:
listproc@online.oreilly.com
Put the following information in the first line of your message (*not* in the Subject field):
subscribe oreilly-events

3. Get Examples from Our Books via FTP

There are two ways to access an archive of example files from our books:

Regular FTP
* ftp to:
  ftp.oreilly.com
  (login: anonymous
  password: your email address)
* Point your web browser to:
  ftp://ftp.oreilly.com/

FTPMAIL
* Send an email message to:
  ftpmail@online.oreilly.com
  (Write "help" in the message body)

4. Contact Us via Email

order@oreilly.com
To place a book or software order online. Good for North American and international customers.

subscriptions@oreilly.com
To place an order for any of our newsletters or periodicals.

books@oreilly.com
General questions about any of our books.

software@oreilly.com
For general questions and product information about our software. Check out O'Reilly Software Online at **http://software.oreilly.com/** for software and technical support information. Registered O'Reilly software users send your questions to:
website-support@oreilly.com

cs@oreilly.com
For answers to problems regarding your order or our products.

booktech@oreilly.com
For book content technical questions or corrections.

proposals@oreilly.com
To submit new book or software proposals to our editors and product managers.

international@oreilly.com
For information about our international distributors or translation queries. For a list of our distributors outside of North America check out:
http://www.oreilly.com/www/order/country.html

O'Reilly & Associates, Inc.
101 Morris Street, Sebastopol, CA 95472 USA
TEL   707-829-0515 or 800-998-9938
       (6am to 5pm PST)
FAX   707-829-0104

O'REILLY™

TO ORDER: **800-998-9938** • *order@oreilly.com* • *http://www.oreilly.com/*
OUR PRODUCTS ARE AVAILABLE AT A BOOKSTORE OR SOFTWARE STORE NEAR YOU.
FOR INFORMATION: **800-998-9938** • **707-829-0515** • *info@oreilly.com*

International Distributors

UK, EUROPE, MIDDLE EAST AND NORTHERN AFRICA (except France, Germany, Switzerland, & Austria)

INQUIRIES
International Thomson Publishing Europe
Berkshire House
168-173 High Holborn
London WC1V 7AA, UK
Telephone: 44-171-497-1422
Fax: 44-171-497-1426
Email: itpint@itps.co.uk

ORDERS
International Thomson Publishing Services, Ltd.
Cheriton House, North Way
Andover, Hampshire SP10 5BE,
United Kingdom
Telephone: 44-264-342-832 (UK)
Telephone: 44-264-342-806 (outside UK)
Fax: 44-264-364418 (UK)
Fax: 44-264-342761 (outside UK)
UK & Eire orders: itpuk@itps.co.uk
International orders: itpint@itps.co.uk

FRANCE

Editions Eyrolles
61 bd Saint-Germain
75240 Paris Cedex 05
France
Fax: 33-01-44-41-11-44

FRENCH LANGUAGE BOOKS
All countries except Canada
Telephone: 33-01-44-41-46-16
Email: geodif@eyrolles.com

ENGLISH LANGUAGE BOOKS
Telephone: 33-01-44-41-11-87
Email: distribution@eyrolles.com

GERMANY, SWITZERLAND, AND AUSTRIA

INQUIRIES
O'Reilly Verlag
Balthasarstr. 81
D-50670 Köln
Germany
Telephone: 49-221-97-31-60-0
Fax: 49-221-97-31-60-8
Email: anfragen@oreilly.de

ORDERS
International Thomson Publishing
Königswinterer Straße 418
53227 Bonn, Germany
Telephone: 49-228-97024 0
Fax: 49-228-441342
Email: order@oreilly.de

JAPAN

O'Reilly Japan, Inc.
Kiyoshige Building 2F
12-Banchi, Sanei-cho
Shinjuku-ku
Tokyo 160 Japan
Tel: 81-3-3356-5227
Fax: 81-3-3356-5261
Email: kenji@oreilly.com

INDIA

Computer Bookshop (India) PVT. Ltd.
190 Dr. D.N. Road, Fort
Bombay 400 001 India
Tel: 91-22-207-0989
Fax: 91-22-262-3551
Email: cbsbom@giasbm01.vsnl.net.in

HONG KONG

City Discount Subscription Service Ltd.
Unit D, 3rd Floor, Yan's Tower
27 Wong Chuk Hang Road
Aberdeen, Hong Kong
Telephone: 852-2580-3539
Fax: 852-2580-6463
Email: citydis@ppn.com.hk

KOREA

Hanbit Publishing, Inc.
Sonyoung Bldg. 202
Yeksam-dong 736-36
Kangnam-ku
Seoul, Korea
Telephone: 822-554-9610
Fax: 822-556-0363
Email: hant93@chollian.dacom.co.kr

TAIWAN

ImageArt Publishing, Inc.
4/fl. No. 65 Shinyi Road Sec. 4
Taipei, Taiwan, R.O.C.
Telephone: 886-2708-5770
Fax: 886-2705-6690
Email: marie@ms1.hinet.net

SINGAPORE, MALAYSIA, AND THAILAND

Longman Singapore
25 First Lok Yan Road
Singapore 2262
Telephone: 65-268-2666
Fax: 65-268-7023
Email: daniel@longman.com.sg

PHILIPPINES

Mutual Books, Inc.
429-D Shaw Boulevard
Mandaluyong City, Metro
Manila, Philippines
Telephone: 632-725-7538
Fax: 632-721-3056
Email: mbikikog@mnl.sequel.net

CHINA

Ron's DataCom Co., Ltd.
79 Dongwu Avenue
Dongxihu District
Wuhan 430040
China
Telephone: 86-27-83892568
Fax: 86-27-83222108
Email: hongfeng@public.wh.hb.cn

AUSTRALIA

WoodsLane Pty. Ltd.
7/5 Vuko Place, Warriewood NSW 2102
P.O. Box 935,
Mona Vale NSW 2103
Australia
Telephone: 61-2-9970-5111
Fax: 61-2-9970-5002
Email: info@woodslane.com.au

ALL OTHER ASIA COUNTRIES

O'Reilly & Associates, Inc.
101 Morris Street
Sebastopol, CA 95472 USA
Telephone: 707-829-0515
Fax: 707-829-0104
Email: order@oreilly.com

THE AMERICAS

McGraw-Hill Interamericana Editores,
S.A. de C.V.
Cedro No. 512
Col. Atlampa 06450
Mexico, D.F.
Telephone: 52-5-541-3155
Fax: 52-5-541-4913
Email: mcgraw-hill@infosel.net.mx

SOUTHERN AFRICA

International Thomson Publishing Southern Africa
Building 18, Constantia Park
138 Sixteenth Road
P.O. Box 2459
Halfway House, 1685 South Africa
Tel: 27-11-805-4819
Fax: 27-11-805-3648

O'REILLY™

TO ORDER: **800-998-9938** • **order@oreilly.com** • **http://www.oreilly.com/**
OUR PRODUCTS ARE AVAILABLE AT A BOOKSTORE OR SOFTWARE STORE NEAR YOU.
FOR INFORMATION: **800-998-9938** • **707-829-0515** • **info@oreilly.com**

O'REILLY™

O'Reilly & Associates, Inc.
101 Morris Street
Sebastopol, CA 95472-9902
1-800-998-9938

Visit us online at:
http://www.o
orders@

O'REILLY WOULD LIKE TO HEAR FROM YOU

Which book did this card come from?

_____

Where did you buy this book?
- ❏ Bookstore
- ❏ Direct from O'Reilly
- ❏ Bundled with hardware/software
- ❏ Computer Store
- ❏ Class/seminar
- ❏ Other _____

What operating system do you use?
- ❏ UNIX
- ❏ Windows NT
- ❏ Macintosh
- ❏ PC(Windows/DOS)
- ❏ Other _____

What is your job description?
- ❏ System Administrator
- ❏ Network Administrator
- ❏ Web Developer
- ❏ Programmer
- ❏ Educator/Teacher
- ❏ Other _____

❏ Please send me O'Reilly's catalog, containing a complete listing of O'Reilly books and software.

Name _____ Company/Organization _____

Address _____

City _____ State _____ Zip/Postal Code _____ Country _____

Telephone _____ Internet or other email address (specify network) _____

Nineteenth century wood engraving
of a bear from the O'Reilly &
Associates Nutshell Handbook®
Using & Managing UUCP.

POST CARD

BUSINESS REPLY MAIL

FIRST CLASS MAIL   PERMIT NO. 80   SEBASTOPOL, CA

Postage will be paid by addressee

O'Reilly & Associates, Inc.
101 Morris Street
Sebastopol, CA 95472-9902